D0029347

On
Strategy

On
Strategy

HARVARD BUSINESS REVIEW PRESS
Boston, Massachusetts

Library of Congress Cataloging-in-Publication Data
HBR's 10 must reads on strategy.
p. cm.
Includes index.
ISBN 978-1-4221-5798-5 (pbk. : alk. paper) 1. Strategic planning.
I. Harvard business review. II. Title: HBR's ten must reads on strategy.
III. Title: Harvard business review's 10 must reads on strategy.
   HD30.28.H395 2010
   658.4 '012—dc22

                                        2010031619

Contents

On
Strategy

What Is Strategy?

by Michael E. Porter

I. Operational Effectiveness Is Not Strategy

For almost two decades, managers have been learning to play by a new set of rules. Companies must be flexible to respond rapidly to competitive and market changes. They must benchmark continuously to achieve best practice. They must outsource aggressively to gain efficiencies. And they must nurture a few core competencies in race to stay ahead of rivals.

Positioning—once the heart of strategy—is rejected as too static for today's dynamic markets and changing technologies. According to the new dogma, rivals can quickly copy any market position, and competitive advantage is, at best, temporary.

But those beliefs are dangerous half-truths, and they are leading more and more companies down the path of mutually destructive competition. True, some barriers to competition are falling as regulation eases and markets become global. True, companies have properly invested energy in becoming leaner and more nimble. In many industries, however, what some call *hypercompetition* is a self-inflicted wound, not the inevitable outcome of a changing paradigm of competition.

The root of the problem is the failure to distinguish between operational effectiveness and strategy. The quest for productivity, quality, and speed has spawned a remarkable number of management tools and techniques: total quality management, benchmarking, time-based competition, outsourcing, partnering, reengineering, change management. Although the resulting operational improvements have often been dramatic, many companies have been frustrated by their inability to translate those gains into sustainable profitability. And bit by bit, almost imperceptibly, management tools have taken the place of strategy. As managers push to improve on all fronts, they move farther away from viable competitive positions.

Operational effectiveness: necessary but not sufficient

Operational effectiveness and strategy are both essential to superior performance, which, after all, is the primary goal of any enterprise. But they work in very different ways.

A company can outperform rivals only if it can establish a difference that it can preserve. It must deliver greater value to customers or create comparable value at a lower cost, or do both. The arithmetic of superior profitability then follows: delivering greater value allows a company to charge higher average unit prices; greater efficiency results in lower average unit costs.

Ultimately, all differences between companies in cost or price derive from the hundreds of activities required to create, produce, sell, and deliver their products or services, such as calling on customers, assembling final products, and training employees. Cost is generated by performing activities, and cost advantage arises from performing particular activities more efficiently than competitors. Similarly, differentiation arises from both the choice of activities and how they are performed. Activities, then, are the basic units of competitive advantage. Overall advantage or disadvantage results from all a company's activities, not only a few.[1]

Operational effectiveness (OE) means performing similar activities *better* than rivals perform them. Operational effectiveness includes but is not limited to efficiency. It refers to any number of practices that allow a company to better utilize its inputs by, for example, reducing defects in products or developing better products faster. In contrast, strategic positioning means performing *different* activities from rivals' or performing similar activities in *different* ways.

Differences in operational effectiveness among companies are pervasive. Some companies are able to get more out of their inputs

Idea in Brief

The myriad activities that go into creating, producing, selling, and delivering a product or service are the basic units of competitive advantage. **Operational effectiveness** means performing these activities better—that is, faster, or with fewer inputs and defects—than rivals. Companies can reap enormous advantages from operational effectiveness, as Japanese firms demonstrated in the 1970s and 1980s with such practices as total quality management and continuous improvement. But from a competitive standpoint, the problem with operational effectiveness is that best practices are easily emulated. As all competitors in an industry adopt them, the **productivity frontier**—the maximum value a company can deliver

at a given cost, given the best available technology, skills, and management techniques—shifts outward, lowering costs and improving value at the same time. Such competition produces absolute improvement in operational effectiveness, but relative improvement for no one. And the more benchmarking that companies do, the more **competitive convergence** you have—that is, the more indistinguishable companies are from one another.

Strategic positioning attempts to achieve sustainable competitive advantage by preserving what is distinctive about a company. It means performing *different* activities from rivals, or performing *similar* activities in different ways.

than others because they eliminate wasted effort, employ more advanced technology, motivate employees better, or have greater insight into managing particular activities or sets of activities. Such differences in operational effectiveness are an important source of differences in profitability among competitors because they directly affect relative cost positions and levels of differentiation.

Differences in operational effectiveness were at the heart of the Japanese challenge to Western companies in the 1980s. The Japanese were so far ahead of rivals in operational effectiveness that they could offer lower cost and superior quality at the same time. It is worth dwelling on this point, because so much recent thinking about competition depends on it. Imagine for a moment a *productivity frontier* that constitutes the sum of all existing best practices at any given time. Think of it as the maximum value that a

Idea in Practice

Three key principles underlie strategic positioning.

1. **Strategy is the creation of a unique and valuable position, involving a different set of activities.** Strategic position emerges from three distinct sources:

   - serving few needs of many customers (Jiffy Lube provides only auto lubricants)

   - serving broad needs of few customers (Bessemer Trust targets only very high-wealth clients)

   - serving broad needs of many customers in a narrow market (Carmike Cinemas operates only in cities with a population under 200,000)

2. **Strategy requires you to make trade-offs in competing—to choose what *not* to do.** Some competitive activities are incompatible; thus, gains in one area can be achieved only at the expense of another area. For example, Neutrogena soap is positioned more as a medicinal product than as a cleansing agent. The company says "no" to sales based on deodorizing, gives up large volume, and sacrifices manufacturing efficiencies. By contrast, Maytag's decision to extend its product line and acquire other brands

represented a failure to make difficult trade-offs: the boost in revenues came at the expense of return on sales.

3. **Strategy involves creating "fit" among a company's activities.** Fit has to do with the ways a company's activities interact and reinforce one another. For example, Vanguard Group aligns all of its activities with a low-cost strategy; it distributes funds directly to consumers and minimizes portfolio turnover. Fit drives both competitive advantage and sustainability: when activities mutually reinforce each other, competitors can't easily imitate them. When Continental Lite tried to match a few of Southwest Airlines' activities, but not the whole interlocking system, the results were disastrous.

Employees need guidance about how to deepen a strategic position rather than broaden or compromise it. About how to extend the company's uniqueness while strengthening the fit among its activities. This work of deciding which target group of customers and needs to serve requires discipline, the ability to set limits, and forthright communication. Clearly, strategy and leadership are inextricably linked.

company delivering a particular product or service can create at a given cost, using the best available technologies, skills, management techniques, and purchased inputs. The productivity frontier can apply to individual activities, to groups of linked activities such as order processing and manufacturing, and to an entire company's activities. When a company improves its operational effectiveness, it moves toward the frontier. Doing so may require capital investment, different personnel, or simply new ways of managing.

The productivity frontier is constantly shifting outward as new technologies and management approaches are developed and as new inputs become available. Laptop computers, mobile communications, the Internet, and software such as Lotus Notes, for example, have redefined the productivity frontier for sales-force operations and created rich possibilities for linking sales with such activities as order processing and after-sales support. Similarly, lean production, which involves a family of activities, has allowed substantial improvements in manufacturing productivity and asset utilization.

Operational effectiveness versus strategic positioning

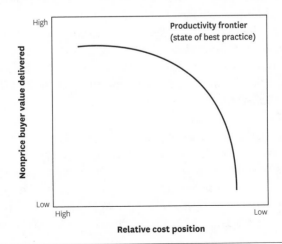

5

For at least the past decade, managers have been preoccupied with improving operational effectiveness. Through programs such as TQM, time-based competition, and benchmarking, they have changed how they perform activities in order to eliminate inefficiencies, improve customer satisfaction, and achieve best practice. Hoping to keep up with shifts in the productivity frontier, managers have embraced continuous improvement, empowerment, change management, and the so-called learning organization. The popularity of outsourcing and the virtual corporation reflect the growing recognition that it is difficult to perform all activities as productively as specialists.

As companies move to the frontier, they can often improve on multiple dimensions of performance at the same time. For example, manufacturers that adopted the Japanese practice of rapid changeovers in the 1980s were able to lower cost and improve differentiation simultaneously. What were once believed to be real trade-offs—between defects and costs, for example—turned out to be illusions created by poor operational effectiveness. Managers have learned to reject such false trade-offs.

Constant improvement in operational effectiveness is necessary to achieve superior profitability. However, it is not usually sufficient. Few companies have competed successfully on the basis of operational effectiveness over an extended period, and staying ahead of rivals gets harder every day. The most obvious reason for that is the rapid diffusion of best practices. Competitors can quickly imitate management techniques, new technologies, input improvements, and superior ways of meeting customers' needs. The most generic solutions—those that can be used in multiple settings—diffuse the fastest. Witness the proliferation of OE techniques accelerated by support from consultants.

OE competition shifts the productivity frontier outward, effectively raising the bar for everyone. But although such competition produces absolute improvement in operational effectiveness, it leads to relative improvement for no one. Consider the $5 billion-plus U.S. commercial-printing industry. The major players— R.R. Donnelley & Sons Company, Quebecor, World Color Press, and

THE 1s FIRST PROFIT NOW IS UPSTREAM.

Big Flower Press—are competing head to head, serving all types of customers, offering the same array of printing technologies (gravure and web offset), investing heavily in the same new equipment, running their presses faster, and reducing crew sizes. But the resulting major productivity gains are being captured by customers and equipment suppliers, not retained in superior profitability. Even industry-leader Donnelley's profit margin, consistently higher than 7% in the 1980s, fell to less than 4.6% in 1995. This pattern is playing itself out in industry after industry. Even the Japanese, pioneers of the new competition, suffer from persistently low profits. (See the sidebar "Japanese Companies Rarely Have Strategies.")

The second reason that improved operational effectiveness is insufficient—competitive convergence—is more subtle and insidious. The more benchmarking companies do, the more they look alike. The more that rivals outsource activities to efficient third parties, often the same ones, the more generic those activities become. As rivals imitate one another's improvements in quality, cycle times, or supplier partnerships, strategies converge and competition becomes a series of races down identical paths that no one can win. Competition based on operational effectiveness alone is mutually destructive, leading to wars of attrition that can be arrested only by limiting competition.

The recent wave of industry consolidation through mergers makes sense in the context of OE competition. Driven by performance pressures but lacking strategic vision, company after company has had no better idea than to buy up its rivals. The competitors left standing are often those that outlasted others, not companies with real advantage.

After a decade of impressive gains in operational effectiveness, many companies are facing diminishing returns. Continuous improvement has been etched on managers' brains. But its tools unwittingly draw companies toward imitation and homogeneity. Gradually, managers have let operational effectiveness supplant strategy. The result is zero-sum competition, static or declining prices, and pressures on costs that compromise companies' ability to invest in the business for the long term.

Japanese Companies Rarely Have Strategies

THE JAPANESE TRIGGERED A GLOBAL revolution in operational effectiveness in the 1970s and 1980s, pioneering practices such as total quality management and continuous improvement. As a result, Japanese manufacturers enjoyed substantial cost and quality advantages for many years.

But Japanese companies rarely developed distinct strategic positions of the kind discussed in this article. Those that did—Sony, Canon, and Sega, for example—were the exception rather than the rule. Most Japanese companies imitate and emulate one another. All rivals offer most if not all product varieties, features, and services; they employ all channels and match one anothers' plant configurations.

The dangers of Japanese-style competition are now becoming easier to recognize. In the 1980s, with rivals operating far from the productivity frontier, it seemed possible to win on both cost and quality indefinitely. Japanese companies were all able to grow in an expanding domestic economy and by penetrating global markets. They appeared unstoppable. But as the gap in operational effectiveness narrows, Japanese companies are increasingly caught in a trap of their own making. If they are to escape the mutually destructive battles now ravaging their performance, Japanese companies will have to learn strategy.

To do so, they may have to overcome strong cultural barriers. Japan is notoriously consensus oriented, and companies have a strong tendency to mediate differences among individuals rather than accentuate them. Strategy, on the other hand, requires hard choices. The Japanese also have a deeply ingrained service tradition that predisposes them to go to great lengths to satisfy any need a customer expresses. Companies that compete in that way end up blurring their distinct positioning, becoming all things to all customers.

This discussion of Japan is drawn from the author's research with Hirotaka Takeuchi, with help from Mariko Sakakibara.

II. Strategy Rests on Unique Activities

Competitive strategy is about being different. It means deliberately choosing a different set of activities to deliver a unique mix of value.

Southwest Airlines Company, for example, offers short-haul, low-cost, point-to-point service between midsize cities and secondary airports in large cities. Southwest avoids large airports and does not fly great distances. Its customers include business travelers, families, and students. Southwest's frequent departures and low fares attract price-sensitive customers who otherwise would travel by bus or car, and convenience-oriented travelers who would choose a full-service airline on other routes.

Most managers describe strategic positioning in terms of their customers: "Southwest Airlines serves price- and convenience-sensitive travelers," for example. But the essence of strategy is in the activities—choosing to perform activities differently or to perform different activities than rivals. Otherwise, a strategy is nothing more than a marketing slogan that will not withstand competition.

A full-service airline is configured to get passengers from almost any point A to any point B. To reach a large number of destinations and serve passengers with connecting flights, full-service airlines employ a hub-and-spoke system centered on major airports. To attract passengers who desire more comfort, they offer first-class or business-class service. To accommodate passengers who must change planes, they coordinate schedules and check and transfer baggage. Because some passengers will be traveling for many hours, full-service airlines serve meals.

Southwest, in contrast, tailors all its activities to deliver low-cost, convenient service on its particular type of route. Through fast turnarounds at the gate of only 15 minutes, Southwest is able to keep planes flying longer hours than rivals and provide frequent departures with fewer aircraft. Southwest does not offer meals, assigned seats, interline baggage checking, or premium classes of service. Automated ticketing at the gate encourages customers to bypass travel agents, allowing Southwest to avoid their commissions. A standardized fleet of 737 aircraft boosts the efficiency of maintenance.

Southwest has staked out a unique and valuable strategic position based on a tailored set of activities. On the routes served by Southwest, a full-service airline could never be as convenient or as low cost.

Ikea, the global furniture retailer based in Sweden, also has a clear strategic positioning. Ikea targets young furniture buyers who want style at low cost. What turns this marketing concept into a strategic

Finding New Positions: The Entrepreneurial Edge

STRATEGIC COMPETITION CAN BE THOUGHT of as the process of perceiving new positions that woo customers from established positions or draw new customers into the market. For example, superstores offering depth of merchandise in a single product category take market share from broad-line department stores offering a more limited selection in many categories. Mail-order catalogs pick off customers who crave convenience. In principle, incumbents and entrepreneurs face the same challenges in finding new strategic positions. In practice, new entrants often have the edge.

Strategic positionings are often not obvious, and finding them requires creativity and insight. New entrants often discover unique positions that have been available but simply overlooked by established competitors. Ikea, for example, recognized a customer group that had been ignored or served poorly. Circuit City Stores' entry into used cars, CarMax, is based on a new way of performing activities—extensive refurbishing of cars, product guarantees, no-haggle pricing, sophisticated use of in-house customer financing—that has long been open to incumbents.

New entrants can prosper by occupying a position that a competitor once held but has ceded through years of imitation and straddling. And entrants coming from other industries can create new positions because of distinctive activities drawn from their other businesses. CarMax borrows heavily from Circuit City's expertise in inventory management, credit, and other activities in consumer electronics retailing.

Most commonly, however, new positions open up because of change. New customer groups or purchase occasions arise; new needs emerge as societies evolve; new distribution channels appear; new technologies are developed; new machinery or information systems become available. When such changes happen, new entrants, unencumbered by a long history in the industry, can often more easily perceive the potential for a new way of competing. Unlike incumbents, newcomers can be more flexible because they face no trade-offs with their existing activities.

---

positioning is the tailored set of activities that make it work. Like Southwest, Ikea has chosen to perform activities differently from its rivals.

Consider the typical furniture store. Showrooms display samples of the merchandise. One area might contain 25 sofas; another will display five dining tables. But those items represent only a fraction of the choices available to customers. Dozens of books displaying fabric swatches or wood samples or alternate styles offer customers thousands of product varieties to choose from. Salespeople often escort customers through the store, answering questions and helping them navigate this maze of choices. Once a customer makes a selection, the order is relayed to a third-party manufacturer. With luck, the furniture will be delivered to the customer's home within six to eight weeks. This is a value chain that maximizes customization and service but does so at high cost.

In contrast, Ikea serves customers who are happy to trade off service for cost. Instead of having a sales associate trail customers around the store, Ikea uses a self-service model based on clear, in-store displays. Rather than rely solely on third-party manufacturers, Ikea designs its own low-cost, modular, ready-to-assemble furniture to fit its positioning. In huge stores, Ikea displays every product it sells in room-like settings, so customers don't need a decorator to help them imagine how to put the pieces together. Adjacent to the furnished showrooms is a warehouse section with the products in boxes on pallets. Customers are expected to do their own pickup and delivery, and Ikea will even sell you a roof rack for your car that you can return for a refund on your next visit.

Although much of its low-cost position comes from having customers "do it themselves," Ikea offers a number of extra services that its competitors do not. In-store child care is one. Extended hours are another. Those services are uniquely aligned with the needs of its customers, who are young, not wealthy, likely to have children (but no nanny), and, because they work for a living, have a need to shop at odd hours.

The origins of strategic positions

Strategic positions emerge from three distinct sources, which are not mutually exclusive and often overlap. First, positioning can be based on producing a subset of an industry's products or services. I call this *variety-based positioning* because it is based on the choice of product or service varieties rather than customer segments.

11

Variety-based positioning makes economic sense when a company can best produce particular products or services using distinctive sets of activities.

Jiffy Lube International, for instance, specializes in automotive lubricants and does not offer other car repair or maintenance services. Its value chain produces faster service at a lower cost than broader line repair shops, a combination so attractive that many customers subdivide their purchases, buying oil changes from the focused competitor, Jiffy Lube, and going to rivals for other services.

The Vanguard Group, a leader in the mutual fund industry, is another example of variety-based positioning. Vanguard provides an array of common stock, bond, and money market funds that offer predictable performance and rock-bottom expenses. The company's investment approach deliberately sacrifices the possibility of extraordinary performance in any one year for good relative performance in every year. Vanguard is known, for example, for its index funds. It avoids making bets on interest rates and steers clear of narrow stock groups. Fund managers keep trading levels low, which holds expenses down; in addition, the company discourages customers from rapid buying and selling because doing so drives up costs and can force a fund manager to trade in order to deploy new capital and raise cash for redemptions. Vanguard also takes a consistent low-cost approach to managing distribution, customer service, and marketing. Many investors include one or more Vanguard funds in their portfolio, while buying aggressively managed or specialized funds from competitors.

The people who use Vanguard or Jiffy Lube are responding to a superior value chain for a particular type of service. A variety-based positioning can serve a wide array of customers, but for most it will meet only a subset of their needs.

A second basis for positioning is that of serving most or all the needs of a particular group of customers. I call this *needs-based positioning*, which comes closer to traditional thinking about targeting a segment of customers. It arises when there are groups of customers with differing needs, and when a tailored set of activities can serve those needs best. Some groups of customers are more price sensitive

The Connection with Generic Strategies

IN COMPETITIVE STRATEGY (The Free Press, 1985), I introduced the concept of generic strategies—cost leadership, differentiation, and focus—to represent the alternative strategic positions in an industry. The generic strategies remain useful to characterize strategic positions at the simplest and broadest level. Vanguard, for instance, is an example of a cost leadership strategy, whereas Ikea, with its narrow customer group, is an example of cost-based focus. Neutrogena is a focused differentiator. The bases for positioning—varieties, needs, and access—carry the understanding of those generic strategies to a greater level of specificity. Ikea and Southwest are both cost-based focusers, for example, but Ikea's focus is based on the needs of a customer group, and Southwest's is based on offering a particular service variety.

The generic strategies framework introduced the need to choose in order to avoid becoming caught between what I then described as the inherent contradictions of different strategies. Trade-offs between the activities of incompatible positions explain those contradictions. Witness Continental Lite, which tried and failed to compete in two ways at once.

than others, demand different product features, and need varying amounts of information, support, and services. Ikea's customers are a good example of such a group. Ikea seeks to meet all the home furnishing needs of its target customers, not just a subset of them.

A variant of needs-based positioning arises when the same customer has different needs on different occasions or for different types of transactions. The same person, for example, may have different needs when traveling on business than when traveling for pleasure with the family. Buyers of cans—beverage companies, for example—will likely have different needs from their primary supplier than from their secondary source.

It is intuitive for most managers to conceive of their business in terms of the customers' needs they are meeting. But a critical element of needs-based positioning is not at all intuitive and is often overlooked. Differences in needs will not translate into meaningful positions unless the best set of activities to satisfy them *also* differs. If that were not the case, every competitor could meet those same needs, and there would be nothing unique or valuable about the positioning.

In private banking, for example, Bessemer Trust Company targets families with a minimum of $5 million in investable assets who want capital preservation combined with wealth accumulation. By assigning one sophisticated account officer for every 14 families, Bessemer has configured its activities for personalized service. Meetings, for example, are more likely to be held at a client's ranch or yacht than in the office. Bessemer offers a wide array of customized services, including investment management and estate administration, oversight of oil and gas investments, and accounting for racehorses and aircraft. Loans, a staple of most private banks, are rarely needed by Bessemer's clients and make up a tiny fraction of its client balances and income. Despite the most generous compensation of account officers and the highest personnel cost as a percentage of operating expenses, Bessemer's differentiation with its target families produces a return on equity estimated to be the highest of any private banking competitor.

Citibank's private bank, on the other hand, serves clients with minimum assets of about $250,000 who, in contrast to Bessemer's clients, want convenient access to loans—from jumbo mortgages to deal financing. Citibank's account managers are primarily lenders. When clients need other services, their account manager refers them to other Citibank specialists, each of whom handles prepackaged products. Citibank's system is less customized than Bessemer's and allows it to have a lower manager-to-client ratio of 1:125. Biannual office meetings are offered only for the largest clients. Both Bessemer and Citibank have tailored their activities to meet the needs of a different group of private banking customers. The same value chain cannot profitably meet the needs of both groups.

The third basis for positioning is that of segmenting customers who are accessible in different ways. Although their needs are similar to those of other customers, the best configuration of activities to reach them is different. I call this *access-based positioning*. Access can be a function of customer geography or customer scale—or of anything that requires a different set of activities to reach customers in the best way.

Segmenting by access is less common and less well understood than the other two bases. Carmike Cinemas, for example, operates movie theaters exclusively in cities and towns with populations under 200,000. How does Carmike make money in markets that are not only small but also won't support big-city ticket prices? It does so through a set of activities that result in a lean cost structure. Carmike's small-town customers can be served through standardized, low-cost theater complexes requiring fewer screens and less sophisticated projection technology than big-city theaters. The company's proprietary information system and management process eliminate the need for local administrative staff beyond a single theater manager. Carmike also reaps advantages from centralized purchasing, lower rent and payroll costs (because of its locations), and rock-bottom corporate overhead of 2% (the industry average is 5%). Operating in small communities also allows Carmike to practice a highly personal form of marketing in which the theater manager knows patrons and promotes attendance through personal contacts. By being the dominant if not the only theater in its markets—the main competition is often the high school football team—Carmike is also able to get its pick of films and negotiate better terms with distributors.

Rural versus urban-based customers are one example of access driving differences in activities. Serving small rather than large customers or densely rather than sparsely situated customers are other examples in which the best way to configure marketing, order processing, logistics, and after-sale service activities to meet the similar needs of distinct groups will often differ.

Positioning is not only about carving out a niche. A position emerging from any of the sources can be broad or narrow. A focused competitor, such as Ikea, targets the special needs of a subset of customers and designs its activities accordingly. Focused competitors thrive on groups of customers who are overserved (and hence overpriced) by more broadly targeted competitors, or underserved (and hence underpriced). A broadly targeted competitor—for example, Vanguard or Delta Air Lines—serves a wide array of customers, performing a set of activities designed to meet their common needs. It

ignores or meets only partially the more idiosyncratic needs of particular customer customer groups.

Whatever the basis—variety, needs, access, or some combination
of the three—positioning requires a tailored set of activities because
it is always a function of differences on the supply side; that is, of
differences in activities. However, positioning is not always a function of differences on the demand, or customer, side. Variety and access positionings, in particular, do not rely on *any* customer
differences. In practice, however, variety or access differences often
accompany needs differences. The tastes—that is, the needs—of
Carmike's small-town customers, for instance, run more toward
comedies, Westerns, action films, and family entertainment.
Carmike does not run any films rated NC-17.

Having defined positioning, we can now begin to answer the
question, "What is strategy?" Strategy is the creation of a unique and
valuable position, involving a different set of activities. If there were
only one ideal position, there would be no need for strategy. Companies would face a simple imperative—win the race to discover and
preempt it. The essence of strategic positioning is to choose activities that are different from rivals'. If the same set of activities were
best to produce all varieties, meet all needs, and access all customers, companies could easily shift among them and operational
effectiveness would determine performance.

III. A Sustainable Strategic Position Requires Trade-offs

Choosing a unique position, however, is not enough to guarantee a
sustainable advantage. A valuable position will attract imitation by
incumbents, who are likely to copy it in one of two ways.

First, a competitor can reposition itself to match the superior per-
former. J.C. Penney, for instance, has been repositioning itself from a
Sears clone to a more upscale, fashion-oriented, soft-goods retailer.
A second and far more common type of imitation is straddling. The
straddler seeks to match the benefits of a successful position while
maintaining its existing position. It grafts new features, services, or
technologies onto the activities it already performs.

For those who argue that competitors can copy any market position, the airline industry is a perfect test case. It would seem that nearly any competitor could imitate any other airline's activities. Any airline can buy the same planes, lease the gates, and match the menus and ticketing and baggage handling services offered by other airlines.

Continental Airlines saw how well Southwest was doing and decided to straddle. While maintaining its position as a full-service airline, Continental also set out to match Southwest on a number of point-to-point routes. The airline dubbed the new service Continental Lite. It eliminated meals and first-class service, increased departure frequency, lowered fares, and shortened turnaround time at the gate. Because Continental remained a full-service airline on other routes, it continued to use travel agents and its mixed fleet of planes and to provide baggage checking and seat assignments.

But a strategic position is not sustainable unless there are trade-offs with other positions. Trade-offs occur when activities are incompatible. Simply put, a trade-off means that more of one thing necessitates less of another. An airline can choose to serve meals—adding cost and slowing turnaround time at the gate—or it can choose not to, but it cannot do both without bearing major inefficiencies.

Trade-offs create the need for choice and protect against repositioners and straddlers. Consider Neutrogena soap. Neutrogena Corporation's variety-based positioning is built on a "kind to the skin," residue-free soap formulated for pH balance. With a large detail force calling on dermatologists, Neutrogena's marketing strategy looks more like a drug company's than a soap maker's. It advertises in medical journals, sends direct mail to doctors, attends medical conferences, and performs research at its own Skincare Institute. To reinforce its positioning, Neutrogena originally focused its distribution on drugstores and avoided price promotions. Neutrogena uses a slow, more expensive manufacturing process to mold its fragile soap.

In choosing this position, Neutrogena said no to the deodorants and skin softeners that many customers desire in their soap. It gave up the large-volume potential of selling through supermarkets and using price promotions. It sacrificed manufacturing efficiencies to achieve the soap's desired attributes. In its original positioning, Neutrogena made a whole raft of trade-offs like those, trade-offs that protected the company from imitators.

Trade-offs arise for three reasons. The first is inconsistencies in image or reputation. A company known for delivering one kind of value may lack credibility and confuse customers—or even undermine its reputation—if it delivers another kind of value or attempts to deliver two inconsistent things at the same time. For example, Ivory soap, with its position as a basic, inexpensive everyday soap, would have a hard time reshaping its image to match Neutrogena's premium "medical" reputation. Efforts to create a new image typically cost tens or even hundreds of millions of dollars in a major industry—a powerful barrier to imitation.

Second, and more important, trade-offs arise from activities themselves. Different positions (with their tailored activities) require different product configurations, different equipment, different employee behavior, different skills, and different management systems. Many trade-offs reflect inflexibilities in machinery, people, or systems. The more Ikea has configured its activities to lower costs by having its customers do their own assembly and delivery, the less able it is to satisfy customers who require higher levels of service.

However, trade-offs can be even more basic. In general, value is destroyed if an activity is overdesigned or underdesigned for its use. For example, even if a given salesperson were capable of providing a high level of assistance to one customer and none to another, the salesperson's talent (and some of his or her cost) would be wasted on the second customer. Moreover, productivity can improve when variation of an activity is limited. By providing a high level of assistance all the time, the salesperson and the entire sales activity can often achieve efficiencies of learning and scale.

Finally, trade-offs arise from limits on internal coordination and control. By clearly choosing to compete in one way and not another, senior management makes organizational priorities clear. Companies that try to be all things to all customers, in contrast, risk confusion in the trenches as employees attempt to make day-to-day operating decisions without a clear framework.

Positioning trade-offs are pervasive in competition and essential to strategy. They create the need for choice and purposefully limit what a company offers. They deter straddling or repositioning, because competitors that engage in those approaches undermine their strategies and degrade the value of their existing activities.

Trade-offs ultimately grounded Continental Lite. The airline lost hundreds of millions of dollars, and the CEO lost his job. Its planes were delayed leaving congested hub cities or slowed at the gate by baggage transfers. Late flights and cancellations generated a thousand complaints a day. Continental Lite could not afford to compete on price and still pay standard travel-agent commissions, but neither could it do without agents for its full-service business. The airline compromised by cutting commissions for all Continental flights across the board. Similarly, it could not afford to offer the same frequent-flier benefits to travelers paying the much lower ticket prices for Lite service. It compromised again by lowering the rewards of Continental's entire frequent-flier program. The results: angry travel agents and full-service customers.

Continental tried to compete in two ways at once. In trying to be low cost on some routes and full service on others, Continental paid an enormous straddling penalty. If there were no trade-offs between the two positions, Continental could have succeeded. But the absence of trade-offs is a dangerous half-truth that managers must unlearn. Quality is not always free. Southwest's convenience, one kind of high quality, happens to be consistent with low costs because its frequent departures are facilitated by a number of low-cost practices—fast gate turnarounds and automated ticketing, for example. However, other dimensions of airline quality—an assigned seat, a meal, or baggage transfer—require costs to provide.

In general, false trade-offs between cost and quality occur primarily when there is redundant or wasted effort, poor control or accuracy, or weak coordination. Simultaneous improvement of cost and differentiation is possible only when a company begins far behind the productivity frontier or when the frontier shifts outward. At the frontier, where companies have achieved current best practice, the trade-off between cost and differentiation is very real indeed.

After a decade of enjoying productivity advantages, Honda Motor Company and Toyota Motor Corporation recently bumped up against the frontier. In 1995, faced with increasing customer resistance to higher automobile prices, Honda found that the only way to produce a less-expensive car was to skimp on features. In the United States, it replaced the rear disk brakes on the Civic with lower-cost drum brakes and used cheaper fabric for the back seat, hoping customers would not notice. Toyota tried to sell a version of its best-selling Corolla in Japan with unpainted bumpers and cheaper seats. In Toyota's case, customers rebelled, and the company quickly dropped the new model.

For the past decade, as managers have improved operational effectiveness greatly, they have internalized the idea that eliminating trade-offs is a good thing. But if there are no trade-offs companies will never achieve a sustainable advantage. They will have to run faster and faster just to stay in place.

As we return to the question, What is strategy? we see that trade-offs add a new dimension to the answer. Strategy is making trade-offs in competing. The essence of strategy is choosing what *not* to do. Without trade-offs, there would be no need for choice and thus no need for strategy. Any good idea could and would be quickly imitated. Again, performance would once again depend wholly on operational effectiveness.

IV. Fit Drives Both Competitive Advantage and Sustainability

Positioning choices determine not only which activities a company will perform and how it will configure individual activities but also how activities relate to one another. While operational effectiveness is about achieving excellence in individual activities, or functions, strategy is about *combining* activities.

Southwest's rapid gate turnaround, which allows frequent departures and greater use of aircraft, is essential to its high-convenience, low-cost positioning. But how does Southwest achieve it? Part of the answer lies in the company's well-paid gate and ground crews, whose productivity in turnarounds is enhanced by flexible union rules. But the bigger part of the answer lies in how Southwest performs other activities. With no meals, no seat assignment, and no interline baggage transfers, Southwest avoids having to perform activities that slow down other airlines. It selects airports and routes to avoid congestion that introduces delays. Southwest's strict limits on the type and length of routes make standardized aircraft possible: every aircraft Southwest turns is a Boeing 737.

What is Southwest's core competence? Its key success factors? The correct answer is that everything matters. Southwest's strategy involves a whole system of activities, not a collection of parts. Its competitive advantage comes from the way its activities fit and reinforce one another.

Fit locks out imitators by creating a chain that is as strong as its *strongest* link. As in most companies with good strategies, Southwest's activities complement one another in ways that create real economic value. One activity's cost, for example, is lowered because of the way other activities are performed. Similarly, one activity's value to customers can be enhanced by a company's other activities. That is the way strategic fit creates competitive advantage and superior profitability.

Types of fit

The importance of fit among functional policies is one of the oldest ideas in strategy. Gradually, however, it has been supplanted on the management agenda. Rather than seeing the company as a whole, managers have turned to "core" competencies, "critical" resources, and "key" success factors. In fact, fit is a far more central component of competitive advantage than most realize.

Fit is important because discrete activities often affect one another. A sophisticated sales force, for example, confers a greater advantage when the company's product embodies premium technology and its marketing approach emphasizes customer assistance and support. A production line with high levels of model variety is more valuable when combined with an inventory and order processing system that minimizes the need for stocking finished goods, a sales process equipped to explain and encourage customization, and an advertising theme that stresses the benefits of product variations that meet a customer's special needs. Such complementarities are pervasive in strategy. Although some fit among activities is generic and applies to many companies, the most valuable fit is strategy-specific because it enhances a position's uniqueness and amplifies trade-offs.[2]

There are three types of fit, although they are not mutually exclusive. First-order fit is *simple consistency* between each activity (function) and the overall strategy. Vanguard, for example, aligns all activities with its low-cost strategy. It minimizes portfolio turnover and does not need highly compensated money managers. The company distributes its funds directly, avoiding commissions to brokers. It also limits advertising, relying instead on public relations and word-of-mouth recommendations. Vanguard ties its employees' bonuses to cost savings.

Consistency ensures that the competitive advantages of activities cumulate and do not erode or cancel themselves out. It makes the strategy easier to communicate to customers, employees, and shareholders, and improves implementation through single-mindedness in the corporation.

Second-order fit occurs when *activities are reinforcing*. Neutrogena, for example, markets to upscale hotels eager to offer their guests a soap recommended by dermatologists. Hotels grant Neutrogena the privilege of using its customary packaging while requiring other soaps to feature the hotel's name. Once guests have tried Neutrogena in a luxury hotel, they are more likely to purchase it at the drugstore or ask their doctor about it. Thus Neutrogena's medical and hotel marketing activities reinforce one another, lowering total marketing costs.

In another example, Bic Corporation sells a narrow line of standard, low-priced pens to virtually all major customer markets (retail, commercial, promotional, and giveaway) through virtually all available channels. As with any variety-based positioning serving a broad group of customers, Bic emphasizes a common need (low price for an acceptable pen) and uses marketing approaches with a broad reach

Mapping activity systems

Activity-system maps, such as this one for Ikea, show how a company's strategic position is contained in a set of tailored activities designed to deliver it. In companies with a clear strategic position, a number of higher-order strategic themes (in dark grey) can be identified and implemented through clusters of tightly linked activities (in light grey).

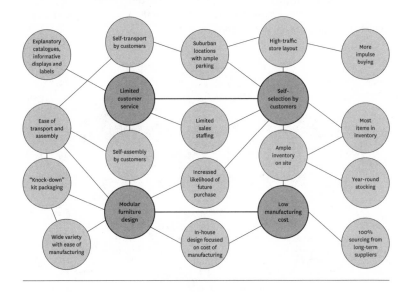

(a large sales force and heavy television advertising). Bic gains the benefits of consistency across nearly all activities, including product design that emphasizes ease of manufacturing, plants configured for low cost, aggressive purchasing to minimize material costs, and in-house parts production whenever the economics dictate.

Yet Bic goes beyond simple consistency because its activities are reinforcing. For example, the company uses point-of-sale displays and frequent packaging changes to stimulate impulse buying. To handle point-of-sale tasks, a company needs a large sales force. Bic's is the largest in its industry, and it handles point-of-sale activities better than its rivals do. Moreover, the combination of point-of-sale

Vanguard's activity system

Activity-system maps can be useful for examining and strengthening strategic fit. A set of basic questions should guide the process. First, is each activity consistent with the overall positioning—the varieties produced, the needs served, and the type of customers accessed? Ask those responsible for each activity to identify how other activities within the company improve or detract from their performance. Second, are there ways to strengthen how activities and groups of activities reinforce one another? Finally, could changes in one activity eliminate the need to perform others?

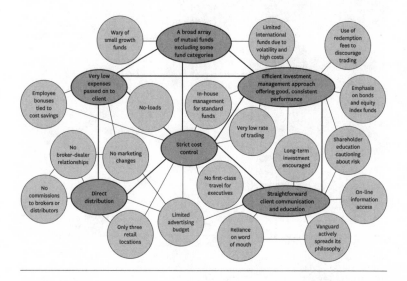

activity, heavy television advertising, and packaging changes yields far more impulse buying than any activity in isolation could.

Third-order fit goes beyond activity reinforcement to what I call *optimization of effort*. The Gap, a retailer of casual clothes, considers product availability in its stores a critical element of its strategy. The Gap could keep products either by holding store inventory or by restocking from warehouses. The Gap has optimized its effort across these activities by restocking its selection of basic clothing almost daily out of three warehouses, thereby minimizing the need to carry

Southwest Airlines' activity system

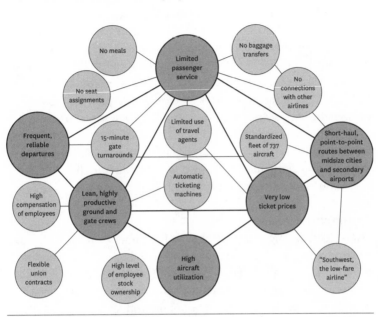

large in-store inventories. The emphasis is on restocking because the Gap's merchandising strategy sticks to basic items in relatively few colors. While comparable retailers achieve turns of three to four times per year, the Gap turns its inventory seven and a half times per year. Rapid restocking, moreover, reduces the cost of implementing the Gap's short model cycle, which is six to eight weeks long.[3]

Coordination and information exchange across activities to eliminate redundancy and minimize wasted effort are the most basic types of effort optimization. But there are higher levels as well. Product design choices, for example, can eliminate the need for after-sale service or make it possible for customers to perform service activities themselves. Similarly, coordination with suppliers or distribution channels can eliminate the need for some in-house activities, such as end-user training.

In all three types of fit, the whole matters more than any individual part. Competitive advantage grows out of the *entire system* of activities. The fit among activities substantially reduces cost or increases differentiation. Beyond that, the competitive value of individual activities—or the associated skills, competencies, or resources—cannot be decoupled from the system or the strategy. Thus in competitive companies it can be misleading to explain success by specifying individual strengths, core competencies, or critical resources. The list of strengths cuts across many functions, and one strength blends into others. It is more useful to think in terms of themes that pervade many activities, such as low cost, a particular notion of customer service, or a particular conception of the value delivered. These themes are embodied in nests of tightly linked activities.

Fit and sustainability

Strategic fit among many activities is fundamental not only to competitive advantage but also to the sustainability of that advantage. It is harder for a rival to match an array of interlocked activities than it is merely to imitate a particular sales-force approach, match a process technology, or replicate a set of product features. Positions built on systems of activities are far more sustainable than those built on individual activities.

Consider this simple exercise. The probability that competitors can match any activity is often less than one. The probabilities then quickly compound to make matching the entire system highly unlikely (.9 x .9 = .81; .9 x .9 x .9 x .9 = .66, and so on). Existing companies that try to reposition or straddle will be forced to reconfigure many activities. And even new entrants, though they do not confront the trade-offs facing established rivals, still face formidable barriers to imitation.

The more a company's positioning rests on activity systems with second- and third-order fit, the more sustainable its advantage will be. Such systems, by their very nature, are usually difficult to untangle from outside the company and therefore hard to imitate. And even if rivals can identify the relevant interconnections, they will have difficulty replicating them. Achieving fit is difficult because it requires the integration of decisions and actions across many independent subunits.

A competitor seeking to match an activity system gains little by imitating only some activities and not matching the whole. Performance does not improve; it can decline. Recall Continental Lite's disastrous attempt to imitate Southwest.

Finally, fit among a company's activities creates pressures and incentives to improve operational effectiveness, which makes imitation even harder. Fit means that poor performance in one activity will degrade the performance in others, so that weaknesses are exposed and more prone to get attention. Conversely, improvements in one activity will pay dividends in others. Companies with strong fit among their activities are rarely inviting targets. Their superiority in strategy and in execution only compounds their advantages and raises the hurdle for imitators.

When activities complement one another, rivals will get little benefit from imitation unless they successfully match the whole system. Such situations tend to promote winner-take-all competition. The company that builds the best activity system—Toys R Us, for instance—wins, while rivals with similar strategies—Child World and Lionel Leisure—fall behind. Thus finding a new strategic position is often preferable to being the second or third imitator of an occupied position.

The most viable positions are those whose activity systems are incompatible because of tradeoffs. Strategic positioning sets the trade-off rules that define how individual activities will be configured and integrated. Seeing strategy in terms of activity systems only makes it clearer why organizational structure, systems, and processes need to be strategy-specific. Tailoring organization to strategy, in turn, makes complementarities more achievable and contributes to sustainability.

One implication is that strategic positions should have a horizon of a decade or more, not of a single planning cycle. Continuity fosters improvements in individual activities and the fit across activities, allowing an organization to build unique capabilities and skills tailored to its strategy. Continuity also reinforces a company's identity.

Conversely, frequent shifts in positioning are costly. Not only must a company reconfigure individual activities, but it must also realign entire systems. Some activities may never catch up to the vacillating strategy. The inevitable result of frequent shifts in strategy, or of failure to choose a distinct position in the first place, is "me-too" or hedged activity configurations, inconsistencies across functions, and organizational dissonance.

What is strategy? We can now complete the answer to this question. Strategy is creating fit among a company's activities. The success of a strategy depends on doing many things well—not just a few—and integrating among them. If there is no fit among activities, there is no distinctive strategy and little sustainability. Management reverts to the simpler task of overseeing independent functions, and operational effectiveness determines an organization's relative performance.

V. Rediscovering Strategy

The failure to choose

Why do so many companies fail to have a strategy? Why do managers avoid making strategic choices? Or, having made them in the past, why do managers so often let strategies decay and blur?

Commonly, the threats to strategy are seen to emanate from outside a company because of changes in technology or the behavior of competitors. Although external changes can be the problem, the greater threat to strategy often comes from within. A sound strategy is undermined by a misguided view of competition, by organizational failures, and, especially, by the desire to grow.

Managers have become confused about the necessity of making choices. When many companies operate far from the productivity frontier, trade-offs appear unnecessary. It can seem that a well-run company should be able to beat its ineffective rivals on all dimensions simultaneously. Taught by popular management thinkers that they do not have to make trade-offs, managers have acquired a macho sense that to do so is a sign of weakness.

Unnerved by forecasts of hypercompetition, managers increase its likelihood by imitating everything about their competitors.

Alternative Views of Strategy

The Implicit Strategy Model of the Past Decade

- One ideal competitive position in the industry
- Benchmarking of all activities and achieving best practice
- Aggressive outsourcing and partnering to gain efficiencies
- Advantages rest on a few key success factors, critical resources, core competencies
- Flexibility and rapid responses to all competitive and market changes

Sustainable Competitive Advantage

- Unique competitive position for the company
- Activities tailored to strategy
- Clear trade-offs and choices vis-à-vis competitors
- Competitive advantage arises from fit across activities
- Sustainability comes from the activity system, not the parts
- Operational effectiveness a given

Exhorted to think in terms of revolution, managers chase every new technology for its own sake.

The pursuit of operational effectiveness is seductive because it is concrete and actionable. Over the past decade, managers have been under increasing pressure to deliver tangible, measurable performance improvements. Programs in operational effectiveness produce reassuring progress, although superior profitability may remain elusive. Business publications and consultants flood the market with information about what other companies are doing, reinforcing the best-practice mentality. Caught up in the race for operational effectiveness, many managers simply do not understand the need to have a strategy.

Companies avoid or blur strategic choices for other reasons as well. Conventional wisdom within an industry is often strong,

Reconnecting with Strategy

MOST COMPANIES OWE THEIR INITIAL success to a unique strategic position involving clear trade-offs. Activities once were aligned with that position. The passage of time and the pressures of growth, however, led to compromises that were, at first, almost imperceptible. Through a succession of incremental changes that each seemed sensible at the time, many established companies have compromised their way to homogeneity with their rivals.

The issue here is not with the companies whose historical position is no longer viable; their challenge is to start over, just as a new entrant would. At issue is a far more common phenomenon: the established company achieving mediocre returns and lacking a clear strategy. Through incremental additions of product varieties, incremental efforts to serve new customer groups, and emulation of rivals' activities, the existing company loses its clear competitive position. Typically, the company has matched many of its competitors' offerings and practices and attempts to sell to most customer groups.

A number of approaches can help a company reconnect with strategy. The first is a careful look at what it already does. Within most well-established companies is a core of uniqueness. It is identified by answering questions such as the following:

- Which of our product or service varieties are the most distinctive?

- Which of our product or service varieties are the most profitable?

homogenizing competition. Some managers mistake "customer focus" to mean they must serve all customer needs or respond to every request from distribution channels. Others cite the desire to preserve flexibility.

Organizational realities also work against strategy. Trade-offs are frightening, and making no choice is sometimes preferred to risking blame for a bad choice. Companies imitate one another in a type of herd behavior, each assuming rivals know something they do not. Newly empowered employees, who are urged to seek every possible source of improvement, often lack a vision of the whole and the perspective to recognize trade-offs. The failure to choose sometimes comes down to the reluctance to disappoint valued managers or employees.

- Which of our customers are the most satisfied?

- Which customers, channels, or purchase occasions are the most profitable?

- Which of the activities in our value chain are the most different and effective?

Around this core of uniqueness are encrustations added incrementally over time. Like barnacles, they must be removed to reveal the underlying strategic positioning. A small percentage of varieties or customers may well account for most of a company's sales and especially its profits. The challenge, then, is to refocus on the unique core and realign the company's activities with it. Customers and product varieties at the periphery can be sold or allowed through inattention or price increases to fade away.

A company's history can also be instructive. What was the vision of the founder? What were the products and customers that made the company? Looking backward, one can reexamine the original strategy to see if it is still valid. Can the historical positioning be implemented in a modern way, one consistent with today's technologies and practices? This sort of thinking may lead to a commitment to renew the strategy and may challenge the organization to recover its distinctiveness. Such a challenge can be galvanizing and can instill the confidence to make the needed trade-offs.

The growth trap

Among all other influences, the desire to grow has perhaps the most perverse effect on strategy. Trade-offs and limits appear to constrain growth. Serving one group of customers and excluding others, for instance, places a real or imagined limit on revenue growth. Broadly targeted strategies emphasizing low price result in lost sales with customers sensitive to features or service. Differentiators lose sales to price-sensitive customers.

Managers are constantly tempted to take incremental steps that surpass those limits but blur a company's strategic position. Eventually, pressures to grow or apparent saturation of the target market lead managers to broaden the position by extending product lines, adding new features, imitating competitors' popular services, matching processes, and even making acquisitions. For years, Maytag Corporation's success was based on its focus on reliable, durable washers and dryers, later extended to include dishwashers. However, conventional wisdom emerging within the industry supported the notion of selling a full line of products. Concerned with slow industry growth and competition from broad-line appliance makers, Maytag was pressured by dealers and encouraged by customers to extend its line. Maytag expanded into refrigerators and cooking products under the Maytag brand and acquired other brands—Jenn-Air, Hardwick Stove, Hoover, Admiral, and Magic Chef—with disparate positions. Maytag has grown substantially from $684 million in 1985 to a peak of $3.4 billion in 1994, but return on sales has declined from 8% to 12% in the 1970s and 1980s to an average of less than 1% between 1989 and 1995. Cost cutting will improve this performance, but laundry and dishwasher products still anchor Maytag's profitability.

Neutrogena may have fallen into the same trap. In the early 1990s, its U.S. distribution broadened to include mass merchandisers such as Wal-Mart Stores. Under the Neutrogena name, the company expanded into a wide variety of products—eye-makeup remover and shampoo, for example—in which it was not unique and which diluted its image, and it began turning to price promotions.

Compromises and inconsistencies in the pursuit of growth will erode the competitive advantage a company had with its original varieties or target customers. Attempts to compete in several ways at once create confusion and undermine organizational motivation and focus. Profits fall, but more revenue is seen as the answer. Managers are unable to make choices, so the company embarks on a new round of broadening and compromises. Often, rivals continue to match each other until desperation breaks the cycle, resulting in a merger or downsizing to the original positioning.

Profitable growth

Many companies, after a decade of restructuring and cost-cutting, are turning their attention to growth. Too often, efforts to grow blur uniqueness, create compromises, reduce fit, and ultimately

Emerging Industries and Technologies

DEVELOPING A STRATEGY IN A newly emerging industry or in a business undergoing revolutionary technological changes is a daunting proposition. In such cases, managers face a high level of uncertainty about the needs of customers, the products and services that will prove to be the most desired, and the best configuration of activities and technologies to deliver them. Because of all this uncertainty, imitation and hedging are rampant: unable to risk being wrong or left behind, companies match all features, offer all new services, and explore all technologies.

During such periods in an industry's development, its basic productivity frontier is being established or reestablished. Explosive growth can make such times profitable for many companies, but profits will be temporary because imitation and strategic convergence will ultimately destroy industry profitability. The companies that are enduringly successful will be those that begin as early as possible to define and embody in their activities a unique competitive position. A period of imitation may be inevitable in emerging industries, but that period reflects the level of uncertainty rather than a desired state of affairs.

In high-tech industries, this imitation phase often continues much longer than it should. Enraptured by technological change itself, companies pack more features—most of which are never used—into their products while slashing prices across the board. Rarely are trade-offs even considered. The drive for growth to satisfy market pressures leads companies into every product area. Although a few companies with fundamental advantages prosper, the majority are doomed to a rat race no one can win.

Ironically, the popular business press, focused on hot, emerging industries, is prone to presenting these special cases as proof that we have entered a new era of competition in which none of the old rules are valid. In fact, the opposite is true.

undermine competitive advantage. In fact, the growth imperative is hazardous to strategy.

What approaches to growth preserve and reinforce strategy? Broadly, the prescription is to concentrate on deepening a strategic position rather than broadening and compromising it. One approach is to look for extensions of the strategy that leverage the existing activity system by offering features or services that rivals would find impossible or costly to match on a stand-alone basis. In other words, managers can ask themselves which activities, features, or forms of competition are feasible or less costly to them because of complementary activities that their company performs.

Deepening a position involves making the company's activities more distinctive, strengthening fit, and communicating the strategy better to those customers who should value it. But many companies succumb to the temptation to chase "easy" growth by adding hot features, products, or services without screening them or adapting them to their strategy. Or they target new customers or markets in which the company has little special to offer. A company can often grow faster—and far more profitably—by better penetrating needs and varieties where it is distinctive than by slugging it out in potentially higher growth arenas in which the company lacks uniqueness. Carmike, now the largest theater chain in the United States, owes its rapid growth to its disciplined concentration on small markets. The company quickly sells any big-city theaters that come to it as part of an acquisition.

Globalization often allows growth that is consistent with strategy, opening up larger markets for a focused strategy. Unlike broadening domestically, expanding globally is likely to leverage and reinforce a company's unique position and identity.

Companies seeking growth through broadening within their industry can best contain the risks to strategy by creating stand-alone units, each with its own brand name and tailored activities. Maytag has clearly struggled with this issue. On the one hand, it has organized its premium and value brands into separate units with different strategic positions. On the other, it has created an umbrella appliance company for all its brands to gain critical mass. With shared design, manufacturing, distribution, and customer service, it will be hard to avoid homogenization. If a given business unit attempts to compete with different positions for different products or customers, avoiding compromise is nearly impossible.

The role of leadership

The challenge of developing or reestablishing a clear strategy is often primarily an organizational one and depends on leadership. With so many forces at work against making choices and tradeoffs in organizations, a clear intellectual framework to guide strategy is a necessary counterweight. Moreover, strong leaders willing to make choices are essential.

In many companies, leadership has degenerated into orchestrating operational improvements and making deals. But the leader's role is broader and far more important. General management is more than the stewardship of individual functions. Its core is strategy: defining and communicating the company's unique position, making trade-offs, and forging fit among activities. The leader must provide the discipline to decide which industry changes and customer needs the company will respond to, while avoiding organizational distractions and maintaining the company's distinctiveness. Managers at lower levels lack the perspective and the confidence to maintain a strategy. There will be constant pressures to compromise, relax trade-offs, and emulate rivals. One of the leader's jobs is to teach others in the organization about strategy—and to say no.

Strategy renders choices about what not to do as important as choices about what to do. Indeed, setting limits is another function of leadership. Deciding which target group of customers, varieties, and needs the company should serve is fundamental to developing a strategy. But so is deciding not to serve other customers or needs and not to offer certain features or services. Thus strategy requires constant discipline and clear communication. Indeed, one of the most important functions of an explicit, communicated strategy is to guide employees in making choices that arise because of trade-offs in their individual activities and in day-to-day decisions.

Improving operational effectiveness is a necessary part of management, but it is *not* strategy. In confusing the two, managers have unintentionally backed into a way of thinking about competition that is driving many industries toward competitive convergence, which is in no one's best interest and is not inevitable.

Managers must clearly distinguish operational effectiveness from strategy. Both are essential, but the two agendas are different.

The operational agenda involves continual improvement everywhere there are no trade-offs. Failure to do this creates vulnerability even for companies with a good strategy. The operational agenda is the proper place for constant change, flexibility, and relentless efforts to achieve best practice. In contrast, the strategic agenda is the right place for defining a unique position, making clear trade-offs, and tightening fit. It involves the continual search for ways to reinforce and extend the company's position. The strategic agenda demands discipline and continuity; its enemies are distraction and compromise.

Strategic continuity does not imply a static view of competition. A company must continually improve its operational effectiveness and actively try to shift the productivity frontier; at the same time, there needs to be ongoing effort to extend its uniqueness while strengthening the fit among its activities. Strategic continuity, in fact, should make an organization's continual improvement more effective.

A company may have to change its strategy if there are major structural changes in its industry. In fact, new strategic positions often arise because of industry changes, and new entrants unencumbered by history often can exploit them more easily. However, a company's choice of a new position must be driven by the ability to find new trade-offs and leverage a new system of complementary activities into a sustainable advantage.

Originally published in November 1996. Reprint 96608.

Notes

1. I first described the concept of activities and its use in understanding competitive advantage in *Competitive Advantage* (New York: The Free Press, 1985). The ideas in this article build on and extend that thinking.

2. Paul Milgrom and John Roberts have begun to explore the economics of systems of complementary functions, activities, and functions. Their focus is on the emergence of "modern manufacturing" as a new set of complementary activities, on the tendency of companies to react to external changes with coherent bundles of internal responses, and on the need for central coordination—a strategy—to align functional managers. In the latter case, they model what has long been a bedrock principle of strategy. See Paul Milgrom and John Roberts, "The Economics of Modern Manufacturing: Technology, Strategy, and Organization," *American Economic Review* 80 (1990): 511–528; Paul Milgrom, Yingyi Qian, and John Roberts, "Complementarities, Momentum, and Evolution of Modern Manufacturing," *American Economic Review* 81 (1991) 84–88; and Paul Milgrom and John Roberts,

"Complementarities and Fit: Strategy, Structure, and Organizational Changes in Manufacturing," *Journal of Accounting and Economics,* vol. 19 (March–May 1995): 179–208.

3. Material on retail strategies is drawn in part from Jan Rivkin, "The Rise of Retail Category Killers," unpublished working paper, January 1995. Nicolaj Siggelkow prepared the case study on the Gap.

The Five
Competitive Forces
That Shape Strategy

by Michael E. Porter

IN ESSENCE, THE JOB of the strategist is to understand and cope with competition. Often, however, managers define competition too narrowly, as if it occurred only among today's direct competitors. Yet competition for profits goes beyond established industry rivals to include four other competitive forces as well: customers, suppliers, potential entrants, and substitute products. The extended rivalry that results from all five forces defines an industry's structure and shapes the nature of competitive interaction within an industry.

As different from one another as industries might appear on the surface, the underlying drivers of profitability are the same. The global auto industry, for instance, appears to have nothing in common with the worldwide market for art masterpieces or the heavily regulated health-care delivery industry in Europe. But to understand industry competition and profitability in each of those three cases, one must analyze the industry's underlying structure in terms of the five forces. (See "The five forces that shape industry competition.")

If the forces are intense, as they are in such industries as airlines, textiles, and hotels, almost no company earns attractive returns on investment. If the forces are benign, as they are in industries such as software, soft drinks, and toiletries, many companies are profitable. Industry structure drives competition and profitability, not whether an industry produces a product or service, is emerging or mature, high tech or low tech, regulated or unregulated. While a myriad of factors can affect industry profitability in the short run—including the weather and the business cycle—industry structure, manifested in the competitive forces, sets industry profitability in the medium and long run. (See "Differences in Industry Profitability.")

Understanding the competitive forces, and their underlying causes, reveals the roots of an industry's current profitability while providing a framework for anticipating and influencing competition (and profitability) over time. A healthy industry structure should be as much a competitive concern to strategists as their company's own position. Understanding industry structure is also essential to effective strategic positioning. As we will see, defending against the competitive forces and shaping them in a company's favor are crucial to strategy.

Forces That Shape Competition

The configuration of the five forces differs by industry. In the market for commercial aircraft, fierce rivalry between dominant producers Airbus and Boeing and the bargaining power of the airlines that place huge orders for aircraft are strong, while the threat of entry, the threat of substitutes, and the power of suppliers are more benign. In the movie theater industry, the proliferation of substitute forms of entertainment and the power of the movie producers and distributors who supply movies, the critical input, are important.

The strongest competitive force or forces determine the profitability of an industry and become the most important to strategy formulation. The most salient force, however, is not always obvious.

For example, even though rivalry is often fierce in commodity industries, it may not be the factor limiting profitability. Low returns in the photographic film industry, for instance, are the result of a superior substitute product—as Kodak and Fuji, the world's leading producers of photographic film, learned with the advent of digital photography. In such a situation, coping with the substitute product becomes the number one strategic priority.

Idea in Brief

You know that to sustain long-term profitability you must respond strategically to competition. And you naturally keep tabs on your **established** rivals. But as you scan the competitive arena, are you also looking *beyond* your direct competitors? As Porter explains in this update of his revolutionary 1979 HBR article, four additional competitive forces can hurt your prospective profits:

- Savvy **customers** can force down prices by playing you and your rivals against one another.

- Powerful **suppliers** may constrain your profits if they charge higher prices.

- Aspiring **entrants,** armed with new capacity and hungry for market share, can ratchet up the investment required for you to stay in the game.

- **Substitute offerings** can lure customers away.

Consider commercial aviation: It's one of the least profitable industries because all five forces are strong. **Established rivals** compete intensely on price. **Customers** are fickle, searching for the best deal regardless of carrier. **Suppliers**—plane and engine manufacturers, along with unionized labor forces—bargain away the lion's share of airlines' profits. **New players** enter the industry in a constant stream. And **substitutes** are readily available—such as train or car travel.

By analyzing all five competitive forces, you gain a complete picture of what's influencing profitability in your industry. You identify game-changing trends early, so you can swiftly exploit them. And you spot ways to work around constraints on profitability—or even reshape the forces in your favor.

Industry structure grows out of a set of economic and technical characteristics that determine the strength of each competitive force. We will examine these drivers in the pages that follow, taking the perspective of an incumbent, or a company already present in the industry. The analysis can be readily extended to understand the challenges facing a potential entrant.

Threat of entry
New entrants to an industry bring new capacity and a desire to gain market share that puts pressure on prices, costs, and the rate of

Idea in Practice

By understanding how the five competitive forces influence profitability in your industry, you can develop a strategy for enhancing your company's long-term profits. Porter suggests the following:

Position Your Company Where the Forces Are Weakest

Example: In the heavy-truck industry, many buyers operate large fleets and are highly motivated to drive down truck prices. Trucks are built to regulated standards and offer similar features, so price competition is stiff; unions exercise considerable supplier power; and buyers can use substitutes such as cargo delivery by rail.

To create and sustain long-term profitability within this industry, heavy-truck maker Paccar chose to focus on one customer group where competitive forces are weakest: individual drivers who own their trucks and contract directly with suppliers. These

operators have limited clout as buyers and are less price sensitive because of their emotional ties to and economic dependence on their own trucks.

For these customers, Paccar has developed such features as luxurious sleeper cabins, plush leather seats, and sleek exterior styling. Buyers can select from thousands of options to put their personal signature on these built-to-order trucks.

Customers pay Paccar a 10% premium, and the company has been profitable for 68 straight years and earned a long-run return on equity above 20%.

Exploit Changes in the Forces

Example: With the advent of the Internet and digital distribution of music, unauthorized downloading created an illegal but potent substitute for record companies' services. The record companies

investment necessary to compete. Particularly when new entrants are diversifying from other markets, they can leverage existing capabilities and cash flows to shake up competition, as Pepsi did when it entered the bottled water industry, Microsoft did when it began to offer internet browsers, and Apple did when it entered the music distribution business.

The threat of entry, therefore, puts a cap on the profit potential of an industry. When the threat is high, incumbents must hold down tried to develop technical platforms for digital distribution themselves, but major labels didn't want to sell their music through a platform owned by a rival.

Into this vacuum stepped Apple, with its iTunes music store supporting its iPod music player. The birth of this powerful new gatekeeper has whittled down the number of major labels from six in 1997 to four today.

Reshape the Forces in Your Favor

Use tactics designed specifically to reduce the share of profits leaking to other players. For example:

- To neutralize **supplier power,** standardize specifications for parts so your company can switch more easily among vendors.

- To counter **customer power,** expand your services so it's

harder for customers to leave you for a rival.

- To temper price wars initiated by **established rivals,** invest more heavily in products that differ significantly from competitors' offerings.

- To scare off **new entrants,** elevate the fixed costs of competing; for instance, by escalating your R&D expenditures.

- To limit the threat of **substitutes,** offer better value through wider product accessibility. Soft-drink producers did this by introducing vending machines and convenience store channels, which dramatically improved the availability of soft drinks relative to other beverages.

their prices or boost investment to deter new competitors. In specialty coffee retailing, for example, relatively low entry barriers mean that Starbucks must invest aggressively in modernizing stores and menus.

The threat of entry in an industry depends on the height of entry barriers that are present and on the reaction entrants can expect from incumbents. If entry barriers are low and newcomers expect little retaliation from the entrenched competitors, the threat of

Q3

entry is high and industry profitability is moderated. It is the *threat* of entry, not whether entry actually occurs, that holds down profitability.

Barriers to entry. Entry barriers are advantages that incumbents have relative to new entrants. There are seven major sources:

1. *Supply-side economies of scale.* These economies arise when firms that produce at larger volumes enjoy lower costs per unit because they can spread fixed costs over more units, employ more efficient technology, or command better terms from suppliers. Supply-side scale economies deter entry by forcing the aspiring entrant either to come into the industry on a large scale, which requires dislodging entrenched competitors, or to accept a cost disadvantage.

Scale economies can be found in virtually every activity in the value chain; which ones are most important varies by industry.[1] In microprocessors, incumbents such as Intel are protected by scale economies in research, chip fabrication, and consumer marketing. For lawn care companies like Scotts Miracle-Gro, the most important scale economies are found in the supply chain and media advertising. In small-package delivery, economies of scale arise in national logistical systems and information technology.

2. *Demand-side benefits of scale.* These benefits, also known as network effects, arise in industries where a buyer's willingness to pay for a company's product increases with the number of other buyers who also patronize the company. Buyers may trust larger companies more for a crucial product: Recall the old adage that no one ever got fired for buying from IBM (when it was the dominant computer maker). Buyers may also value being in a "network" with a larger number of fellow customers. For instance, online auction participants are attracted to eBay because it offers the most potential trading partners. Demand-side benefits of scale discourage entry by limiting the willingness of customers to buy from a newcomer and by reducing the price the newcomer can command until it builds up a large base of customers.

3. *Customer switching costs.* Switching costs are fixed costs that buyers face when they change suppliers. Such costs may arise

because a buyer who switches vendors must, for example, alter product specifications, retrain employees to use a new product, or modify processes or information systems. The larger the switching costs, the harder it will be for an entrant to gain customers. Enterprise resource planning (ERP) software is an example of a product with very high switching costs. Once a company has installed SAP's ERP system, for example, the costs of moving to a new vendor are astronomical because of embedded data, the fact that internal processes have been adapted to SAP, major retraining needs, and the mission-critical nature of the applications.

4. *Capital requirements.* The need to invest large financial resources in order to compete can deter new entrants. Capital may be necessary not only for fixed facilities but also to extend customer credit, build inventories, and fund start-up losses. The barrier is particularly great if the capital is required for unrecoverable and therefore harder-to-finance expenditures, such as up-front advertising or research and development. While major corporations have the financial resources to invade almost any industry, the huge capital requirements in certain fields limit the pool of likely entrants. Conversely, in such fields as tax preparation services or short-haul trucking, capital requirements are minimal and potential entrants plentiful.

It is important not to overstate the degree to which capital requirements alone deter entry. If industry returns are attractive and are expected to remain so, and if capital markets are efficient, investors will provide entrants with the funds they need. For aspiring air carriers, for instance, financing is available to purchase expensive aircraft because of their high resale value, one reason why there have been numerous new airlines in almost every region.

5. *Incumbency advantages independent of size.* No matter what their size, incumbents may have cost or quality advantages not available to potential rivals. These advantages can stem from such sources as proprietary technology, preferential access to the best raw material sources, preemption of the most favorable geographic locations, established brand identities, or cumulative experience that has allowed incumbents to learn how to produce more efficiently.

The five forces that shape industry competition

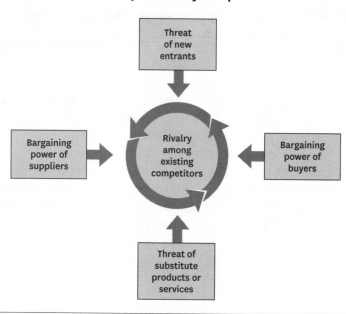

Entrants try to bypass such advantages. Upstart discounters such as Target and Wal-Mart, for example, have located stores in freestanding sites rather than regional shopping centers where established department stores were well entrenched.

6. *Unequal access to distribution channels.* The new entrant must, of course, secure distribution of its product or service. A new food item, for example, must displace others from the supermarket shelf via price breaks, promotions, intense selling efforts, or some other means. The more limited the wholesale or retail channels are and the more that existing competitors have tied them up, the tougher entry into an industry will be. Sometimes access to distribution is so high a barrier that new entrants must bypass distribution channels altogether or create their own. Thus, upstart low-cost airlines have avoided distribution through travel agents (who tend to favor

established higher-fare carriers) and have encouraged passengers to book their own flights on the internet.

7. *Restrictive government policy.* Government policy can hinder or aid new entry directly, as well as amplify (or nullify) the other entry barriers. Government directly limits or even forecloses entry into industries through, for instance, licensing requirements and restrictions on foreign investment. Regulated industries like liquor retailing, taxi services, and airlines are visible examples. Government policy can heighten other entry barriers through such means as expansive patenting rules that protect proprietary technology from imitation or environmental or safety regulations that raise scale economies facing newcomers. Of course, government policies may also make entry easier—directly through subsidies, for instance, or indirectly by funding basic research and making it available to all firms, new and old, reducing scale economies.

Entry barriers should be assessed relative to the capabilities of potential entrants, which may be start-ups, foreign firms, or companies in related industries. And, as some of our examples illustrate, the strategist must be mindful of the creative ways newcomers might find to circumvent apparent barriers.

Expected retaliation. How potential entrants believe incumbents may react will also influence their decision to enter or stay out of an industry. If reaction is vigorous and protracted enough, the profit potential of participating in the industry can fall below the cost of capital. Incumbents often use public statements and responses to one entrant to send a message to other prospective entrants about their commitment to defending market share.

Newcomers are likely to fear expected retaliation if:

- Incumbents have previously responded vigorously to new entrants.

- Incumbents possess substantial resources to fight back, including excess cash and unused borrowing power, available productive capacity, or clout with distribution channels and customers.

Differences in Industry Profitability

THE AVERAGE RETURN on invested capital varies markedly from industry to industry. Between 1992 and 2006, for example, average return on invested capital in U.S. industries ranged as low as zero or even negative to more than 50%. At the high end are industries like soft drinks and prepackaged software, which have been almost six times more profitable than the airline industry over the period.

Average return on invested capital in U.S. industries, 1992–2006

Return on invested capital (ROIC) is the appropriate measure of profitability for strategy formulation, not to mention for equity investors. Return on sales or the growth rate of profits fail to account for the capital required to compete in the industry. Here, we utilize earnings before interest and taxes divided by average invested capital less excess cash as the measure of ROIC. This measure controls for idiosyncratic differences in capital structure and tax rates across companies and industries.

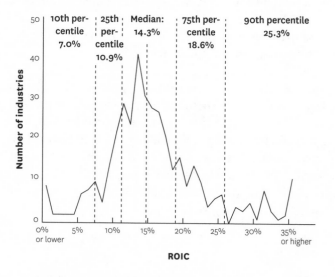

Source: Standard & Poor's, Compustat, and author's calculations

Profitability of selected U.S. industries

Average ROIC, 1992–2006

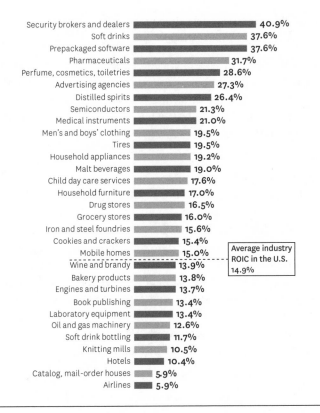

Industry	ROIC
Security brokers and dealers	40.9%
Soft drinks	37.6%
Prepackaged software	37.6%
Pharmaceuticals	31.7%
Perfume, cosmetics, toiletries	28.6%
Advertising agencies	27.3%
Distilled spirits	26.4%
Semiconductors	21.3%
Medical instruments	21.0%
Men's and boys' clothing	19.5%
Tires	19.5%
Household appliances	19.2%
Malt beverages	19.0%
Child day care services	17.6%
Household furniture	17.0%
Drug stores	16.5%
Grocery stores	16.0%
Iron and steel foundries	15.6%
Cookies and crackers	15.4%
Mobile homes	15.0%
Wine and brandy	13.9%
Bakery products	13.8%
Engines and turbines	13.7%
Book publishing	13.4%
Laboratory equipment	13.4%
Oil and gas machinery	12.6%
Soft drink bottling	11.7%
Knitting mills	10.5%
Hotels	10.4%
Catalog, mail-order houses	5.9%
Airlines	5.9%

Average industry ROIC in the U.S. 14.9%

- Incumbents seem likely to cut prices because they are committed to retaining market share at all costs or because the industry has high fixed costs, which create a strong motivation to drop prices to fill excess capacity.

- Industry growth is slow so newcomers can gain volume only by taking it from incumbents.

An analysis of barriers to entry and expected retaliation is obviously crucial for any company contemplating entry into a new industry. The challenge is to find ways to surmount the entry barriers without nullifying, through heavy investment, the profitability of participating in the industry.

The power of suppliers

Powerful suppliers capture more of the value for themselves by charging higher prices, limiting quality or services, or shifting costs to industry participants. Powerful suppliers, including suppliers of labor, can squeeze profitability out of an industry that is unable to pass on cost increases in its own prices. Microsoft, for instance, has contributed to the erosion of profitability among personal computer makers by raising prices on operating systems. PC makers, competing fiercely for customers who can easily switch among them, have limited freedom to raise their prices accordingly.

Companies depend on a wide range of different supplier groups for inputs. A supplier group is powerful if:

- It is more concentrated than the industry it sells to. Microsoft's near monopoly in operating systems, coupled with the fragmentation of PC assemblers, exemplifies this situation.

- The supplier group does not depend heavily on the industry for its revenues. Suppliers serving many industries will not hesitate to extract maximum profits from each one. If a particular industry accounts for a large portion of a supplier group's volume or profit, however, suppliers will want to

Industry Analysis in Practice

Good industry analysis looks rigorously at the structural underpinnings of profitability. A first step is to understand the appropriate time horizon. One of the essential tasks in industry analysis is to distinguish temporary or cyclical changes from structural changes. A good guideline for the appropriate time horizon is the full business cycle for the particular industry. For most industries, a three-to-five-year horizon is appropriate, although in some industries with long lead times, such as mining, the appropriate horizon might be a decade or more. It is average profitability over this period, not profitability in any particular year, that should be the focus of analysis.

The point of industry analysis is not to declare the industry attractive or unattractive but to understand the underpinnings of competition and the root causes of profitability. As much as possible, analysts should look at industry structure quantitatively, rather than be satisfied with lists of qualitative factors. Many elements of the five forces can be quantified: the percentage of the buyer's total cost accounted for by the industry's product (to understand buyer price sensitivity); the percentage of industry sales required to fill a plant or operate a logistical network of efficient scale (to help assess barriers to entry); the buyer's switching cost (determining the inducement an entrant or rival must offer customers).

The strength of the competitive forces affects prices, costs, and the investment required to compete; thus the forces are directly tied to the income statements and balance sheets of industry participants. Industry structure defines the gap between revenues and costs. For example, intense rivalry drives down prices or elevates the costs of marketing, R&D, or customer service, reducing margins. How much? Strong suppliers drive up input costs. How much? Buyer power lowers prices or elevates the costs of meeting buyers' demands, such as the requirement to hold more inventory or provide financing. How much? Low barriers to entry or close substitutes limit the level of sustainable prices. How much? It is these economic relationships that sharpen the strategist's understanding of industry competition.

Finally, good industry analysis does not just list pluses and minuses but sees an industry in overall, systemic terms. Which forces are underpinning (or constraining) today's profitability? How might shifts in one competitive force trigger reactions in others? Answering such questions is often the source of true strategic insights.

protect the industry through reasonable pricing and assist in activities such as R&D and lobbying.

- Industry participants face switching costs in changing suppliers. For example, shifting suppliers is difficult if companies have invested heavily in specialized ancillary equipment or in learning how to operate a supplier's equipment (as with Bloomberg terminals used by financial professionals). Or firms may have located their production lines adjacent to a supplier's manufacturing facilities (as in the case of some beverage companies and container manufacturers). When switching costs are high, industry participants find it hard to play suppliers off against one another. (Note that suppliers may have switching costs as well. This limits their power.)

- Suppliers offer products that are differentiated. Pharmaceutical companies that offer patented drugs with distinctive medical benefits have more power over hospitals, health maintenance organizations, and other drug buyers, for example, than drug companies offering me-too or generic products.

- There is no substitute for what the supplier group provides. Pilots' unions, for example, exercise considerable supplier power over airlines partly because there is no good alternative to a well-trained pilot in the cockpit.

- The supplier group can credibly threaten to integrate forward into the industry. In that case, if industry participants make too much money relative to suppliers, they will induce suppliers to enter the market.

The power of buyers

Powerful customers—the flip side of powerful suppliers—can capture more value by forcing down prices, demanding better quality or more service (thereby driving up costs), and generally playing industry participants off against one another, all at the expense of industry profitability. Buyers are powerful if they have negotiating leverage relative to industry participants, especially if they are price sensitive, using their clout primarily to pressure price reductions.

As with suppliers, there may be distinct groups of customers who differ in bargaining power. A customer group has negotiating leverage if:

- There are few buyers, or each one purchases in volumes that are large relative to the size of a single vendor. Large-volume buyers are particularly powerful in industries with high fixed costs, such as telecommunications equipment, offshore drilling, and bulk chemicals. High fixed costs and low marginal costs amplify the pressure on rivals to keep capacity filled through discounting.

- The industry's products are standardized or undifferentiated. If buyers believe they can always find an equivalent product, they tend to play one vendor against another.

- Buyers face few switching costs in changing vendors.

- Buyers can credibly threaten to integrate backward and produce the industry's product themselves if vendors are too profitable. Producers of soft drinks and beer have long controlled the power of packaging manufacturers by threatening to make, and at times actually making, packaging materials themselves.

A buyer group is price sensitive if:

- The product it purchases from the industry represents a significant fraction of its cost structure or procurement budget. Here buyers are likely to shop around and bargain hard, as consumers do for home mortgages. Where the product sold by an industry is a small fraction of buyers' costs or expenditures, buyers are usually less price sensitive.

- The buyer group earns low profits, is strapped for cash, or is otherwise under pressure to trim its purchasing costs. Highly profitable or cash-rich customers, in contrast, are generally less price sensitive (that is, of course, if the item does not represent a large fraction of their costs).

- The quality of buyers' products or services is little affected by the industry's product. Where quality is very much affected by the industry's product, buyers are generally less price sensitive. When purchasing or renting production quality cameras, for instance, makers of major motion pictures opt for highly reliable equipment with the latest features. They pay limited attention to price.

- The industry's product has little effect on the buyer's other costs. Here, buyers focus on price. Conversely, where an industry's product or service can pay for itself many times over by improving performance or reducing labor, material, or other costs, buyers are usually more interested in quality than in price. Examples include products and services like tax accounting or well logging (which measures below-ground conditions of oil wells) that can save or even make the buyer money. Similarly, buyers tend not to be price sensitive in services such as investment banking, where poor performance can be costly and embarrassing.

Most sources of buyer power apply equally to consumers and to business-to-business customers. Like industrial customers, consumers tend to be more price sensitive if they are purchasing products that are undifferentiated, expensive relative to their incomes, and of a sort where product performance has limited consequences. The major difference with consumers is that their needs can be more intangible and harder to quantify.

Intermediate customers, or customers who purchase the product but are not the end user (such as assemblers or distribution channels), can be analyzed the same way as other buyers, with one important addition. Intermediate customers gain significant bargaining power when they can influence the purchasing decisions of customers downstream. Consumer electronics retailers, jewelry retailers, and agricultural-equipment distributors are examples of distribution channels that exert a strong influence on end customers. Producers often attempt to diminish channel clout through exclusive arrangements with particular distributors or retailers or by marketing directly to end users. Component manufacturers seek to develop power over assemblers by creating preferences for their components with downstream customers. Such is the case with bicycle parts and with sweeteners. DuPont has created enormous clout by advertising its Stainmaster brand of carpet fibers not only to the carpet manufacturers that actually buy them but also to downstream consumers. Many consumers request Stainmaster carpet even though DuPont is not a carpet manufacturer.

The threat of substitutes

A substitute performs the same or a similar function as an industry's product by a different means. Videoconferencing is a substitute for travel. Plastic is a substitute for aluminum. E-mail is a substitute for express mail. Sometimes, the threat of substitution is downstream or indirect, when a substitute replaces a buyer industry's product. For example, lawn-care products and services are threatened when multifamily homes in urban areas substitute for single-family homes in the suburbs. Software sold to agents is threatened when airline and travel websites substitute for travel agents.

Substitutes are always present, but they are easy to overlook because they may appear to be very different from the industry's product: To someone searching for a Father's Day gift, neckties and power tools may be substitutes. It is a substitute to do without, to purchase a used product rather than a new one, or to do it yourself (bring the service or product in-house).

When the threat of substitutes is high, industry profitability suffers. Substitute products or services limit an industry's profit potential by placing a ceiling on prices. If an industry does not distance itself from substitutes through product performance, marketing, or other means, it will suffer in terms of profitability—and often growth potential.

Substitutes not only limit profits in normal times, they also reduce the bonanza an industry can reap in good times. In emerging economies, for example, the surge in demand for wired telephone lines has been capped as many consumers opt to make a mobile telephone their first and only phone line.

The threat of a substitute is high if:

- It offers an attractive price-performance trade-off to the industry's product. The better the relative value of the substitute, the tighter is the lid on an industry's profit potential. For example, conventional providers of long-distance telephone service have suffered from the advent of inexpensive internet-based phone services such as Vonage and Skype. Similarly, video rental outlets are struggling with the emergence of cable and satellite video-on-demand services, online video rental services such as Netflix, and the rise of internet video sites like Google's YouTube.

- The buyer's cost of switching to the substitute is low. Switching from a proprietary, branded drug to a generic drug usually involves minimal costs, for example, which is why the shift to generics (and the fall in prices) is so substantial and rapid.

Strategists should be particularly alert to changes in other industries that may make them attractive substitutes when they were not before. Improvements in plastic materials, for example, allowed them to substitute for steel in many automobile components. In this way, technological changes or competitive discontinuities in seemingly unrelated businesses can have major impacts on industry profitability. Of course the substitution threat can also shift in favor of an industry, which bodes well for its future profitability and growth potential.

Rivalry among existing competitors

Rivalry among existing competitors takes many familiar forms, including price discounting, new product introductions, advertising campaigns, and service improvements. High rivalry limits the profitability of an industry. The degree to which rivalry drives down an industry's profit potential depends, first, on the *intensity* with which companies compete and, second, on the *basis* on which they compete.

The intensity of rivalry is greatest if:

- Competitors are numerous or are roughly equal in size and power. In such situations, rivals find it hard to avoid poaching business. Without an industry leader, practices desirable for the industry as a whole go unenforced.

- Industry growth is slow. Slow growth precipitates fights for market share.

- Exit barriers are high. Exit barriers, the flip side of entry barriers, arise because of such things as highly specialized assets or management's devotion to a particular business. These barriers keep companies in the market even though they may be earning low or negative returns. Excess capacity remains in use, and the profitability of healthy competitors suffers as the sick ones hang on.

- Rivals are highly committed to the business and have aspirations for leadership, especially if they have goals that go beyond economic performance in the particular industry. High commitment to a business arises for a variety of reasons. For example, state-owned competitors may have goals that include employment or prestige. Units of larger companies may participate in an industry for image reasons or to offer a full line. Clashes of personality and ego have sometimes exaggerated rivalry to the detriment of profitability in fields such as the media and high technology.

- Firms cannot read each other's signals well because of lack of familiarity with one another, diverse approaches to competing, or differing goals.

The strength of rivalry reflects not just the intensity of competition but also the basis of competition. The *dimensions* on which competition takes place, and whether rivals converge to compete on the *same dimensions,* have a major influence on profitability.

Rivalry is especially destructive to profitability if it gravitates solely to price because price competition transfers profits directly from an industry to its customers. Price cuts are usually easy for competitors to see and match, making successive rounds of retaliation likely. Sustained price competition also trains customers to pay less attention to product features and service.

Price competition is most liable to occur if:

- Products or services of rivals are nearly identical and there are few switching costs for buyers. This encourages competitors to cut prices to win new customers. Years of airline price wars reflect these circumstances in that industry.

- Fixed costs are high and marginal costs are low. This creates intense pressure for competitors to cut prices below their average costs, even close to their marginal costs, to steal incremental customers while still making some contribution to covering fixed costs. Many basic-materials businesses, such as paper and aluminum, suffer from this problem, especially if demand is not growing. So do delivery companies with fixed networks of routes that must be served regardless of volume.

- Capacity must be expanded in large increments to be efficient. The need for large capacity expansions, as in the polyvinyl chloride business, disrupts the industry's supply-demand balance and often leads to long and recurring periods of overcapacity and price cutting.

- The product is perishable. Perishability creates a strong temptation to cut prices and sell a product while it still has value. More products and services are perishable than is commonly thought. Just as tomatoes are perishable because they rot, models of computers are perishable because they soon become obsolete, and information may be perishable if it diffuses rapidly or becomes outdated, thereby losing its value.

Services such as hotel accommodations are perishable in the sense that unused capacity can never be recovered.

Competition on dimensions other than price—on product features, support services, delivery time, or brand image, for instance— is less likely to erode profitability because it improves customer value and can support higher prices. Also, rivalry focused on such dimensions can improve value relative to substitutes or raise the barriers facing new entrants. While nonprice rivalry sometimes escalates to levels that undermine industry profitability, this is less likely to occur than it is with price rivalry.

As important as the dimensions of rivalry is whether rivals compete on the *same* dimensions. When all or many competitors aim to meet the same needs or compete on the same attributes, the result is zero-sum competition. Here, one firm's gain is often another's loss, driving down profitability. While price competition runs a stronger risk than nonprice competition of becoming zero sum, this may not happen if companies take care to segment their markets, targeting their low-price offerings to different customers.

Rivalry can be positive sum, or actually increase the average profitability of an industry, when each competitor aims to serve the needs of different customer segments, with different mixes of price, products, services, features, or brand identities. Such competition can not only support higher average profitability but also expand the industry, as the needs of more customer groups are better met. The opportunity for positive-sum competition will be greater in industries serving diverse customer groups. With a clear understanding of the structural underpinnings of rivalry, strategists can sometimes take steps to shift the nature of competition in a more positive direction.

Factors, Not Forces

Industry structure, as manifested in the strength of the five competitive forces, determines the industry's long-run profit potential because it determines how the economic value created by the industry is divided—how much is retained by companies in the industry versus bargained away by customers and suppliers, limited by substitutes, or constrained by potential new entrants. By considering all five forces, a strategist keeps overall structure in mind instead of gravitating to any one element. In addition, the strategist's attention remains focused on structural conditions rather than on fleeting factors.

It is especially important to avoid the common pitfall of mistaking certain visible attributes of an industry for its underlying structure. Consider the following:

Industry growth rate

A common mistake is to assume that fast-growing industries are always attractive. Growth does tend to mute rivalry, because an expanding pie offers opportunities for all competitors. But fast growth can put suppliers in a powerful position, and high growth with low entry barriers will draw in entrants. Even without new entrants, a high growth rate will not guarantee profitability if customers are powerful or substitutes are attractive. Indeed, some fast-growth businesses, such as personal computers, have been among the least profitable industries in recent years. A narrow focus on growth is one of the major causes of bad strategy decisions.

Technology and innovation

Advanced technology or innovations are not by themselves enough to make an industry structurally attractive (or unattractive). Mundane, low-technology industries with price-insensitive buyers, high switching costs, or high entry barriers arising from scale economies are often far more profitable than sexy industries, such as software and internet technologies, that attract competitors.[2]

Government

Government is not best understood as a sixth force because government involvement is neither inherently good nor bad for industry profitability. The best way to understand the influence of government on competition is to analyze how specific government policies affect the five competitive forces. For instance, patents raise barriers to entry, boosting industry profit potential. Conversely, government policies favoring unions may raise supplier power and diminish profit potential. Bankruptcy rules that allow failing companies to reorganize rather than exit can lead to excess capacity and intense rivalry. Government operates at multiple levels and through many different policies, each of which will affect structure in different ways.

Complementary products and services

Complements are products or services used together with an industry's product. Complements arise when the customer benefit of two products combined is greater than the sum of each product's value in isolation. Computer hardware and software, for instance, are valuable together and worthless when separated.

In recent years, strategy researchers have highlighted the role of complements, especially in high-technology industries where they are most obvious.[3] By no means, however, do complements appear only there. The value of a car, for example, is greater when the driver also has access to gasoline stations, roadside assistance, and auto insurance.

Complements can be important when they affect the overall demand for an industry's product. However, like government policy, complements are not a sixth force determining industry profitability since the presence of strong complements is not necessarily bad (or good) for industry profitability. Complements affect profitability through the way they influence the five forces.

The strategist must trace the positive or negative influence of complements on all five forces to ascertain their impact on profitability. The presence of complements can raise or lower barriers to entry. In application software, for example, barriers to entry were lowered when producers of complementary operating system software, notably Microsoft, provided tool sets making it easier to write applications. Conversely, the need to attract producers of complements can raise barriers to entry, as it does in video game hardware.

The presence of complements can also affect the threat of substitutes. For instance, the need for appropriate fueling stations makes it difficult for cars using alternative fuels to substitute for conventional vehicles. But complements can also make substitution easier.

For example, Apple's iTunes hastened the substitution from CDs to digital music.

Complements can factor into industry rivalry either positively (as when they raise switching costs) or negatively (as when they neutralize product differentiation). Similar analyses can be done for buyer and supplier power. Sometimes companies compete by altering conditions in complementary industries in their favor, such as when videocassette-recorder producer JVC persuaded movie studios to favor its standard in issuing prerecorded tapes even though rival Sony's standard was probably superior from a technical standpoint.

Identifying complements is part of the analyst's work. As with government policies or important technologies, the strategic significance of complements will be best understood through the lens of the five forces.

Changes in Industry Structure

So far, we have discussed the competitive forces at a single point in time. Industry structure proves to be relatively stable, and industry profitability differences are remarkably persistent over time in practice. However, industry structure is constantly undergoing modest adjustment—and occasionally it can change abruptly.

Shifts in structure may emanate from outside an industry or from within. They can boost the industry's profit potential or reduce it. They may be caused by changes in technology, changes in customer needs, or other events. The five competitive forces provide a framework for identifying the most important industry developments and for anticipating their impact on industry attractiveness.

Shifting threat of new entry

Changes to any of the seven barriers described above can raise or lower the threat of new entry. The expiration of a patent, for instance, may unleash new entrants. On the day that Merck's patents for the cholesterol reducer Zocor expired, three pharmaceutical makers entered the market for the drug. Conversely, the proliferation of products in the ice cream industry has gradually filled up the limited freezer space in grocery stores, making it harder for new ice cream makers to gain access to distribution in North America and Europe.

Strategic decisions of leading competitors often have a major impact on the threat of entry. Starting in the 1970s, for example, retailers such as Wal-Mart, Kmart, and Toys "R" Us began to adopt new procurement, distribution, and inventory control technologies with large fixed costs, including automated distribution centers, bar coding, and point-of-sale terminals. These investments increased the economies of scale and made it more difficult for small retailers to enter the business (and for existing small players to survive).

Changing supplier or buyer power

As the factors underlying the power of suppliers and buyers change with time, their clout rises or declines. In the global appliance industry, for instance, competitors including Electrolux, General Electric, and Whirlpool have been squeezed by the consolidation of retail channels (the decline of appliance specialty stores, for instance, and the rise of big-box retailers like Best Buy and Home Depot in the United States). Another example is travel agents, who depend on airlines as a key supplier. When the internet allowed airlines to sell tickets directly to customers, this significantly increased their power to bargain down agents' commissions.

Shifting threat of substitution

The most common reason substitutes become more or less threatening over time is that advances in technology create new substitutes or shift price-performance comparisons in one direction or the other. The earliest microwave ovens, for example, were large and priced above $2,000, making them poor substitutes for conventional ovens. With technological advances, they became serious substitutes. Flash computer memory has improved enough recently to become a meaningful substitute for low-capacity hard-disk drives.

Trends in the availability or performance of complementary producers also shift the threat of substitutes.

New bases of rivalry

Rivalry often intensifies naturally over time. As an industry matures, growth slows. Competitors become more alike as industry conventions emerge, technology diffuses, and consumer tastes converge. Industry profitability falls, and weaker competitors are driven from the business. This story has played out in industry after industry; televisions, snowmobiles, and telecommunications equipment are just a few examples.

A trend toward intensifying price competition and other forms of rivalry, however, is by no means inevitable. For example, there has been enormous competitive activity in the U.S. casino industry in recent decades, but most of it has been positive-sum competition directed toward new niches and geographic segments (such as riverboats, trophy properties, Native American reservations, international expansion, and novel customer groups like families). Head-to-head rivalry that lowers prices or boosts the payouts to winners has been limited.

The nature of rivalry in an industry is altered by mergers and acquisitions that introduce new capabilities and ways of competing. Or, technological innovation can reshape rivalry. In the retail brokerage industry, the advent of the internet lowered marginal costs and reduced differentiation, triggering far more intense competition on commissions and fees than in the past.

In some industries, companies turn to mergers and consolidation not to improve cost and quality but to attempt to stop intense competition. Eliminating rivals is a risky strategy, however. The five competitive forces tell us that a profit windfall from removing today's competitors often attracts new competitors and backlash from customers and suppliers. In New York banking, for example, the 1980s and 1990s saw escalating consolidations of commercial and savings banks, including Manufacturers Hanover, Chemical, Chase, and Dime Savings. But today the retail-banking landscape of

Manhattan is as diverse as ever, as new entrants such as Wachovia, Bank of America, and Washington Mutual have entered the market.

Implications for Strategy

Understanding the forces that shape industry competition is the starting point for developing strategy. Every company should already know what the average profitability of its industry is and how that has been changing over time. The five forces reveal *why* industry profitability is what it is. Only then can a company incorporate industry conditions into strategy.

The forces reveal the most significant aspects of the competitive environment. They also provide a baseline for sizing up a company's strengths and weaknesses: Where does the company stand versus buyers, suppliers, entrants, rivals, and substitutes? Most importantly, an understanding of industry structure guides managers toward fruitful possibilities for strategic action, which may include any or all of the following: positioning the company to better cope with the current competitive forces; anticipating and exploiting shifts in the forces; and shaping the balance of forces to create a new industry structure that is more favorable to the company. The best strategies exploit more than one of these possibilities.

Positioning the company

Strategy can be viewed as building defenses against the competitive forces or finding a position in the industry where the forces are weakest. Consider, for instance, the position of Paccar in the market for heavy trucks. The heavy-truck industry is structurally challenging. Many buyers operate large fleets or are large leasing companies, with both the leverage and the motivation to drive down the price of one of their largest purchases. Most trucks are built to regulated standards and offer similar features, so price competition is rampant. Capital intensity causes rivalry to be fierce, especially during the recurring cyclical downturns. Unions exercise considerable supplier power. Though there are few direct substitutes for an

18-wheeler, truck buyers face important substitutes for their services, such as cargo delivery by rail.

In this setting, Paccar, a Bellevue, Washington–based company with about 20% of the North American heavy-truck market, has chosen to focus on one group of customers: owner-operators—drivers who own their trucks and contract directly with shippers or serve as subcontractors to larger trucking companies. Such small operators have limited clout as truck buyers. They are also less price sensitive because of their strong emotional ties to and economic dependence on the product. They take great pride in their trucks, in which they spend most of their time.

Paccar has invested heavily to develop an array of features with owner-operators in mind: luxurious sleeper cabins, plush leather seats, noise-insulated cabins, sleek exterior styling, and so on. At the company's extensive network of dealers, prospective buyers use software to select among thousands of options to put their personal signature on their trucks. These customized trucks are built to order, not to stock, and delivered in six to eight weeks. Paccar's trucks also have aerodynamic designs that reduce fuel consumption, and they maintain their resale value better than other trucks. Paccar's roadside assistance program and IT-supported system for distributing spare parts reduce the time a truck is out of service. All these are crucial considerations for an owner-operator. Customers pay Paccar a 10% premium, and its Kenworth and Peterbilt brands are considered status symbols at truck stops.

Paccar illustrates the principles of positioning a company within a given industry structure. The firm has found a portion of its industry where the competitive forces are weaker—where it can avoid buyer power and price-based rivalry. And it has tailored every single part of the value chain to cope well with the forces in its segment. As a result, Paccar has been profitable for 68 years straight and has earned a long-run return on equity above 20%.

In addition to revealing positioning opportunities within an existing industry, the five forces framework allows companies to rigorously analyze entry and exit. Both depend on answering the difficult question: "What is the potential of this business?" Exit is indicated when industry structure is poor or declining and the company has no prospect of a superior positioning. In considering entry into a new industry, creative strategists can use the framework to spot an industry with a good future before this good future is reflected in the prices of acquisition candidates. Five forces analysis may also reveal industries that are not necessarily attractive for the average entrant but in which a company has good reason to believe it can surmount entry barriers at lower cost than most firms or has a unique ability to cope with the industry's competitive forces.

Exploiting industry change

Industry changes bring the opportunity to spot and claim promising new strategic positions if the strategist has a sophisticated understanding of the competitive forces and their underpinnings. Consider, for instance, the evolution of the music industry during the past decade. With the advent of the internet and the digital distribution of music, some analysts predicted the birth of thousands of music labels (that is, record companies that develop artists and bring their music to market). This, the analysts argued, would break a pattern that had held since Edison invented the phonograph: Between three and six major record companies had always dominated the industry. The internet would, they predicted, remove distribution as a barrier to entry, unleashing a flood of new players into the music industry.

A careful analysis, however, would have revealed that physical distribution was not the crucial barrier to entry. Rather, entry was barred by other benefits that large music labels enjoyed. Large labels could pool the risks of developing new artists over many bets, cushioning the impact of inevitable failures. Even more important, they had advantages in breaking through the clutter and getting their new artists heard. To do so, they could promise radio stations and record stores access to well-known artists in exchange for promotion of new artists. New labels would find this nearly impossible to match. The major labels stayed the course, and new music labels have been rare.

This is not to say that the music industry is structurally unchanged by digital distribution. Unauthorized downloading created an illegal but potent substitute. The labels tried for years to develop technical platforms for digital distribution themselves, but major companies hesitated to sell their music through a platform owned by a rival. Into this vacuum stepped Apple with its iTunes music store, launched in 2003 to support its iPod music player. By permitting the creation of a powerful new gatekeeper, the major labels allowed industry structure to shift against them. The number of major record companies has actually declined—from six in 1997 to four today—as companies struggled to cope with the digital phenomenon.

When industry structure is in flux, new and promising competitive positions may appear. Structural changes open up new needs and new ways to serve existing needs. Established leaders may overlook these or be constrained by past strategies from pursuing them. Smaller competitors in the industry can capitalize on such changes, or the void may well be filled by new entrants.

Shaping industry structure

When a company exploits structural change, it is recognizing, and reacting to, the inevitable. However, companies also have the ability to shape industry structure. A firm can lead its industry toward new ways of competing that alter the five forces for the better. In reshaping structure, a company wants its competitors to follow so that the entire industry will be transformed. While many industry participants may benefit in the process, the innovator can benefit most if it can shift competition in directions where it can excel.

An industry's structure can be reshaped in two ways: by redividing profitability in favor of incumbents or by expanding the overall profit pool. Redividing the industry pie aims to increase the share of profits to industry competitors instead of to suppliers, buyers, substitutes, and keeping out potential entrants. Expanding the profit pool involves increasing the overall pool of economic value generated by the industry in which rivals, buyers, and suppliers can all share.

Redividing profitability. To capture more profits for industry rivals, the starting point is to determine which force or forces are currently constraining industry profitability and address them.

A company can potentially influence all of the competitive forces. The strategist's goal here is to reduce the share of profits that leak to suppliers, buyers, and substitutes or are sacrificed to deter entrants.

To neutralize supplier power, for example, a firm can standardize specifications for parts to make it easier to switch among suppliers. It can cultivate additional vendors, or alter technology to avoid a powerful supplier group altogether. To counter customer power, companies may expand services that raise buyers' switching costs or find alternative means of reaching customers to neutralize powerful channels. To temper profit-eroding price rivalry, companies can invest more heavily in unique products, as pharmaceutical firms have done, or expand support services to customers. To scare off entrants, incumbents can elevate the fixed cost of competing—for instance, by escalating their R&D or marketing expenditures. To limit the threat of substitutes, companies can offer better value through new features or wider product accessibility. When soft-drink producers introduced vending machines and convenience store channels, for example, they dramatically improved the availability of soft drinks relative to other beverages.

Sysco, the largest food-service distributor in North America, offers a revealing example of how an industry leader can change the structure of an industry for the better. Food-service distributors purchase food and related items from farmers and food processors. They then warehouse and deliver these items to restaurants, hospitals, employer cafeterias, schools, and other food-service institutions. Given low barriers to entry, the food-service distribution industry has historically been highly fragmented, with numerous local competitors. While rivals try to cultivate customer relationships, buyers are price sensitive because food represents a large share of their costs. Buyers can also choose the substitute approaches of purchasing directly from manufacturers or using retail sources, avoiding distributors altogether. Suppliers wield bargaining power: They are often large companies with strong brand names that food preparers and consumers recognize. Average profitability in the industry has been modest.

Defining the Relevant Industry

DEFINING THE INDUSTRY IN WHICH competition actually takes place is important for good industry analysis, not to mention for developing strategy and setting business unit boundaries. Many strategy errors emanate from mistaking the relevant industry, defining it too broadly or too narrowly. Defining the industry too broadly obscures differences among products, customers, or geographic regions that are important to competition, strategic positioning, and profitability. Defining the industry too narrowly overlooks commonalities and linkages across related products or geographic markets that are crucial to competitive advantage. Also, strategists must be sensitive to the possibility that industry boundaries can shift.

The boundaries of an industry consist of two primary dimensions. First is the *scope of products or services.* For example, is motor oil used in cars part of the same industry as motor oil used in heavy trucks and stationary engines, or are these different industries? The second dimension is *geographic scope.* Most industries are present in many parts of the world. However, is competition contained within each state, or is it national? Does competition take place within regions such as Europe or North America, or is there a single global industry?

The five forces are the basic tool to resolve these questions. If industry structure for two products is the same or very similar (that is, if they have the same buyers, suppliers, barriers to entry, and so forth), then the products are best treated as being part of the same industry. If industry structure differs markedly, however, the two products may be best understood as separate industries.

In lubricants, the oil used in cars is similar or even identical to the oil used in trucks, but the similarity largely ends there. Automotive motor oil is sold to fragmented, generally unsophisticated customers through numerous and often powerful channels, using extensive advertising. Products are packaged

Sysco recognized that, given its size and national reach, it might change this state of affairs. It led the move to introduce private-label distributor brands with specifications tailored to the food-service market, moderating supplier power. Sysco emphasized value-added services to buyers such as credit, menu planning, and inventory management to shift the basis of competition away from just price. These moves, together with stepped-up investments in information technology and regional distribution centers, substantially raised in small containers and logistical costs are high, necessitating local production. Truck and power generation lubricants are sold to entirely different buyers in entirely different ways using a separate supply chain. Industry structure (buyer power, barriers to entry, and so forth) is substantially different. Automotive oil is thus a distinct industry from oil for truck and stationary engine uses. Industry profitability will differ in these two cases, and a lubricant company will need a separate strategy for competing in each area.

Differences in the five competitive forces also reveal the geographic scope of competition. If an industry has a similar structure in every country (rivals, buyers, and so on), the presumption is that competition is global, and the five forces analyzed from a global perspective will set average profitability. A single global strategy is needed. If an industry has quite different structures in different geographic regions, however, each region may well be a distinct industry. Otherwise, competition would have leveled the differences. The five forces analyzed for each region will set profitability there.

The extent of differences in the five forces for related products or across geographic areas is a matter of degree, making industry definition often a matter of judgment. A rule of thumb is that where the differences in any one force are large, and where the differences involve more than one force, distinct industries may well be present.

Fortunately, however, even if industry boundaries are drawn incorrectly, careful five forces analysis should reveal important competitive threats. A closely related product omitted from the industry definition will show up as a substitute, for example, or competitors overlooked as rivals will be recognized as potential entrants. At the same time, the five forces analysis should reveal major differences within overly broad industries that will indicate the need to adjust industry boundaries or strategies.

the bar for new entrants while making the substitutes less attractive. Not surprisingly, the industry has been consolidating, and industry profitability appears to be rising.

Industry leaders have a special responsibility for improving industry structure. Doing so often requires resources that only large players possess. Moreover, an improved industry structure is a public good because it benefits every firm in the industry, not just the company that initiated the improvement. Often, it is more in the

Typical Steps in Industry Analysis

Define the relevant industry:

- What products are in it? Which ones are part of another distinct industry?
- What is the geographic scope of competition?

Identify the participants and segment them into groups, if appropriate:

Who are

- the buyers and buyer groups?
- the suppliers and supplier groups?
- the competitors?
- the substitutes?
- the potential entrants?

Assess the underlying drivers of each competitive force to determine which forces are strong and which are weak and why.

Determine overall industry structure, and test the analysis for consistency:

- *Why* is the level of profitability what it is?
- Which are the *controlling* forces for profitability?
- Is the industry analysis consistent with actual long-run profitability?
- Are more-profitable players better positioned in relation to the five forces?

Analyze recent and likely future changes in each force, both positive and negative.

Identify aspects of industry structure that might be influenced by competitors, by new entrants, or by your company.

---

interests of an industry leader than any other participant to invest for the common good because leaders will usually benefit the most. Indeed, improving the industry may be a leader's most profitable strategic opportunity, in part because attempts to gain further market share can trigger strong reactions from rivals, customers, and even suppliers.

There is a dark side to shaping industry structure that is equally important to understand. Ill-advised changes in competitive positioning and operating practices can *undermine* industry structure. Faced with pressures to gain market share or enamored with innovation for its own sake, managers may trigger new kinds of competition that no incumbent can win. When taking actions to improve their own company's competitive advantage, then, strategists should ask whether they are setting in motion dynamics that will undermine industry structure in the long run. In the early days of the personal computer industry, for instance, IBM tried to make up for its late entry by offering an open architecture that would set industry standards and attract complementary makers of application software and peripherals. In the process, it ceded ownership of the critical components of the PC—the operating system and the microprocessor—to Microsoft and Intel. By standardizing PCs, it encouraged price-based rivalry and shifted power to suppliers. Consequently, IBM became the temporarily dominant firm in an industry with an enduringly unattractive structure.

Expanding the profit pool. When overall demand grows, the industry's quality level rises, intrinsic costs are reduced, or waste is eliminated, the pie expands. The total pool of value available to competitors, suppliers, and buyers grows. The total profit pool expands, for example, when channels become more competitive or when an industry discovers latent buyers for its product that are not currently being served. When soft-drink producers rationalized their independent bottler networks to make them more efficient and effective, both the soft-drink companies and the bottlers benefited. Overall value can also expand when firms work collaboratively with suppliers to improve coordination and limit unnecessary costs incurred in the supply chain. This lowers the inherent cost structure of the industry, allowing higher profit, greater demand through lower prices, or both. Or, agreeing on quality standards can bring up industrywide quality and service levels, and hence prices, benefiting rivals, suppliers, and customers.

Expanding the overall profit pool creates win-win opportunities for multiple industry participants. It can also reduce the risk of destructive rivalry that arises when incumbents attempt to shift bargaining power or capture more market share. However, expanding the pie does not reduce the importance of industry structure. How the expanded pie is divided will ultimately be determined by the five forces. The most successful companies are those that expand the industry profit pool in ways that allow them to share disproportionately in the benefits.

Defining the industry

The five competitive forces also hold the key to defining the relevant industry (or industries) in which a company competes. Drawing industry boundaries correctly, around the arena in which competition actually takes place, will clarify the causes of profitability and the appropriate unit for setting strategy. A company needs a separate strategy for each distinct industry. Mistakes in industry definition made by competitors present opportunities for staking out superior strategic positions. (See the sidebar "Defining the Relevant Industry.")

Competition and Value

The competitive forces reveal the drivers of industry competition. A company strategist who understands that competition extends well beyond existing rivals will detect wider competitive threats and be better equipped to address them. At the same time, thinking comprehensively about an industry's structure can uncover opportunities: differences in customers, suppliers, substitutes, potential entrants, and rivals that can become the basis for distinct strategies yielding superior performance. In a world of more open competition and relentless change, it is more important than ever to think structurally about competition.

Understanding industry structure is equally important for investors as for managers. The five competitive forces reveal whether

Common Pitfalls

In conducting the analysis avoid the following common mistakes:

- Defining the industry too broadly or too narrowly.
- Making lists instead of engaging in rigorous analysis.
- Paying equal attention to all of the forces rather than digging deeply into the most important ones.
- Confusing effect (price sensitivity) with cause (buyer economics).
- Using static analysis that ignores industry trends.
- Confusing cyclical or transient changes with true structural changes.
- Using the framework to declare an industry attractive or unattractive rather than using it to guide strategic choices.

an industry is truly attractive, and they help investors anticipate positive or negative shifts in industry structure before they are obvious. The five forces distinguish short-term blips from structural changes and allow investors to take advantage of undue pessimism or optimism. Those companies whose strategies have industry-transforming potential become far clearer. This deeper thinking about competition is a more powerful way to achieve genuine investment success than the financial projections and trend extrapolation that dominate today's investment analysis.

If both executives and investors looked at competition this way, capital markets would be a far more effective force for company success and economic prosperity. Executives and investors would both be focused on the same fundamentals that drive sustained profitability. The conversation between investors and executives would focus on the structural, not the transient. Imagine the improvement in company performance—and in the economy as a whole—if all the energy expended in "pleasing the Street" were redirected toward the factors that create true economic value.

Originally published in January 2008. Reprint R0801E.

Notes

1. For a discussion of the value chain framework, see Michael E. Porter, *Competitive Advantage: Creating and Sustaining Superior Performance* (The Free Press, 1998).

2. For a discussion of how internet technology improves the attractiveness of some industries while eroding the profitability of others, see Michael E. Porter, "Strategy and the Internet" (HBR, March 2001).

3. See, for instance, Adam M. Brandenburger and Barry J. Nalebuff, *Co-opetition* (Currency Doubleday, 1996).

Building Your Company's Vision

by James C. Collins and Jerry I. Porras

We shall not cease from exploration/And the end of all our exploring/Will be to arrive where we started/And know the place for the first time.
—T.S. Eliot, *Four Quartets*

COMPANIES THAT ENJOY ENDURING success have core values and a core purpose that remain fixed while their business strategies and practices endlessly adapt to a changing world. The dynamic of preserving the core while stimulating progress is the reason that companies such as Hewlett-Packard, 3M, Johnson & Johnson, Procter & Gamble, Merck, Sony, Motorola, and Nordstrom became elite institutions able to renew themselves and achieve superior long-term performance. Hewlett-Packard employees have long known that radical change in operating practices, cultural norms, and business strategies does not mean losing the spirit of the HP Way—the company's core principles. Johnson & Johnson continually questions its structure and revamps its processes while preserving the ideals embodied in its credo. In 1996, 3M sold off several of its large mature businesses—a dramatic move that surprised the business press—to refocus on its enduring core purpose of solving unsolved problems innovatively. We studied companies such as these in our research for *Built to Last: Successful Habits of Visionary Companies* and found that they have outperformed the general stock market by a factor of 12 since 1925.

Truly great companies understand the difference between what should never change and what should be open for change, between what is genuinely sacred and what is not. This rare ability to manage continuity and change—requiring a consciously practiced discipline—is closely linked to the ability to develop a vision. Vision provides guidance about what core to preserve and what future to stimulate progress toward. But *vision* has become one of the most overused and least understood words in the language, conjuring up different images for different people: of deeply held values, outstanding achievement, societal bonds, exhilarating goals, motivating forces, or raisons d'être. We recommend a conceptual framework to define vision, add clarity and rigor to the vague and fuzzy concepts swirling around that trendy term, and give practical guidance for articulating a coherent vision within an organization. It is a prescriptive framework rooted in six years of research and refined and tested by our ongoing work with executives from a great variety of organizations around the world.

A well-conceived vision consists of two major components: *core ideology* and *envisioned future*. (See the exhibit "Articulating a vision.") Core ideology, the yin in our scheme, defines what we stand for and why we exist. Yin is unchanging and complements yang, the envisioned future. The envisioned future is what we aspire to become, to achieve, to create—something that will require significant change and progress to attain.

Core Ideology

Core ideology defines the enduring character of an organization—a consistent identity that transcends product or market life cycles, technological breakthroughs, management fads, and individual leaders. In fact, the most lasting and significant contribution of those who build visionary companies is the core ideology. As Bill Hewlett said about his longtime friend and business partner David Packard upon Packard's death not long ago, "As far as the company is concerned, the greatest thing he left behind him was a code of ethics known as the HP Way." HP's core ideology, which has guided the company since its inception more than 50 years ago, includes a deep respect for the individual, a dedication to affordable quality and reliability, a commitment to community responsibility (Packard

Idea in Brief

Hewlett-Packard. 3M. Sony. Companies with exceptionally durable visions that are "built to last." What distinguishes their visions from most others, those empty muddles that get revised with every passing business fad, but never prompt anything more than a yawn? Enduring companies have clear plans for how they will advance into an uncertain future. But they are equally clear about how they will remain steadfast, about the values and purposes they will always stand for. This *Harvard Business Review* article describes the two components of any lasting vision: **core ideology** and an **envisioned future.**

himself bequeathed his $4.3 billion of Hewlett-Packard stock to a charitable foundation), and a view that the company exists to make technical contributions for the advancement and welfare of humanity. Company builders such as David Packard, Masaru Ibuka of Sony, George Merck of Merck, William McKnight of 3M, and Paul Galvin of Motorola understood that it is more important to know who you are than where you are going, for where you are going will change as the world around you changes. Leaders die, products become obsolete, markets change, new technologies emerge, and management fads come and go, but core ideology in a great company endures as a source of guidance and inspiration.

Core ideology provides the glue that holds an organization together as it grows, decentralizes, diversifies, expands globally, and develops workplace diversity. Think of it as analogous to the principles of Judaism that held the Jewish people together for centuries without a homeland, even as they spread throughout the Diaspora. Or think of the truths held to be self-evident in the Declaration of Independence, or the enduring ideals and principles of the scientific community that bond scientists from every nationality together in the common purpose of advancing human knowledge. Any effective vision must embody the core ideology of the organization, which in turn consists of two distinct parts: core values, a system of guiding principles and tenets; and core purpose, the organization's most fundamental reason for existence.

Q3

Idea in Practice

A company's practices and strategies should change continually; its core ideology should not. Core ideology defines a company's timeless character. It's the glue that holds the enterprise together even when everything else is up for grabs. Core ideology is something you *discover*—by looking inside. It's not something you can invent, much less fake.

A core ideology has two parts:

1. **Core values are the handful of guiding principles by which a company navigates.** They require no external justification. For example, Disney's core values of imagination and wholesomeness stem from the founder's belief that these should be nurtured for their own sake, not merely to capitalize on a business opportunity. Instead of changing its core values, a great company will change its markets—seek out different customers—in order to remain true to its core values.

2. **Core purpose is an organization's most fundamental reason for being.** It should not be confused with the company's current product lines or customer segments. Rather, it reflects people's idealistic motivations for doing the company's work. Disney's core purpose is to make people happy—not to build theme parks and make cartoons.

An envisioned future, the second component of an effective vision, has two elements:

1. **Big, Hairy, Audacious Goals (BHAGs) are ambitious plans that rev up the entire organization.** They typically require 10 to 30 years' work to complete.

2. **Vivid descriptions paint a picture of what it will be like to achieve the BHAGs.** They make the goals vibrant, engaging—and tangible.

Example: In the 1950s, Sony's goal was to "become the company most known for changing the worldwide poor-quality image of Japanese products." It made this BHAG vivid by adding, "Fifty years from now, our brand name will be as well known as any in the world . . . and will signify innovation and quality. . . . 'Made in Japan' will mean something fine, not something shoddy."

Don't confuse your company's core ideology with its envisioned future—in particular, don't confuse a BHAG with a core purpose. A BHAG is a clearly articulated goal that is reachable within 10 to 30 years. But your core purpose can never be completed.

Core values

Core values are the essential and enduring tenets of an organization. A small set of timeless guiding principles, core values require no external justification; they have *intrinsic* value and importance to those inside the organization. The Walt Disney Company's core values of imagination and wholesomeness stem not from market requirements but from the founder's inner belief that imagination and wholesomeness should be nurtured for their own sake. William Procter and James Gamble didn't instill in P&G's culture a focus on product excellence merely as a strategy for success but as an almost religious tenet. And that value has been passed down for more than 15 decades by P&G people. Service to the customer—even to the point of subservience—is a way of life at Nordstrom that traces its roots back to 1901, eight decades before customer service programs became stylish. For Bill Hewlett and David Packard, respect for the individual was first and foremost a deep personal value; they didn't get it from a book or hear it from a management guru. And Ralph S. Larsen, CEO of Johnson & Johnson, puts it this way: "The core values embodied in our credo might be a competitive advantage, but that is not *why* we have them. We have them because they define for us what we stand for, and we would hold them even if they became a competitive *dis*advantage in certain situations."

The point is that a great company decides for itself what values it holds to be core, largely independent of the current environment, competitive requirements, or management fads. Clearly, then, there is no universally right set of core values. A company need not have as its core value customer service (Sony doesn't) or respect for the individual (Disney doesn't) or quality (Wal-Mart Stores doesn't) or market focus (HP doesn't) or teamwork (Nordstrom doesn't). A company might have operating practices and business strategies around those qualities without having them at the essence of its being. Furthermore, great companies need not have likable or humanistic core values, although many do. The key is not *what* core values an organization has but that it has core values at all.

Companies tend to have only a few core values, usually between three and five. In fact, we found that none of the visionary companies we studied in our book had more than five: most had only three or four. (See the sidebar "Core Values Are a Company's Essential Tenets.") And, indeed, we should expect that. Only a few values can be truly *core*—that is, so fundamental and deeply held that they will change seldom, if ever.

To identify the core values of your own organization, push with relentless honesty to define what values are truly central. If you articulate more than five or six, chances are that you are confusing core values (which do not change) with operating practices, business strategies, or cultural norms (which should be open to change). Remember, the values must stand the test of time. After you've drafted a preliminary list of the core values, ask about each one, If the circumstances changed and *penalized* us for holding this core value, would we still keep it? If you can't honestly answer yes, then the value is not core and should be dropped from consideration.

A high-technology company wondered whether it should put quality on its list of core values. The CEO asked, "Suppose in ten years quality doesn't make a hoot of difference in our markets. Suppose the only thing that matters is sheer speed and horsepower but

Articulating a vision

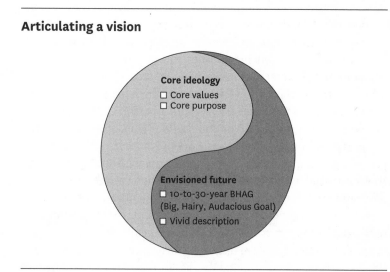

Core ideology
□ Core values
□ Core purpose

Envisioned future
□ 10-to-30-year BHAG
(Big, Hairy, Audacious Goal)
□ Vivid description

not quality. Would we still want to put quality on our list of core values?" The members of the management team looked around at one another and finally said no. Quality stayed in the *strategy* of the company, and quality-improvement programs remained in place as a mechanism for stimulating progress; but quality did not make the list of core values.

The same group of executives then wrestled with leading-edge innovation as a core value. The CEO asked, "Would we keep innovation on the list as a core value, no matter how the world around us changed?" This time, the management team gave a resounding yes. The managers' outlook might be summarized as, "We always want to do leading-edge innovation. That's who we are. It's really important to us and always will be. No matter what. And if our current markets don't value it, we will find markets that do." Leading-edge innovation went on the list and will stay there. A company should not change its core values in response to market changes; rather, it should change markets, if necessary, to remain true to its core values.

Who should be involved in articulating the core values varies with the size, age, and geographic dispersion of the company, but in many situations we have recommended what we call a *Mars Group*. It works like this: Imagine that you've been asked to re-create the very best attributes of your organization on another planet but you have seats on the rocket ship for only five to seven people. Whom should you send? Most likely, you'll choose the people who have a gut-level understanding of your core values, the highest level of credibility with their peers, and the highest levels of competence. We'll often ask people brought together to work on core values to nominate a Mars Group of five to seven individuals (not necessarily all from the assembled group). Invariably, they end up selecting highly credible representatives who do a super job of articulating the core values precisely because they are exemplars of those values—a representative slice of the company's genetic code.

Even global organizations composed of people from widely diverse cultures can identify a set of shared core values. The secret is to work from the individual to the organization. People involved in articulating the core values need to answer several questions: What

Core Values Are a Company's Essential Tenets

Merck

- Corporate social responsibility
- Unequivocal excellence in all aspects of the company
- Science-based innovation
- Honesty and integrity
- Profit, but profit from work that benefits humanity

Nordstrom

- Service to the customer above all else
- Hard work and individual productivity
- Never being satisfied
- Excellence in reputation; being part of something special

Philip Morris

- The right to freedom of choice
- Winning—beating others in a good fight
- Encouraging individual initiative
- Opportunity based on merit; no one is entitled to anything
- Hard work and continuous self-improvement

Sony

- Elevation of the Japanese culture and national status
- Being a pioneer—not following others; doing the impossible
- Encouraging individual ability and creativity

Walt Disney

- No cynicism
- Nurturing and promulgation of "wholesome American values"
- Creativity, dreams, and imagination
- Fanatical attention to consistency and detail
- Preservation and control of the Disney magic

core values do you personally bring to your work? (These should be so fundamental that you would hold them regardless of whether or not they were rewarded.) What would you tell your children are the core values that you hold at work and that you hope *they* will hold when they become working adults? If you awoke tomorrow morning with enough money to retire for the rest of your life, would you continue to live those core values? Can you envision them being as valid for you 100 years from now as they are today? Would you want to hold those core values, even if at some point one or more of them became a competitive *dis*advantage? If you werc to start a new organization tomorrow in a different line of work, what core values would you build into the new organization regardless of its industry? The last three questions are particularly important because they make the crucial distinction between enduring core values that should not change and practices and strategies that should be changing all the time.

Core purpose

Core purpose, the second part of core ideology, is the organization's reason for being. An effective purpose reflects people's idealistic motivations for doing the company's work. It doesn't just describe the organization's output or target customers; it captures the soul of the organization. (See the sidebar "Core Purpose Is a Company's Reason for Being.") Purpose, as illustrated by a speech David Packard gave to HP employees in 1960, gets at the deeper reasons for an organization's existence beyond just making money. Packard said,

> I want to discuss why a company exists in the first place. In other words, why are we here? I think many people assume, wrongly, that a company exists simply to make money. While this is an important result of a company's existence, we have to go deeper and find the real reasons for our being. As we investigate this, we inevitably come to the conclusion that a group of people get together and exist as an institution that we call a company so they are able to accomplish something collectively that they could not accomplish separately—they make a contribution

to society, a phrase which sounds trite but is fundamental . . .
You can look around [in the general business world and] see people who are interested in money and nothing else, but the underlying drives come largely from a desire to do something else:
to make a product, to give a service—generally to do something
which is of value.[1]

Purpose (which should last at least 100 years) should not be confused with specific goals or business strategies (which should
change many times in 100 years). Whereas you might achieve a goal
or complete a strategy, you cannot fulfill a purpose; it is like a guiding star on the horizon—forever pursued but never reached. Yet although purpose itself does not change, it does inspire change. The
very fact that purpose can never be fully realized means that an organization can never stop stimulating change and progress.

In identifying purpose, some companies make the mistake of
simply describing their current product lines or customer segments.
We do not consider the following statement to reflect an effective
purpose: "We exist to fulfill our government charter and participate
in the secondary mortgage market by packaging mortgages into investment securities." The statement is merely descriptive. A far
more effective statement of purpose would be that expressed by the
executives of the Federal National Mortgage Association, Fannie
Mae: "To strengthen the social fabric by continually democratizing
home ownership." The secondary mortgage market as we know it
might not even exist in 100 years, but strengthening the social fabric
by continually democratizing home ownership can be an enduring
purpose, no matter how much the world changes. Guided and in-
spired by this purpose, Fannie Mae launched in the early 1990s a series of bold initiatives, including a program to develop new systems
for reducing mortgage underwriting costs by 40% in five years; programs to eliminate discrimination in the lending process (backed by
$5 billion in underwriting experiments); and an audacious goal to
provide, by the year 2000, $1 trillion targeted at 10 million families
that had traditionally been shut out of home ownership—minorities,
immigrants, and low-income groups.

Similarly, 3M defines its purpose not in terms of adhesives and abrasives but as the perpetual quest to solve unsolved problems innovatively—a purpose that is always leading 3M into new fields. McKinsey & Company's purpose is not to do management consulting but to help corporations and governments be more successful: in 100 years, it might involve methods other than consulting. Hewlett-Packard doesn't exist to make electronic test and measurement equipment but to make technical contributions that improve people's lives—a purpose that has led the company far afield from its origins in electronic instruments. Imagine if Walt Disney had conceived of his company's purpose as to make cartoons, rather than to make people happy; we probably wouldn't have Mickey Mouse, Disneyland, EPCOT Center, or the Anaheim Mighty Ducks Hockey Team.

One powerful method for getting at purpose is the *five whys.* Start with the descriptive statement We make X products or We deliver X services, and then ask, Why is that important? five times. After a few whys, you'll find that you're getting down to the fundamental purpose of the organization.

We used this method to deepen and enrich a discussion about purpose when we worked with a certain market-research company. The executive team first met for several hours and generated the following statement of purpose for their organization: To provide the best market-research data available. We then asked the following question: Why is it important to provide the best market-research data available? After some discussion, the executives answered in a way that reflected a deeper sense of their organization's purpose: To provide the best market-research data available so that our customers will understand their markets better than they could otherwise. A further discussion let team members realize that their sense of self-worth came not just from helping customers understand their markets better but also from making a *contribution* to their customers' success. This introspection eventually led the company to identify its purpose as: To contribute to our customers' success by helping them understand their markets. With this purpose in mind, the company now frames its product decisions not with the

Core Purpose Is a Company's Reason for Being

3M: To solve unsolved problems innovatively

Cargill: To improve the standard of living around the world

Fannie Mae: To strengthen the social fabric by continually democratizing home ownership

Hewlett-Packard: To make technical contributions for the advancement and welfare of humanity

Lost Arrow Corporation: To be a role model and a tool for social change

Pacific Theatres: To provide a place for people to flourish and to enhance the community

Mary Kay Cosmetics: To give unlimited opportunity to women

McKinsey & Company: To help leading corporations and governments be more successful

Merck: To preserve and improve human life

Nike: To experience the emotion of competition, winning, and crushing competitors

Sony: To experience the joy of advancing and applying technology for the benefit of the public

Telecare Corporation: To help people with mental impairments realize their full potential

Wal-Mart: To give ordinary folk the chance to buy the same things as rich people

Walt Disney: To make people happy

---

question Will it sell? but with the question Will it make a contribution to our customers' success?

The five whys can help companies in any industry frame their work in a more meaningful way. An asphalt and gravel company might begin by saying, We make gravel and asphalt products. After a few whys, it could conclude that making asphalt and gravel is important because the quality of the infrastructure plays a vital role in people's safety and experience; because driving on a pitted road is annoying and dangerous; because 747s cannot land safely on runways built with poor workmanship or inferior concrete; because buildings with substandard materials weaken with time and crumble in earthquakes. From such introspection may emerge this purpose: To make people's lives better by improving the quality of man-made structures. With a sense of purpose very much along those lines, Granite Rock Company of Watsonville, California, won the Malcolm Baldrige National Quality Award—not an easy feat for a small rock quarry and asphalt company. And Granite Rock has gone on to be one of the most progressive and exciting companies we've encountered in *any* industry.

Notice that none of the core purposes fall into the category "maximize shareholder wealth." A primary role of core purpose is to guide and inspire. Maximizing shareholder wealth does not inspire people at all levels of an organization, and it provides precious little guidance. Maximizing shareholder wealth is the standard off-the-shelf purpose for those organizations that have not yet identified their true core purpose. It is a substitute—and a weak one at that.

When people in great organizations talk about their achievements, they say very little about earnings per share. Motorola people talk about impressive quality improvements and the effect of the products they create on the world. Hewlett-Packard people talk about their technical contributions to the marketplace. Nordstrom people talk about heroic customer service and remarkable individual performance by star salespeople. When a Boeing engineer talks about launching an exciting and revolutionary new aircraft, she does not say, "I put my heart and soul into this project because it would add 37 cents to our earnings per share."

One way to get at the purpose that lies beyond merely maximizing shareholder wealth is to play the "Random Corporate Serial Killer" game. It works like this: Suppose you could sell the company to someone who would pay a price that everyone inside and outside the company agrees is more than fair (even with a very generous set of assumptions about the expected future cash flows of the company). Suppose further that this buyer would guarantee stable employment for all employees at the same pay scale after the purchase but with no guarantee that those jobs would be in the same industry. Finally, suppose the buyer plans to kill the company after the purchase—its products or services would be discontinued, its operations would be shut down, its brand names would be shelved forever, and so on. The company would utterly and completely cease to exist. Would you accept the offer? Why or why not? What would be lost if the company ceased to exist? Why is it important that the company continue to exist? We've found this exercise to be very powerful for helping hard-nosed, financially focused executives reflect on their organization's deeper reasons for being.

Another approach is to ask each member of the Mars Group, How could we frame the purpose of this organization so that if you woke up tomorrow morning with enough money in the bank to retire, you would nevertheless keep working here? What deeper sense of purpose would motivate you to continue to dedicate your precious creative energies to this company's efforts?

As they move into the twenty-first century, companies will need to draw on the full creative energy and talent of their people. But why should people give full measure? As Peter Drucker has pointed out, the best and most dedicated people are ultimately volunteers, for they have the opportunity to do something else with their lives. Confronted with an increasingly mobile society, cynicism about corporate life, and an expanding entrepreneurial segment of the economy, companies more than ever need to have a clear understanding of their purpose in order to make work meaningful and thereby attract, motivate, and retain outstanding people.

Discovering Core Ideology

You do not create or set core ideology. You *discover* core ideology. You do not deduce it by looking at the external environment. You understand it by looking inside. Ideology has to be authentic. You cannot fake it. Discovering core ideology is not an intellectual exercise. Do not ask, What core values should we hold? Ask instead, What core values do we truly and passionately hold? You should not confuse values that you think the organization ought to have—but does not—with authentic core values. To do so would create cynicism throughout the organization. ("Who're they trying to kid? We all know that isn't a core value around here!") Aspirations are more appropriate as part of your envisioned future or as part of your strategy, not as part of the core ideology. However, authentic core values that have weakened over time can be considered a legitimate part of the core ideology—as long as you acknowledge to the organization that you must work hard to revive them.

Also be clear that the role of core ideology is to guide and inspire, not to differentiate. Two companies can have the same core values or purpose. Many companies could have the purpose to make technical contributions, but few live it as passionately as Hewlett-Packard. Many companies could have the purpose to preserve and improve human life, but few hold it as deeply as Merck. Many companies could have the core value of heroic customer service, but few create as intense a culture around that value as Nordstrom. Many companies could have the core value of innovation, but few create the powerful alignment mechanisms that stimulate the innovation we see at 3M. The authenticity, the discipline, and the consistency with which the ideology is lived—not the content of the ideology—differentiate visionary companies from the rest of the pack.

Core ideology needs to be meaningful and inspirational only to people inside the organization; it need not be exciting to outsiders. Why not? Because it is the people inside the organization who need to commit to the organizational ideology over the long term. Core ideology can also play a role in determining who *is* inside and who is not. A clear and well-articulated ideology attracts to the company people whose personal values are compatible with the company's core values; conversely, it repels those whose personal values are incompatible. You cannot impose new core values or purpose on people. Nor are core values and purpose things people can buy into. Executives often ask, How do we get people to share our core ideology? You don't. You can't. Instead, find people who are predisposed to share your core values and purpose; attract and retain those people; and let those who do not share your core values go elsewhere.

91

Indeed, the very process of articulating core ideology may cause some people to leave when they realize that they are not personally compatible with the organization's core. Welcome that outcome. It is certainly desirable to retain within the core ideology a diversity of people and viewpoints. People who share the same core values and purpose do not necessarily all think or look the same.

Don't confuse core ideology itself with core-ideology statements. A company can have a very strong core ideology without a formal statement. For example, Nike has not (to our knowledge) formally articulated a statement of its core purpose. Yet, according to our observations, Nike has a powerful core purpose that permeates the entire organization: to experience the emotion of competition, winning, and crushing competitors. Nike has a campus that seems more like a shrine to the competitive spirit than a corporate office complex. Giant photos of Nike heroes cover the walls, bronze plaques of Nike athletes hang along the Nike Walk of Fame, statues of Nike athletes stand alongside the running track that rings the campus, and buildings honor champions such as Olympic marathoner Joan Benoit, basketball superstar Michael Jordan, and tennis pro John McEnroe. Nike people who do not feel stimulated by the competitive spirit and the urge to be ferocious simply do not last long in the culture. Even the company's name reflects a sense of competition: Nike is the Greek goddess of victory. Thus, although Nike has not formally articulated its purpose, it clearly has a strong one.

Identifying core values and purpose is therefore not an exercise in wordsmithery. Indeed, an organization will generate a variety of statements over time to describe the core ideology. In Hewlett-Packard's archives, we found more than half a dozen distinct versions of the HP Way, drafted by David Packard between 1956 and 1972. All versions stated the same principles, but the words used varied depending on the era and the circumstances. Similarly, Sony's core ideology has been stated many different ways over the company's history. At its founding, Masaru Ibuka described two key elements of Sony's ideology: "We shall welcome technical difficulties and focus on highly sophisticated technical products that have great usefulness for society regardless of the quantity involved; we shall place our main emphasis on ability, performance, and personal character so that each individual can show the best in ability and skill."[2] Four decades later, this same concept appeared in a statement of core ideology called Sony Pioneer Spirit: "Sony is a pioneer and never intends to follow others. Through progress, Sony wants to serve the whole world. It shall be always a seeker of the unknown. . . . Sony has a principle of respecting and encouraging one's ability . . . and always tries to bring out the best in a person. This is the vital force of Sony."[3] Same core values, different words.

You should therefore focus on getting the content right—on capturing the essence of the core values and purpose. The point is not to create a perfect statement but to gain a deep understanding of your organization's core values and purpose, which can then be expressed in a multitude of ways. In fact, we often suggest that once the core has been identified, managers should generate their own statements of the core values and purpose to share with their groups.

Finally, don't confuse core ideology with the concept of core competence. Core competence is a strategic concept that defines your organization's capabilities—what you are particularly good at—whereas core ideology captures what you stand for and why you exist. Core competencies should be well aligned with a company's core ideology and are often rooted in it; but they are not the same thing. For example, Sony has a core competence of miniaturization—a strength that can be strategically applied to a wide array of products and markets. But it does not have a core *ideology* of miniaturization. Sony might not even have miniaturization as part of its strategy in 100 years, but to remain a great company, it will still have the same core values described in the Sony Pioneer Spirit and the same fundamental reason for being—namely, to advance technology for the benefit of the general public. In a visionary company like Sony, core competencies change over the decades, whereas core ideology does not.

Once you are clear about the core ideology, you should feel free to change absolutely *anything* that is not part of it. From then on, whenever someone says something should not change because "it's part of our culture" or "we've always done it that way" or any such excuse, mention this simple rule: If it's not core, it's up for change. The strong version of the rule is, *If it's not core, change it!* Articulating core ideology is just a starting point, however. You also must determine what type of progress you want to stimulate.

Envisioned Future

The second primary component of the vision framework is *envisioned future*. It consists of two parts: a 10-to-30-year audacious goal plus vivid descriptions of what it will be like to achieve the goal. We recognize that the phrase *envisioned future* is somewhat paradoxical. On the one hand, it conveys concreteness—something visible, vivid, and real. On the other hand, it involves a time yet unrealized—with its dreams, hopes, and aspirations.

Vision-level BHAG

We found in our research that visionary companies often use bold missions—or what we prefer to call *BHAGs* (pronounced BEE-hags and shorthand for Big, Hairy, Audacious Goals)—as a powerful way to stimulate progress. All companies have goals. But there is a difference between merely having a goal and becoming committed to a huge, daunting challenge—such as climbing Mount Everest. A true BHAG is clear and compelling, serves as a unifying focal point of effort, and acts as a catalyst for team spirit. It has a clear finish line, so the organization can know when it has achieved the goal; people like to shoot for finish lines. A BHAG engages people—it reaches out and grabs them. It is tangible, energizing, highly focused. People get it right away; it takes little or no explanation. For example, NASA's 1960s moon mission didn't need a committee of wordsmiths to spend endless hours turning the goal into a verbose, impossible-to-remember mission statement. The goal itself was so easy to grasp—so compelling in its own right—that it could be said 100 different ways yet be easily understood by everyone. Most corporate statements we've seen do little to spur forward movement because they do not contain the powerful mechanism of a BHAG.

Although organizations may have many BHAGs at different levels operating at the same time, vision requires a special type of BHAG— a vision-level BHAG that applies to the entire organization and requires 10 to 30 years of effort to complete. Setting the BHAG that far into the future requires thinking beyond the current capabilities of the organization and the current environment. Indeed, inventing such a goal forces an executive team to be visionary, rather than just strategic or tactical. A BHAG should not be a sure bet—it will have perhaps only a 50% to 70% probability of success—but the organization must believe that it can reach the goal anyway. A BHAG should require extraordinary effort and perhaps a little luck. We have helped companies create a vision-level BHAG by advising them to think in terms of four broad categories: target BHAGs, common-enemy BHAGs, role-model BHAGs, and internal-transformation BHAGs. (See the sidebar "Big, Hairy, Audacious Goals Aid Long-Term Vision.")

Vivid description

In addition to vision-level BHAGs, an envisioned future needs what we call vivid description—that is, a vibrant, engaging, and specific description of what it will be like to achieve the BHAG. Think of it as translating the vision from words into pictures, of creating an image that people can carry around in their heads. It is a question of painting a picture with your words. Picture painting is essential for making the 10-to-30-year BHAG tangible in people's minds.

For example, Henry Ford brought to life the goal of democratizing the automobile with this vivid description: "I will build a motor car for the great multitude. . . . It will be so low in price that no man making a good salary will be unable to own one and enjoy with his family the blessing of hours of pleasure in God's great open spaces. . . . When I'm through, everybody will be able to afford one, and everyone will have one. The horse will have disappeared from our highways, the automobile will be taken for granted . . . [and we will] give a large number of men employment at good wages."

The components-support division of a computer-products company had a general manager who was able to describe vividly the

Big, Hairy, Audacious Goals Aid Long-Term Vision

Target BHAGs can be quantitative or qualitative

- Become a $125 billion company by the year 2000 (Wal-Mart, 1990)

- Democratize the automobile (Ford Motor Company, early 1900s)

- Become the company most known for changing the worldwide poor-quality image of Japanese products (Sony, early 1950s)

- Become the most powerful, the most serviceable, the most far-reaching world financial institution that has ever been (City Bank, predecessor to Citicorp, 1915)

- Become the dominant player in commercial aircraft and bring the world into the jet age (Boeing, 1950)

Common-enemy BHAGs involve David-versus-Goliath thinking

- Knock off RJR as the number one tobacco company in the world (Philip Morris, 1950s)

- Crush Adidas (Nike, 1960s)

- *Yamaha wo tsubusu!* We will destroy Yamaha! (Honda, 1970s)

Role-model BHAGs suit up-and-coming organizations

- Become the Nike of the cycling industry (Giro Sport Design, 1986)

- Become as respected in 20 years as Hewlett-Packard is today (Watkins-Johnson, 1996)

- Become the Harvard of the West (Stanford University, 1940s)

Internal-transformation BHAGs suit large, established organizations

- Become number one or number two in every market we serve and revolutionize this company to have the strengths of a big company combined with the leanness and agility of a small company (General Electric Company, 1980s)

- Transform this company from a defense contractor into the best diversified high-technology company in the world (Rockwell, 1995)

- Transform this division from a poorly respected internal products supplier to one of the most respected, exciting, and sought-after divisions in the company (Components Support Division of a computer products company, 1989) goal of becoming one of the most sought-after divisions in the company: "We will be respected and admired by our peers. . . . Our solutions will be actively sought by the end-product divisions, who will achieve significant product 'hits' in the marketplace largely because of our technical contribution. . . . We will have pride in ourselves. . . . The best up-and-coming people in the company will seek to work in our division. . . . People will give unsolicited feedback that they love what they are doing. . . . [Our own] people will walk on the balls of their feet. . . . [They] will willingly work hard because they want to. . . . Both employees and customers will feel that our division has contributed to their life in a positive way."

In the 1930s, Merck had the BHAG to transform itself from a chemical manufacturer into one of the preeminent drug-making companies in the world, with a research capability to rival any major university. In describing this envisioned future, George Merck said at the opening of Merck's research facility in 1933, "We believe that research work carried on with patience and persistence will bring to industry and commerce new life; and we have faith that in this new laboratory, with the tools we have supplied, science will be advanced, knowledge increased, and human life win ever a greater freedom from suffering and disease. . . . We pledge our every aid that this enterprise shall merit the faith we have in it. Let your light so shine—that those who seek the Truth, that those who toil that this world may be a better place to live in, that those who hold aloft that torch of science and knowledge through these social and economic dark ages, shall take new courage and feel their hands supported."

Passion, emotion, and conviction are essential parts of the vivid description. Some managers are uncomfortable expressing emotion about their dreams, but that's what motivates others. Churchill understood that when he described the BHAG facing Great Britain in 1940. He did not just say, "Beat Hitler." He said, "Hitler knows he will have to break us on this island or lose the war. If we can stand up to him, all Europe may be free, and the life of the world may move forward into broad, sunlit uplands. But if we fail, the whole world, including the United States, including all we have known and cared for, will sink into the abyss of a new Dark Age, made more sinister and perhaps more protracted by the lights of perverted science. Let us therefore brace ourselves to our duties and so bear ourselves that if the British Empire and its Commonwealth last for a thousand years, men will still say, 'This was their finest hour.'"

A few key points

Don't confuse core ideology and envisioned future. In particular, don't confuse core purpose and BHAGs. Managers often exchange one for the other, mixing the two together or failing to articulate both as distinct items. Core purpose—not some specific goal—is the reason why the organization exists. A BHAG is a clearly articulated goal. Core purpose can never be completed, whereas the BHAG is reachable in 10 to 30 years. Think of the core purpose as the star on the horizon to be chased forever; the BHAG is the mountain to be climbed. Once you have reached its summit, you move on to other mountains.

Identifying core ideology is a discovery process, but setting the envisioned future is a creative process. We find that executives often have a great deal of difficulty coming up with an exciting BHAG. They want to analyze their way into the future. We have found, therefore, that some executives make more progress by starting first with the vivid description and backing from there into the BHAG. This approach involves starting with questions such as, We're sitting here in 20 years; what would we love to see? What should this company look like? What should it feel like to employees? What should it have achieved? If someone writes an article for a major business magazine about this company in 20 years, what will it say? One biotechnology company we worked with had trouble envisioning its future. Said one member of the executive team, "Every time we come up with something for the entire company, it is just too generic to be exciting—something banal like 'advance biotechnology worldwide.'" Asked to paint a picture of the company in 20 years, the executives mentioned such things as "on the cover of *Business Week* as a model success story . . . the *Fortune* most admired top-ten list . . . the best science and business graduates want to work here . . . people on airplanes rave about one of our products to seatmates . . . 20

consecutive years of profitable growth . . . an entrepreneurial culture that has spawned half a dozen new divisions from within . . . management gurus use us as an example of excellent management and progressive thinking," and so on. From this, they were able to set the goal of becoming as well respected as Merck or as Johnson & Johnson in biotechnology.

It makes no sense to analyze whether an envisioned future is the right one. With a creation—and the task is creation of a future, not prediction—there can be no right answer. Did Beethoven create the right Ninth Symphony? Did Shakespeare create the right *Hamlet*? We can't answer these questions; they're nonsense. The envisioned future involves such essential questions as Does it get our juices flowing? Do we find it stimulating? Does it spur forward momentum? Does it get people going? The envisioned future should be so exciting in its own right that it would continue to keep the organization motivated even if the leaders who set the goal disappeared. City Bank, the predecessor of Citicorp, had the BHAG "to become the most powerful, the most serviceable, the most far-reaching world financial institution that has ever been"—a goal that generated excitement through multiple generations until it was achieved. Similarly, the NASA moon mission continued to galvanize people even though President John F. Kennedy (the leader associated with setting the goal) died years before its completion.

To create an effective envisioned future requires a certain level of unreasonable confidence and commitment. Keep in mind that a BHAG is not just a goal; it is a Big, Hairy, Audacious Goal. It's not reasonable for a small regional bank to set the goal of becoming "the most powerful, the most serviceable, the most far-reaching world financial institution that has ever been," as City Bank did in 1915. It's not a tepid claim that "we will democratize the automobile," as Henry Ford said. It was almost laughable for Philip Morris—as the sixth-place player with 9% market share in the 1950s—to take on the goal of defeating Goliath RJ Reynolds Tobacco Company and becoming number one. It was hardly modest for Sony, as a small, cash-strapped venture, to proclaim the goal of changing the poor-quality image of Japanese products around the world. (See the sidebar

"Putting It All Together: Sony in the 1950s.") Of course, it's not only the audacity of the goal but also the level of commitment to the goal that counts. Boeing didn't just envision a future dominated by its commercial jets; it bet the company on the 707 and, later, on the 747. Nike's people didn't just talk about the idea of crushing Adidas; they went on a crusade to fulfill the dream. Indeed, the envisioned future should produce a bit of the "gulp factor": when it dawns on people what it will take to achieve the goal, there should be an almost audible gulp.

But what about failure to realize the envisioned future? In our research, we found that the visionary companies displayed a remarkable ability to achieve even their most audacious goals. Ford did democratize the automobile; Citicorp did become the most far-reaching bank in the world; Philip Morris did rise from sixth to first and beat RJ Reynolds worldwide; Boeing did become the dominant commercial aircraft company; and it looks like Wal-Mart will achieve its $125 billion goal, even without Sam Walton. In contrast, the comparison companies in our research frequently did not achieve their BHAGs, if they set them at all. The difference does not lie in setting easier goals: the visionary companies tended to have even more audacious ambitions. The difference does not lie in charismatic, visionary leadership: the visionary companies often achieved their BHAGs without such larger-than-life leaders at the helm. Nor does the difference lie in better strategy: the visionary companies often realized their goals more by an organic process of "let's try a lot of stuff and keep what works" than by well-laid strategic plans. Rather, their success lies in building the strength of their organization as their primary way of creating the future.

Why did Merck become the preeminent drug-maker in the world? Because Merck's architects built the best pharmaceutical research and development organization in the world. Why did Boeing become the dominant commercial aircraft company in the world? Because of its superb engineering and marketing organization, which had the ability to make projects like the 747 a reality. When asked to name the most important decisions that have contributed to the growth and success of Hewlett-Packard, David Packard answered

Putting It All Together: Sony in the 1950s

Core Ideology

Core Values

- Elevation of the Japanese culture and national status
- Being a pioneer—not following others; doing the impossible
- Encouraging individual ability and creativity

Purpose

To experience the sheer joy of innovation and the application of technology for the benefit and pleasure of the general public

Envisioned Future

BHAG

Become the company most known for changing the worldwide poor-quality image of Japanese products

Vivid Description

We will create products that become pervasive around the world. . . . We will be the first Japanese company to go into the U.S. market and distribute directly. . . . We will succeed with innovations that U.S. companies have failed at—such as the transistor radio. . . . Fifty years from now, our brand name will be as well known as any in the world . . . and will signify innovation and quality that rival the most innovative companies anywhere. . . . "Made in Japan" will mean something fine, not something shoddy.

---

entirely in terms of decisions to build the strength of the organization and its people.

Finally, in thinking about the envisioned future, beware of the We've Arrived Syndrome—a complacent lethargy that arises once an organization has achieved one BHAG and fails to replace it with another. NASA suffered from that syndrome after the successful moon landings. After you've landed on the moon, what do you do for an encore? Ford suffered from the syndrome when, after it succeeded in democratizing the automobile, it failed to set a new goal of equal significance and gave General Motors the opportunity to jump ahead in the 1930s. Apple Computer suffered from the syndrome after achieving the goal of creating a computer that nontechies could use. Start-up companies frequently suffer from the We've Arrived Syndrome after going public or after reaching a stage in which survival no longer seems in question. An envisioned future helps an organization only as long as it hasn't yet been achieved. In our work with companies, we frequently hear executives say, "It's just not as exciting around here as it used to be; we seem to have lost our momentum." Usually, that kind of remark signals that the organization has climbed one mountain and not yet picked a new one to climb.

Many executives thrash about with mission statements and vision statements. Unfortunately, most of those statements turn out to be a muddled stew of values, goals, purposes, philosophies, beliefs, aspirations, norms, strategies, practices, and descriptions. They are usually a boring, confusing, structurally unsound stream of words that evoke the response "True, but who cares?" Even more problematic, seldom do these statements have a direct link to the fundamental dynamic of visionary companies: preserve the core and stimulate progress. That dynamic, not vision or mission statements, is the primary engine of enduring companies. Vision simply provides the context for bringing this dynamic to life. Building a visionary company requires 1% vision and 99% alignment. When you have superb alignment, a visitor could drop in from outer space and infer your vision from the operations and activities of the company without ever reading it on paper or meeting a single senior executive.

Creating alignment may be your most important work. But the first step will always be to recast your vision or mission into an effective context for building a visionary company. If you do it right, you shouldn't have to do it again for at least a decade.

Originally published in September 1996. Reprint 96501.

Notes

1. David Packard, speech given to Hewlett-Packard's training group on March 8, 1960; courtesy of Hewlett-Packard Archives.

2. See Nick Lyons, *The Sony Vision* (New York: Crown Publishers, 1976). We also used a translation by our Japanese student Tsuneto Ikeda.

3. Akio Morita, *Made in Japan* (New York: E.P. Dutton, 1986), p. 147.

Reinventing Your Business Model

by Mark W. Johnson, Clayton M. Christensen, and Henning Kagermann

IN 2003, APPLE INTRODUCED the iPod with the iTunes store, revolutionizing portable entertainment, creating a new market, and transforming the company. In just three years, the iPod/iTunes combination became a nearly $10 billion product, accounting for almost 50% of Apple's revenue. Apple's market capitalization catapulted from around $1 billion in early 2003 to over $150 billion by late 2007.

This success story is well known; what's less well known is that Apple was not the first to bring digital music players to market. A company called Diamond Multimedia introduced the Rio in 1998. Another firm, Best Data, introduced the Cabo 64 in 2000. Both products worked well and were portable and stylish. So why did the iPod, rather than the Rio or Cabo, succeed?

Apple did something far smarter than take a good technology and wrap it in a snazzy design. It took a good technology and wrapped it in a great business model. Apple's true innovation was to make downloading digital music easy and convenient. To do that, the company built a groundbreaking business model that combined hardware, software, and service. This approach worked like Gillette's famous blades-and-razor model in reverse: Apple essentially gave away the "blades" (low-margin iTunes music) to lock in purchase of the "razor" (the high-margin iPod). That model defined value in a new way and provided game-changing convenience to the consumer.

Business model innovations have reshaped entire industries and redistributed billions of dollars of value. Retail discounters such as Wal-Mart and Target, which entered the market with pioneering business models, now account for 75% of the total valuation of the retail sector. Low-cost U.S. airlines grew from a blip on the radar screen to 55% of the market value of all carriers. Fully 11 of the 27 companies born in the last quarter century that grew their way into the *Fortune* 500 in the past 10 years did so through business model innovation.

Stories of business model innovation from well-established companies like Apple, however, are rare. An analysis of major innovations within existing corporations in the past decade shows that precious few have been business-model related. And a recent American Management Association study determined that no more than 10% of innovation investment at global companies is focused on developing new business models.

Yet everyone's talking about it. A 2005 survey by the Economist Intelligence Unit reported that over 50% of executives believe business model innovation will become even more important for success than product or service innovation. A 2008 IBM survey of corporate CEOs echoed these results. Nearly all of the CEOs polled reported the need to adapt their business models; more than two-thirds said that extensive changes were required. And in these tough economic times, some CEOs are already looking to business model innovation to address permanent shifts in their market landscapes.

Senior managers at incumbent companies thus confront a frustrating question: Why is it so difficult to pull off the new growth that business model innovation can bring? Our research suggests two problems. The first is a lack of definition: Very little formal study has been done into the dynamics and processes of business model development. Second, few companies understand their existing business model well enough—the premise behind its development, its natural interdependencies, and its strengths and limitations. So they don't know when they can leverage their core business and when success requires a new business model.

Idea in Brief

When Apple introduced the iPod, it did something far smarter than wrap a good technology in a snazzy design. It wrapped a good technology in a **great business model**. Combining hardware, software, and service, the model provided game-changing convenience for consumers *and* record-breaking profits for Apple.

Great business models can reshape industries and drive spectacular growth. Yet many companies find business-model innovation difficult. Managers don't understand their existing model well enough to know when it needs changing—or how.

To determine whether your firm should alter its business model, Johnson, Christensen, and Kagermann advise these steps:

1. Articulate what makes your existing model successful. For example, what customer problem does it solve? How does it make money for your firm?

2. Watch for signals that your model needs changing, such as tough new competitors on the horizon.

3. Decide whether reinventing your model is worth the effort. The answer's yes only if the new model changes the industry or market.

After tackling these problems with dozens of companies, we have found that new business models often look unattractive to internal and external stakeholders—at the outset. To see past the borders of what is and into the land of the new, companies need a road map.

Ours consists of three simple steps. The first is to realize that success starts by not thinking about business models at all. It starts with thinking about the opportunity to satisfy a real customer who needs a job done. The second step is to construct a blueprint laying out how your company will fulfill that need at a profit. In our model, that plan has four elements. The third is to compare that model to your existing model to see how much you'd have to change it to capture the opportunity. Once you do, you will know if you can use your existing model and organization or need to separate out a new unit to execute a new model. Every successful company is already fulfilling a real customer need with an effective business model, whether that model is explicitly understood or not. Let's take a look at what that entails.

Idea in Practice

Understand Your Current Business Model

A successful model has these components:

- **Customer value proposition.** The model helps customers perform a specific "job" that alternative offerings don't address.

Example: MinuteClinics enable people to visit a doctor's office without appointments by making nurse practitioners available to treat minor health issues.

- **Profit formula.** The model generates value for your company through factors such as revenue model, cost structure, margins, and inventory turnover.

Example: The Tata Group's inexpensive car, the Nano, is profitable because the company has reduced many cost structure elements, accepted lower-than-standard gross margins, and sold the Nano in large volumes to its target market: first-time car buyers in emerging markets.

- **Key resources and processes.** Your company has the people, technology, products, facilities, equipment, and brand required to deliver the value proposition to your targeted customers. And it has processes (training, manufacturing, service) to leverage those resources.

Example: For Tata Motors to fulfill the requirements of the Nano's profit formula, it had to reconceive how a car is designed, manufactured, and distributed. It redefined its supplier strategy, choosing to outsource a remarkable 85% of the Nano's components and to use nearly 60% fewer vendors than normal to reduce transaction costs.

Identify When a New Model May Be Needed

These circumstances often require business model change:

Business Model: A Definition

A business model, from our point of view, consists of four interlocking elements that, taken together, create and deliver value. The most important to get right, by far, is the first.

Customer value proposition (CVP)

A successful company is one that has found a way to create value for customers—that is, a way to help customers get an important job

An *opportunity* to . . .	Example
Address needs of large groups who find existing solutions too expensive or complicated.	The Nano's goal is to open car ownership to low-income consumers in emerging markets.
Capitalize on new technology, or leverage existing technologies in new markets.	A company develops a commercial application for a technology originally developed for military use.
Bring a job-to-be-done focus where it doesn't exist.	FedEx focused on performing customers' unmet "job": Receive packages faster and more reliably than any other service could.

A *need* to . . .	Example
Fend off low-end disruptors.	Mini-mills threatened the integrated steel mills a generation ago by making steel at significantly lower prices.
Respond to shifts in competition.	Power-tool maker Hilti switched from selling to renting its tools in part because "good enough" low-end entrants had begun chipping away at the market for selling high-quality tools.

done. By "job" we mean a fundamental problem in a given situation that needs a solution. Once we understand the job and all its dimensions, including the full process for how to get it done, we can design the offering. The more important the job is to the customer, the lower the level of customer satisfaction with current options for getting the job done, and the better your solution is than existing alternatives at getting the job done (and, of course, the lower the price), the greater the CVP. Opportunities for creating a CVP are at their most potent, we have found, when alternative products and services have not been designed with the real job in mind and you can design an offering that gets that job—and only that job—done perfectly. We'll come back to that point later.

Profit formula

The profit formula is the blueprint that defines how the company creates value for itself while providing value to the customer. It consists of the following:

- *Revenue model:* price x volume

- *Cost structure:* direct costs, indirect costs, economies of scale. Cost structure will be predominantly driven by the cost of the key resources required by the business model.

- *Margin model:* given the expected volume and cost structure, the contribution needed from each transaction to achieve desired profits.

- *Resource velocity:* how fast we need to turn over inventory, fixed assets, and other assets—and, overall, how well we need to utilize resources—to support our expected volume and achieve our anticipated profits.

People often think the terms "profit formulas" and "business models" are interchangeable. But how you make a profit is only one piece of the model. We've found it most useful to start by setting the price required to deliver the CVP and then work backwards from there to determine what the variable costs and gross margins must be. This then determines what the scale and resource velocity needs to be to achieve the desired profits.

Key resources

The key resources are assets such as the people, technology, products, facilities, equipment, channels, and brand required to deliver the value proposition to the targeted customer. The focus here is on the *key* elements that create value for the customer and the company, and the way those elements interact. (Every company also has generic resources that do not create competitive differentiation.)

Key processes
Successful companies have operational and managerial processes that allow them to deliver value in a way they can successfully repeat and increase in scale. These may include such recurrent tasks as training, development, manufacturing, budgeting, planning, sales, and service. Key processes also include a company's rules, metrics, and norms.

These four elements form the building blocks of any business. The customer value proposition and the profit formula define value for the customer and the company, respectively; key resources and key processes describe how that value will be delivered to both the customer and the company.

As simple as this framework may seem, its power lies in the complex interdependencies of its parts. Major changes to any of these four elements affect the others and the whole. Successful businesses devise a more or less stable system in which these elements bond to one another in consistent and complementary ways.

How Great Models Are Built

To illustrate the elements of our business model framework, we will look at what's behind two companies' game-changing business model innovations.

Creating a customer value proposition
It's not possible to invent or reinvent a business model without first identifying a clear customer value proposition. Often, it starts as a quite simple realization. Imagine, for a moment, that you are standing on a Mumbai road on a rainy day. You notice the large number of motor scooters snaking precariously in and out around the cars. As you look more closely, you see that most bear whole families—both parents and several children. Your first thought might be "That's

The Elements of a Successful Business Model

EVERY SUCCESSFUL COMPANY ALREADY operates according to an effective business model. By systematically identifying all of its constituent parts, executives can understand how the model fulfills a potent value proposition in a profitable way using certain key resources and key processes. With that understanding, they can then judge how well the same model could be used to fulfill a radically different CVP—and what they'd need to do to construct a new one, if need be, to capitalize on that opportunity.

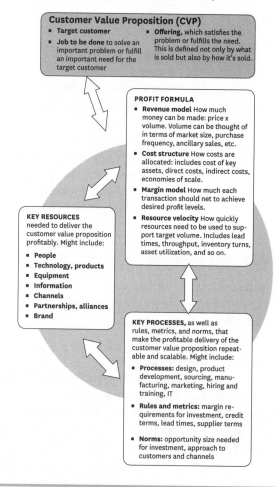

Customer Value Proposition (CVP)
- **Target customer**
- **Job to be done** to solve an important problem or fulfill an important need for the target customer
- **Offering**, which satisfies the problem or fulfills the need. This is defined not only by what is sold but also by how it's sold.

PROFIT FORMULA
- **Revenue model** How much money can be made: price x volume. Volume can be thought of in terms of market size, purchase frequency, ancillary sales, etc.
- **Cost structure** How costs are allocated: includes cost of key assets, direct costs, indirect costs, economies of scale.
- **Margin model** How much each transaction should net to achieve desired profit levels.
- **Resource velocity** How quickly resources need to be used to support target volume. Includes lead times, throughput, inventory turns, asset utilization, and so on.

KEY RESOURCES needed to deliver the customer value proposition profitably. Might include:
- **People**
- **Technology, products**
- **Equipment**
- **Information**
- **Channels**
- **Partnerships, alliances**
- **Brand**

KEY PROCESSES, as well as rules, metrics, and norms, that make the profitable delivery of the customer value proposition repeatable and scalable. Might include:
- **Processes:** design, product development, sourcing, manufacturing, marketing, hiring and training, IT
- **Rules and metrics:** margin requirements for investment, credit terms, lead times, supplier terms
- **Norms:** opportunity size needed for investment, approach to customers and channels

crazy!" or "That's the way it is in developing countries—people get by as best they can."

When Ratan Tata of Tata Group looked out over this scene, he saw a critical job to be done: providing a safer alternative for scooter families. He understood that the cheapest car available in India cost easily five times what a scooter did and that many of these families could not afford one. Offering an affordable, safer, all-weather alternative for scooter families was a powerful value proposition, one with the potential to reach tens of millions of people who were not yet part of the car-buying market. Ratan Tata also recognized that Tata Motors' business model could not be used to develop such a product at the needed price point.

At the other end of the market spectrum, Hilti, a Liechtenstein-based manufacturer of high-end power tools for the construction industry, reconsidered the real job to be done for many of its current customers. A contractor makes money by finishing projects; if the required tools aren't available and functioning properly, the job doesn't get done. Contractors don't make money by *owning* tools; they make it by using them as efficiently as possible. Hilti could help contractors get the job done by selling tool *use* instead of the tools themselves—managing its customers' tool inventory by providing the best tool at the right time and quickly furnishing tool repairs, replacements, and upgrades, all for a monthly fee. To deliver on that value proposition, the company needed to create a fleet-management program for tools and in the process shift its focus from manufacturing and distribution to service. That meant Hilti had to construct a new profit formula and develop new resources and new processes.

The most important attribute of a customer value proposition is its precision: how perfectly it nails the customer job to be done—and nothing else. But such precision is often the most difficult thing to achieve. Companies trying to create the new often neglect to focus on *one* job; they dilute their efforts by attempting to do lots of things. In doing lots of things, they do nothing *really* well.

One way to generate a precise customer value proposition is to think about the four most common barriers keeping people from getting particular jobs done: insufficient wealth, access, skill, or time. Software maker Intuit devised QuickBooks to fulfill small-business owners' need to avoid running out of cash. By fulfilling that job with greatly simplified accounting software, Intuit broke the *skills barrier* that kept untrained small-business owners from using more-complicated accounting packages. MinuteClinic, the drugstore-based basic health care provider, broke the *time barrier* that kept people from visiting a doctor's office with minor health issues by making nurse practitioners available without appointments.

Designing a profit formula
Ratan Tata knew the only way to get families off their scooters and into cars would be to break the *wealth barrier* by drastically decreasing the price of the car. "What if I can change the game and make a car for one lakh?" Tata wondered, envisioning a price point of around US$2,500, less than half the price of the cheapest car available. This, of course, had dramatic ramifications for the profit formula: It required both a significant drop in gross margins and a radical reduction in many elements of the cost structure. He knew, however, he could still make money if he could increase sales volume dramatically, and he knew that his target base of consumers was potentially huge.

For Hilti, moving to a contract management program required shifting assets from customers' balance sheets to its own and generating revenue through a lease/subscription model. For a monthly fee, customers could have a full complement of tools at their fingertips, with repair and maintenance included. This would require a fundamental shift in all major components of the profit formula: the revenue stream (pricing, the staging of payments, and how to think about volume), the cost structure (including added sales development and contract management costs), and the supporting margins and transaction velocity.

Identifying key resources and processes
Having articulated the value proposition for both the customer and the business, companies must then consider the key resources and

Hilti Sidesteps Commoditization

HILTI IS CAPITALIZING ON a game-changing opportunity to increase profitability by turning products into a service. Rather than sell tools (at lower and lower prices), it's selling a "just-the-tool-you-need-when-you-need-it, no-repair-or-storage-hassles" service. Such a radical change in customer value proposition required a shift in all parts of its business model.

Traditional power tool company		Hilti's tool fleet management service
Sales of industrial and professional power tools and accessories	Customer value proposition	Leasing a comprehensive fleet of tools to increase contractors's on-site productivity
Low margins, high inventory turnover	Profit formula	Higher margins; asset heavy; monthly payments for tool maintenance, repair, and replacement
Distribution channel, low-cost manufacturing plants in developing countries, R&D	Key resources and processes	Strong direct-sales approach, contract management, IT systems for inventory management and repair, warehousing

processes needed to deliver that value. For a professional services firm, for example, the key resources are generally its people, and the key processes are naturally people related (training and development, for instance). For a packaged goods company, strong brands and well-selected channel retailers might be the key resources, and associated brand-building and channel-management processes among the critical processes.

Oftentimes, it's not the individual resources and processes that make the difference but their relationship to one another. Companies will almost always need to integrate their key resources and processes in a unique way to get a job done perfectly for a set of customers. When they do, they almost always create enduring competitive advantage. Focusing first on the value proposition and the profit formula makes clear how those resources and processes need to interrelate. For example, most general hospitals offer a value proposition that might be described as, "We'll do anything for anybody." Being all things to all people requires these hospitals to have a vast collection of resources (specialists, equipment, and so on) that can't be knit together in any proprietary way. The result is not just a lack of differentiation but dissatisfaction.

By contrast, a hospital that focuses on a specific value proposition can integrate its resources and processes in a unique way that delights customers. National Jewish Health in Denver, for example, is organized around a focused value proposition we'd characterize as, "If you have a disease of the pulmonary system, bring it here. We'll define its root cause and prescribe an effective therapy." Narrowing its focus has allowed National Jewish to develop processes that integrate the ways in which its specialists and specialized equipment work together.

For Tata Motors to fulfill the requirements of its customer value proposition and profit formula for the Nano, it had to reconceive how a car is designed, manufactured, and distributed. Tata built a small team of fairly young engineers who would not, like the company's more-experienced designers, be influenced and constrained in their thinking by the automaker's existing profit formulas. This team dramatically minimized the number of parts in the vehicle, resulting in a significant cost saving. Tata also reconceived its supplier strategy, choosing to outsource a remarkable 85% of the Nano's components and use nearly 60% fewer vendors than normal to reduce transaction costs and achieve better economies of scale.

At the other end of the manufacturing line, Tata is envisioning an entirely new way of assembling and distributing its cars. The ultimate plan is to ship the modular components of the vehicles to a combined network of company-owned and independent entrepreneur-owned assembly plants, which will build them to order. The Nano will be designed, built, distributed, and serviced in a radically new way—one that could not be accomplished without a new business model. And while the jury is still out, Ratan Tata may solve a traffic safety problem in the process.

For Hilti, the greatest challenge lay in training its sales representatives to do a thoroughly new task. Fleet management is not a half-hour sale; it takes days, weeks, even months of meetings to persuade customers to buy a program instead of a product. Suddenly, field reps accustomed to dealing with crew leaders and on-site purchasing managers in mobile trailers found themselves staring down CEOs and CFOs across conference tables.

Additionally, leasing required new resources—new people, more robust IT systems, and other new technologies—to design and develop the appropriate packages and then come to an agreement on monthly payments. Hilti needed a process for maintaining large arsenals of tools more inexpensively and effectively than its customers had. This required warehousing, an inventory management system, and a supply of replacement tools. On the customer management side, Hilti developed a website that enabled construction managers to view all the tools in their fleet and their usage rates. With that information readily available, the managers could easily handle the cost accounting associated with those assets.

Rules, norms, and metrics are often the last element to emerge in a developing business model. They may not be fully envisioned until the new product or service has been road tested. Nor should they be. Business models need to have the flexibility to change in their early years.

When a New Business Model Is Needed

Established companies should not undertake business-model innovation lightly. They can often create new products that disrupt competitors without fundamentally changing their own business model. Procter & Gamble, for example, developed a number of what it calls "disruptive market innovations" with such products as the Swiffer disposable mop and duster and Febreze, a new kind of air freshener. Both innovations built on P&G's existing business model and its established dominance in household consumables.

There are clearly times, however, when creating new growth requires venturing not only into unknown market territory but also into unknown business model territory. When? The short answer is "When significant changes are needed to all four elements of your existing model." But it's not always that simple. Management judgment is clearly required. That said, we have observed five strategic circumstances that often require business model change:

1. The opportunity to address through disruptive innovation the needs of large groups of potential customers who are shut out of a market entirely because existing solutions are too expensive or complicated for them. This includes the opportunity to democratize products in emerging markets (or reach the bottom of the pyramid), as Tata's Nano does.

2. The opportunity to capitalize on a brand-new technology by wrapping a new business model around it (Apple and MP3 players) or the opportunity to leverage a tested technology by bringing it to a whole new market (say, by offering military technologies in the commercial space or vice versa).

3. The opportunity to bring a job-to-be-done focus where one does not yet exist. That's common in industries where companies focus on products or customer segments, which leads them to refine existing products more and more, increasing commoditization over time. A jobs focus allows companies to redefine industry profitability. For example, when FedEx entered the package delivery market, it did not try to compete through lower prices or better marketing. Instead, it concentrated on fulfilling an entirely unmet customer need to receive packages far, far faster, and more reliably, than any service then could. To do so, it had to integrate its key processes and resources in a vastly more efficient way. The business model that resulted from this job-to-be-done emphasis gave FedEx a significant competitive advantage that took UPS many years to copy.

4. The need to fend off low-end disrupters. If the Nano is successful, it will threaten other automobile makers, much as minimills threatened the integrated steel mills a generation ago by making steel at significantly lower cost.

5. The need to respond to a shifting basis of competition. Inevitably, what defines an acceptable solution in a market will change over time, leading core market segments to

commoditize. Hilti needed to change its business model in part because of lower global manufacturing costs; "good enough" low-end entrants had begun chipping away at the market for high-quality power tools.

Of course, companies should not pursue business model reinvention unless they are confident that the opportunity is large enough to warrant the effort. And, there's really no point in instituting a new business model unless it's not only new to the company but in some way new or game-changing to the industry or market. To do otherwise would be a waste of time and money.

These questions will help you evaluate whether the challenge of business model innovation will yield acceptable results. Answering "yes" to all four greatly increases the odds of successful execution:

- Can you nail the job with a focused, compelling customer value proposition?

- Can you devise a model in which all the elements—the customer value proposition, the profit formula, the key resources, and the key processes—work together to get the job done in the most efficient way possible?

- Can you create a new business development process unfettered by the often negative influences of your core business?

- Will the new business model disrupt competitors?

Creating a new model for a new business does not mean the current model is threatened or should be changed. A new model often reinforces and complements the core business, as Dow Corning discovered.

How Dow Corning Got Out of Its Own Way

When business model innovation is clearly called for, success lies not only in getting the model right but also in making sure the incumbent business doesn't in some way prevent the new model from creating value or thriving. That was a problem for Dow Corning when it built a new business unit—with a new profit formula—from scratch.

Dow Corning Embraces the Low End

TRADITIONALLY HIGH-MARGIN DOW CORNING found new opportunities in low-margin offerings by setting up a separate business unit that operates in an entirely different way. By fundamentally differentiating its low-end and high-end offerings, the company avoided cannibalizing its traditional business even as it found new profits at the low end.

Established business		New business unit
Customized solutions, negotiated contracts	**Customer value proposition**	No frills, bulk prices, sold through the internet
High-margin, high-overhead retail prices pay for value-added services	**Profit formula**	Spot-market pricing, low overhead to accommodate lower margins, high throughput
R&D, sales, and services orientation	**Key resources and processes**	IT system, lowest-cost processes, maximum automation

For many years, Dow Corning had sold thousands of silicone-based products and provided sophisticated technical services to an array of industries. After years of profitable growth, however, a number of product areas were stagnating. A strategic review uncovered a critical insight: Its low-end product segment was commoditizing. Many customers experienced in silicone application no longer needed technical services; they needed basic products at low prices. This shift created an opportunity for growth, but to exploit that opportunity Dow Corning had to figure out a way to serve these customers with a lower-priced product. The problem was that both the business model and the culture were built on high-priced, innovative product and service packages. In 2002, in pursuit of what was essentially a commodity business for low-end customers, Dow Corning CEO Gary Anderson asked executive Don Sheets to form a team to start a new business.

The team began by formulating a customer value proposition that it believed would fulfill the job to be done for these price-driven customers. It determined that the price point had to drop 15% (which for a commoditizing material was a huge reduction). As the team analyzed what that new customer value proposition would require, it

When the Old Model Will Work

YOU DON'T ALWAYS NEED a new business model to capitalize on a game-changing opportunity. Sometimes, as P&G did with its Swiffer, a company finds that its current model is revolutionary in a new market. When will the old model do? When you can fulfill the new customer value proposition:

- With your current profit formula
- Using most, if not all, of your current key resources and processes
- Using the same core metrics, rules, and norms you now use to run your business

---

realized reaching that point was going to take a lot more than merely eliminating services. Dramatic price reduction would call for a different profit formula with a fundamentally lower cost structure, which depended heavily on developing a new IT system. To sell more products faster, the company would need to use the internet to automate processes and reduce overhead as much as possible.

Breaking the rules

As a mature and successful company, Dow Corning was full of highly trained employees used to delivering its high-touch, customized value proposition. To automate, the new business would have to be far more standardized, which meant instituting different and, overall, much stricter rules. For example, order sizes would be limited to a few, larger-volume options; order lead times would fall between two and four weeks (exceptions would cost extra); and credit terms would be fixed. There would be charges if a purchaser required customer service. The writing was on the wall: The new venture would be low-touch, self-service, and standardized. To succeed, Dow Corning would have to break the rules that had previously guided its success.

Sheets next had to determine whether this new venture, with its new rules, could succeed within the confines of Dow Corning's core enterprise. He set up an experimental war game to test how existing staff and systems would react to the requirements of the new customer value proposition. He got crushed as entrenched habits and existing processes thwarted any attempt to change the game. It became clear that the corporate antibodies would kill the initiative before it got off the ground. The way forward was clear: The new venture had to be free from existing rules and free to decide what rules would be appropriate in order for the new commodity line of business to thrive. To nurture the opportunity—and also protect the existing model—a new business unit with a new brand identity was needed. Xiameter was born.

Identifying new competencies

Following the articulation of the new customer value proposition and new profit formula, the Xiameter team focused on the new competencies it would need, its key resources and processes. Information technology, just a small part of Dow Corning's core competencies at that time, emerged as an essential part of the now web-enabled business. Xiameter also needed employees who could make smart decisions very quickly and who would thrive in a fast-changing environment, filled initially with lots of ambiguity. Clearly, new abilities would have to be brought into the business.

Although Xiameter would be established and run as a separate business unit, Don Sheets and the Xiameter team did not want to give up the incumbency advantage that deep knowledge of the industry and of their own products gave them. The challenge was to tap into the expertise without importing the old-rules mind-set. Sheets conducted a focused HR search within Dow Corning for risk takers. During the interview process, when he came across candidates with the right skills, he asked them to take the job on the spot, before they left the room. This approach allowed him to cherry-pick those who could make snap decisions and take big risks.

The secret sauce: patience

Successful new businesses typically revise their business models four times or so on the road to profitability. While a well-considered business-model-innovation process can often shorten this cycle, successful incumbents must tolerate initial failure and grasp the need for course correction. In effect, companies have to focus on learning and adjusting as much as on executing. We recommend companies with new business models be patient for growth (to allow

What Rules, Norms, and Metrics Are Standing in Your Way?

In any business, a fundamental understanding of the core model often fades into the mists of institutional memory, but it lives on in rules, norms, and metrics put in place to protect the status quo (for example, "Gross margins must be at 40%"). They are the first line of defense against any new model's taking root in an existing enterprise.

Financial

- Gross margins
- Opportunity size
- Unit pricing
- Unit margin
- Time to breakeven
- Net present value calculations
- Fixed cost investment
- Credit items

Operational

- End-product quality
- Supplier quality
- Owned versus outsourced manufacturing
- Customer service
- Channels
- Lead times
- Throughput

Other

- Pricing
- Performance demands
- Product-development life cycles
- Basis for individuals' rewards and incentives
- Brand parameters

the market opportunity to unfold) but impatient for profit (as an early validation that the model works). A profitable business is the best early indication of a viable model.

Accordingly, to allow for the trial and error that naturally accompanies the creation of the new while also constructing a development cycle that would produce results and demonstrate feasibility with minimal resource outlay, Dow Corning kept the scale of Xiameter's operation small but developed an aggressive timetable for launch and set the goal of becoming profitable by the end of year one.

Xiameter paid back Dow Corning's investment in just three months and went on to become a major, transformative success. Beforehand, Dow Corning had had no online sales component; now 30% of sales originate online, nearly three times the industry average. Most of these customers are new to the company. Far from cannibalizing existing customers, Xiameter has actually supported the main business, allowing Dow Corning's salespeople to more easily enforce premium pricing for their core offerings while providing a viable alternative for the price-conscious.

Established companies' attempts at transformative growth typically spring from product or technology innovations. Their efforts are often characterized by prolonged development cycles and fitful attempts to find a market. As the Apple iPod story that opened this article suggests, truly transformative businesses are never exclusively about the discovery and commercialization of a great technology. Their success comes from enveloping the new technology in an appropriate, powerful business model.

Bob Higgins, the founder and general partner of Highland Capital Partners, has seen his share of venture success and failure in his 20 years in the industry. He sums up the importance and power of business model innovation this way: "I think historically where we [venture capitalists] fail is when we back technology. Where we succeed is when we back new business models."

Originally published in December 2008. Reprint R0812C.

Blue Ocean Strategy

by W. Chan Kim and Renée Mauborgne

A ONETIME ACCORDION PLAYER, stilt walker, and fire-eater, Guy La-
liberté is now CEO of one of Canada's largest cultural exports, Cirque
du Soleil. Founded in 1984 by a group of street performers, Cirque
has staged dozens of productions seen by some 40 million people in
90 cities around the world. In 20 years, Cirque has achieved revenues that Ringling Bros. and Barnum & Bailey—the world's leading
circus—took more than a century to attain.

Cirque's rapid growth occurred in an unlikely setting. The circus
business was (and still is) in long-term decline. Alternative forms of
entertainment—sporting events, TV, and video games—were casting
a growing shadow. Children, the mainstay of the circus audience,
preferred PlayStations to circus acts. There was also rising senti-
ment, fueled by animal rights groups, against the use of animals, traditionally an integral part of the circus. On the supply side, the star
performers that Ringling and the other circuses relied on to draw in
the crowds could often name their own terms. As a result, the industry was hit by steadily decreasing audiences and increasing costs.
What's more, any new entrant to this business would be competing
against a formidable incumbent that for most of the last century had
set the industry standard.

How did Cirque profitably increase revenues by a factor of 22 over
the last ten years in such an unattractive environment? The tagline
for one of the first Cirque productions is revealing: "We reinvent the
circus." Cirque did not make its money by competing within the

confines of the existing industry or by stealing customers from Ringling and the others. Instead it created uncontested market space that made the competition irrelevant. It pulled in a whole new group of customers who were traditionally noncustomers of the industry— adults and corporate clients who had turned to theater, opera, or ballet and were, therefore, prepared to pay several times more than the price of a conventional circus ticket for an unprecedented entertainment experience.

To understand the nature of Cirque's achievement, you have to realize that the business universe consists of two distinct kinds of space, which we think of as red and blue oceans. Red oceans represent all the industries in existence today—the known market space. In red oceans, industry boundaries are defined and accepted, and the competitive rules of the game are well understood. Here, companies try to outperform their rivals in order to grab a greater share of existing demand. As the space gets more and more crowded, prospects for profits and growth are reduced. Products turn into commodities, and increasing competition turns the water bloody.

Blue oceans denote all the industries *not* in existence today—the unknown market space, untainted by competition. In blue oceans, demand is created rather than fought over. There is ample opportunity for growth that is both profitable and rapid. There are two ways to create blue oceans. In a few cases, companies can give rise to completely new industries, as eBay did with the online auction industry. But in most cases, a blue ocean is created from within a red ocean when a company alters the boundaries of an existing industry. As will become evident later, this is what Cirque did. In breaking through the boundary traditionally separating circus and theater, it made a new and profitable blue ocean from within the red ocean of the circus industry.

Cirque is just one of more than 150 blue ocean creations that we have studied in over 30 industries, using data stretching back more than 100 years. We analyzed companies that created those blue oceans and their less successful competitors, which were caught in red oceans. In studying these data, we have observed a consistent pattern of strategic thinking behind the creation of new markets and

Idea in Brief

The best way to drive profitable growth? Stop competing in over-crowded industries. In those **red oceans,** companies try to outperform rivals to grab bigger slices of existing demand. As the space gets increasingly crowded, profit and growth prospects shrink. Products become commoditized. Ever-more-intense competition turns the water bloody.

How to avoid the fray? Kim and Mauborgne recommend creating **blue oceans**—uncontested market spaces where the competition is irrelevant. In blue oceans, you invent and capture new demand, and you offer customers a leap in value while also streamlining your costs. Results? Handsome profits, speedy growth—and brand equity that lasts for decades while rivals scramble to catch up.

Consider Cirque du Soleil—which invented a new industry that combined elements from traditional circus with elements drawn from sophisticated theater. In just 20 years, Cirque raked in revenues that Ringling Bros. and Barnum & Bailey—the world's leading circus—needed more than a century to attain.

industries, what we call blue ocean strategy. The logic behind blue ocean strategy parts with traditional models focused on competing in existing market space. Indeed, it can be argued that managers' failure to realize the differences between red and blue ocean strategy lies behind the difficulties many companies encounter as they try to break from the competition.

In this article, we present the concept of blue ocean strategy and describe its defining characteristics. We assess the profit and growth consequences of blue oceans and discuss why their creation is a rising imperative for companies in the future. We believe that an understanding of blue ocean strategy will help today's companies as they struggle to thrive in an accelerating and expanding business universe.

Blue and Red Oceans

Although the term may be new, blue oceans have always been with us. Look back 100 years and ask yourself which industries known

Idea in Practice

How to begin creating blue oceans? Kim and Mauborgne offer these suggestions:

Understand the Logic Behind Blue Ocean Strategy

The logic behind blue ocean strategy is counterintuitive:

- **It's not about technology innovation.** Blue oceans seldom result from technological innovation. Often, the underlying technology already exists—and blue ocean creators link it to what buyers value. Compaq, for example, used existing technologies to create its ProSignia server, which gave buyers twice the file and print capability of the minicomputer at one-third the price.

- **You don't have to venture into distant waters to create blue oceans.** Most blue oceans are created from within, not beyond, the red oceans of existing industries. Incumbents often create blue oceans within their core businesses. Consider the megaplexes introduced by AMC—an established player in the movie-theater industry. Megaplexes provided movie-goers spectacular viewing experiences in stadium-size theater complexes at lower costs to theater owners.

Apply Blue Ocean Strategic Moves

To apply blue ocean strategic moves:

- **Never use the competition as a benchmark.** Instead, make the competition irrelevant by creating a leap in value for both

today were then unknown. The answer: Industries as basic as automobiles, music recording, aviation, petrochemicals, pharmaceuticals, and management consulting were unheard-of or had just begun to emerge. Now turn the clock back only 30 years and ask yourself the same question. Again, a plethora of multibillion-dollar industries jump out: mutual funds, cellular telephones, biotechnology, discount retailing, express package delivery, snowboards, coffee bars, and home videos, to name a few. Just three decades ago, none of these industries existed in a meaningful way.

This time, put the clock forward 20 years. Ask yourself: How many industries that are unknown today will exist then? If history is any predictor of the future, the answer is many. Companies have a yourself and your customers. Ford did this with the Model T. Ford could have tried besting the fashionable, customized cars that wealthy people bought for weekend jaunts in the countryside. Instead, it offered a car for everyday use that was far more affordable, durable, and easy to use and fix than rivals' offerings. Model T sales boomed, and Ford's market share surged from 9% in 1908 to 61% in 1921.

- **Reduce your costs while also offering customers more value.** Cirque du Soleil omitted costly elements of traditional circus, such as animal acts and aisle concessions. Its reduced cost structure enabled it to provide sophisticated elements from theater that appealed to adult audiences—such as themes, original scores, and enchanting sets, all of which change year to year. The added value lured adults who had not gone to a circus for years and enticed them to come back more frequently—thereby increasing revenues. By offering the best of circus and theater, Cirque created a market space that, as yet, has no name—and no equals.

huge capacity to create new industries and re-create existing ones, a fact that is reflected in the deep changes that have been necessary in the way industries are classified. The half-century-old Standard Industrial Classification (SIC) system was replaced in 1997 by the North American Industry Classification System (NAICS). The new system expanded the ten SIC industry sectors into 20 to reflect the emerging realities of new industry territories—blue oceans. The services sector under the old system, for example, is now seven sectors ranging from information to health care and social assistance. Given that these classification systems are designed for standardization and continuity, such a replacement shows how significant a source of economic growth the creation of blue oceans has been.

Looking forward, it seems clear to us that blue oceans will remain the engine of growth. Prospects in most established market spaces—red oceans—are shrinking steadily. Technological advances have substantially improved industrial productivity, permitting suppliers to produce an unprecedented array of products and services. And as trade barriers between nations and regions fall and information on products and prices becomes instantly and globally available, niche markets and monopoly havens are continuing to disappear. At the same time, there is little evidence of any increase in demand, at least in the developed markets, where recent United Nations statistics even point to declining populations. The result is that in more and more industries, supply is overtaking demand.

This situation has inevitably hastened the commoditization of products and services, stoked price wars, and shrunk profit margins. According to recent studies, major American brands in a variety of product and service categories have become more and more alike. And as brands become more similar, people increasingly base purchase choices on price. People no longer insist, as in the past, that their laundry detergent be Tide. Nor do they necessarily stick to Colgate when there is a special promotion for Crest, and vice versa. In overcrowded industries, differentiating brands becomes harder both in economic upturns and in downturns.

The Paradox of Strategy

Unfortunately, most companies seem becalmed in their red oceans. In a study of business launches in 108 companies, we found that 86% of those new ventures were line extensions—incremental improvements to existing industry offerings—and a mere 14% were aimed at creating new markets or industries. While line extensions did account for 62% of the total revenues, they delivered only 39% of the total profits. By contrast, the 14% invested in creating new markets and industries delivered 38% of total revenues and a startling 61% of total profits.

So why the dramatic imbalance in favor of red oceans? Part of the explanation is that corporate strategy is heavily influenced by its roots in military strategy. The very language of strategy is deeply imbued with military references—chief executive "officers" in "headquarters," "troops" on the "front lines." Described this way, strategy is all about red ocean competition. It is about confronting an opponent and driving him off a battlefield of limited territory. Blue ocean strategy, by contrast, is about doing business where there is no competitor. It is about creating new land, not dividing up existing land. Focusing on the red ocean therefore means accepting the key constraining factors of war—limited terrain and the need to beat an enemy to succeed. And it means denying the distinctive strength of the business world—the capacity to create new market space that is uncontested.

The tendency of corporate strategy to focus on winning against rivals was exacerbated by the meteoric rise of Japanese companies in the 1970s and 1980s. For the first time in corporate history, customers were deserting Western companies in droves. As competition mounted in the global marketplace, a slew of red ocean strategies emerged, all arguing that competition was at the core of corporate success and failure. Today, one hardly talks about strategy without using the language of competition. The term that best symbolizes this is "competitive advantage." In the competitive-advantage worldview, companies are often driven to outperform rivals and capture greater shares of existing market space.

Of course competition matters. But by focusing on competition, scholars, companies, and consultants have ignored two very important—and, we would argue, far more lucrative—aspects of strategy: One is to find and develop markets where there is little or no competition—blue oceans—and the other is to exploit and protect blue oceans. These challenges are very different from those to which strategists have devoted most of their attention.

Toward Blue Ocean Strategy

What kind of strategic logic is needed to guide the creation of blue oceans? To answer that question, we looked back over 100 years of data on blue ocean creation to see what patterns could be discerned. Some of our data are presented in "A snapshot of blue ocean creation." It shows an overview of key blue ocean creations in three

A snapshot of blue ocean creation

This table identifies the strategic elements that were common to blue ocean creations in three different industries in different eras. It is not intended to be comprehensive in coverage or exhaustive in content. We chose to show American industries because they represented the largest and least-regulated market during our study period. The pattern of blue ocean creations exemplified by these three industries is consistent with what we observed in the other industries in our study.

Key blue ocean creations	Was the blue ocean created by a new entrant or an incumbent?	Was it driven by technology pioneering or value pioneering?	At the time of the blue ocean creation, was the industry attractive or unattractive?
Automobiles			
Ford Model T Unveiled in 1908, the Model T was the first mass-produced car, priced so that many Americans could afford it.	New entrant	Value pioneering* (mostly existing technologies)	Unattractive
GM's "car for every purse and purpose" GM created a blue ocean in 1924 by injecting fun and fashion into the car.	Incumbent	Value pioneering (some new technologies)	Attractive
Japanese fuel-efficient autos Japanese automakers created a blue ocean in the mid-1970s with small, reliable lines of cars.	Incumbent	Value pioneering (some new technologies)	Unattractive
Chrysler minivan With its 1984 minivan, Chrysler created a new class of automobile that was as easy to use as a car but had the passenger space of a van.	Incumbent	Value pioneering (mostly existing technologies)	Unattractive

Key blue ocean creations	Was the blue ocean created by a new entrant or an incumbent?	Was it driven by technology pioneering or value pioneering?	At the time of the blue ocean creation, was the industry attractive or unattractive?
Computers			
CTR's tabulating machine In 1914, CTR created the business machine industry by simplifying, modularizing, and leasing tabulating machines. CTR later changed its name to IBM.	Incumbent	Value pioneering (some new technologies)	Unattractive
IBM 650 electronic computer and System/360 In 1952, IBM created the business computer industry by simplifying and reducing the power and price of existing technology. And it exploded the blue ocean created by the 650 when in 1964 it unveiled the System/360, the first modularized computer system.	Incumbent	Value pioneering (650: mostly existing technologies) Value and technology pioneering (System/360: new and existing technologies)	Nonexistent
Apple personal computer Although it was not the first home computer, the all-in-one, simple-to-use Apple II was a blue ocean creation when it appeared in 1978.	New entrant	Value pioneering (mostly existing technologies)	Unattractive
Compaq PC servers Compaq created a blue ocean in 1992 with its ProSignia server, which gave buyers twice the file and print capability of the minicomputer at one-third the price.	Incumbent	Value pioneering (mostly existing technologies)	Nonexistent

(continued)

Key blue ocean creations	Was the blue ocean created by a new entrant or an incumbent?	Was it driven by technology pioneering or value pioneering?	At the time of the blue ocean creation, was the industry attractive or unattractive?
Dell built-to-order computers In the mid-1990s, Dell created a blue ocean in a highly competitive industry by creating a new purchase and delivery experience for buyers.	New entrant	Value pioneering (mostly existing technologies)	Unattractive
Movie theaters			
Nickelodeon The first Nickelodeon opened its doors in 1905, showing short films around-the-clock to working-class audiences for five cents.	New entrant	Value pioneering (mostly existing technologies)	Nonexistent
Palace theaters Created by Roxy Rothapfel in 1914, these theaters provided an operalike environment for cinema viewing at an affordable price.	Incumbent	Value pioneering (mostly existing technologies)	Attractive
AMC multiplex In the 1960s, the number of multiplexes in America's suburban shopping malls mushroomed. The multiplex gave viewers greater choice while reducing owners' costs.	Incumbent	Value pioneering (mostly existing technologies)	Unattractive
AMC megaplex Megaplexes, introduced in 1995, offered every current blockbuster and provided spectacular viewing experiences in theater complexes as big as stadiums, at a lower cost to theater owners.	Incumbent	Value pioneering (mostly existing technologies)	Unattractive

*Driven by value pioneering does not mean that technologies were not involved. Rather, it means that the defining technologies used had largely been in existence, whether in that industry or elsewhere.

industries that closely touch people's lives: autos—how people get to work; computers—what people use at work; and movie theaters—where people go after work for enjoyment. We found that:

Blue oceans are not about technology innovation

Leading-edge technology is sometimes involved in the creation of blue oceans, but it is not a defining feature of them. This is often true even in industries that are technology intensive. As the exhibit reveals, across all three representative industries, blue oceans were seldom the result of technological innovation per se; the underlying technology was often already in existence. Even Ford's revolutionary assembly line can be traced to the meatpacking industry in America. Like those within the auto industry, the blue oceans within the computer industry did not come about through technology innovations alone but by linking technology to what buyers valued. As with the IBM 650 and the Compaq PC server, this often involved simplifying the technology.

Incumbents often create blue oceans—and usually within their core businesses

GM, the Japanese automakers, and Chrysler were established players when they created blue oceans in the auto industry. So were CTR and its later incarnation, IBM, and Compaq in the computer industry. And in the cinema industry, the same can be said of palace theaters and AMC. Of the companies listed here, only Ford, Apple, Dell, and Nickelodeon were new entrants in their industries; the first three were start-ups, and the fourth was an established player entering an industry that was new to it. This suggests that incumbents are not at a disadvantage in creating new market spaces. Moreover, the blue oceans made by incumbents were usually within their core businesses. In fact, as the exhibit shows, most blue oceans are created from within, not beyond, red oceans of existing industries. This challenges the view that new markets are in distant waters. Blue oceans are right next to you in every industry.

Company and industry are the wrong units of analysis

The traditional units of strategic analysis—company and industry—have little explanatory power when it comes to analyzing how and why blue oceans are created. There is no consistently excellent company; the same company can be brilliant at one time and wrong-headed at another. Every company rises and falls over time. Likewise, there is no perpetually excellent industry; relative attractiveness is driven largely by the creation of blue oceans from within them.

The most appropriate unit of analysis for explaining the creation of blue oceans is the strategic move—the set of managerial actions and decisions involved in making a major market-creating business offering. Compaq, for example, is considered by many people to be "unsuccessful" because it was acquired by Hewlett-Packard in 2001 and ceased to be a company. But the firm's ultimate fate does not invalidate the smart strategic move Compaq made that led to the creation of the multibillion-dollar market in PC servers, a move that was a key cause of the company's powerful comeback in the 1990s.

Creating blue oceans builds brands

So powerful is blue ocean strategy that a blue ocean strategic move can create brand equity that lasts for decades. Almost all of the companies listed in the exhibit are remembered in no small part for the blue oceans they created long ago. Very few people alive today were around when the first Model T rolled off Henry Ford's assembly line in 1908, but the company's brand still benefits from that blue ocean move. IBM, too, is often regarded as an "American institution" largely for the blue oceans it created in computing; the 360 series was its equivalent of the Model T.

Our findings are encouraging for executives at the large, established corporations that are traditionally seen as the victims of new market space creation. For what they reveal is that large R&D budgets are not the key to creating new market space. The key is making the right strategic moves. What's more, companies that understand what drives a good strategic move will be well placed to create multiple blue oceans over time, thereby continuing to deliver high growth and profits over a sustained period. The creation of blue oceans, in other words, is a product of strategy and as such is very much a product of managerial action.

The Defining Characteristics

Our research shows several common characteristics across strategic moves that create blue oceans. We found that the creators of blue oceans, in sharp contrast to companies playing by traditional rules, never use the competition as a benchmark. Instead they make it irrelevant by creating a leap in value for both buyers and the company itself. (The exhibit "Red ocean versus blue ocean strategy" compares the chief characteristics of these two strategy models.)

Perhaps the most important feature of blue ocean strategy is that it rejects the fundamental tenet of conventional strategy: that a trade-off exists between value and cost. According to this thesis, companies can either create greater value for customers at a higher cost or create reasonable value at a lower cost. In other words, strategy is essentially a choice between differentiation and low cost. But when it comes to creating blue oceans, the evidence shows that successful companies pursue differentiation and low cost simultaneously.

To see how this is done, let us go back to Cirque du Soleil. At the time of Cirque's debut, circuses focused on benchmarking one another and maximizing their shares of shrinking demand by tweaking traditional circus acts. This included trying to secure more and better-known clowns and lion tamers, efforts that raised circuses' cost structure without substantially altering the circus experience. The result was rising costs without rising revenues and a downward spiral in overall circus demand. Enter Cirque. Instead of following the conventional logic of outpacing the competition by offering a better solution to the given problem—creating a circus with even greater fun and thrills—it redefined the problem itself by offering people the fun and thrill of the circus *and* the intellectual sophistication and artistic richness of the theater.

In designing performances that landed both these punches, Cirque had to reevaluate the components of the traditional circus

Red ocean versus blue ocean strategy

The imperatives for red ocean and blue ocean strategies are starkly different.

Red ocean strategy	Blue ocean strategy
Compete in existing market space.	Create uncontested market space.
Beat the competition.	Make the competition irrelevant.
Exploit existing demand.	Create and capture new demand.
Make the value/cost trade-off.	Break the value/cost trade-off.
Align the whole system of a company's activities with its strategic choice of differentiation *or* low cost.	Align the whole system of a company's activities in pursuit of differentiation *and* low cost.

offering. What the company found was that many of the elements considered essential to the fun and thrill of the circus were unnecessary and in many cases costly. For instance, most circuses offer animal acts. These are a heavy economic burden, because circuses have to shell out not only for the animals but also for their training, medical care, housing, insurance, and transportation. Yet Cirque found that the appetite for animal shows was rapidly diminishing because of rising public concern about the treatment of circus animals and the ethics of exhibiting them.

Similarly, although traditional circuses promoted their performers as stars, Cirque realized that the public no longer thought of circus artists as stars, at least not in the movie star sense. Cirque did away with traditional three-ring shows, too. Not only did these create confusion among spectators forced to switch their attention from one ring to another, they also increased the number of performers needed, with obvious cost implications. And while aisle concession sales appeared to be a good way to generate revenue, the high prices discouraged parents from making purchases and made them feel they were being taken for a ride.

Cirque found that the lasting allure of the traditional circus came down to just three factors: the clowns, the tent, and the classic acrobatic acts. So Cirque kept the clowns, while shifting their humor away from slapstick to a more enchanting, sophisticated style. It glamorized the tent, which many circuses had abandoned in favor of rented venues. Realizing that the tent, more than anything else, captured the magic of the circus, Cirque designed this classic symbol with a glorious external finish and a high level of audience comfort. Gone were the sawdust and hard benches. Acrobats and other thrilling performers were retained, but Cirque reduced their roles and made their acts more elegant by adding artistic flair.

Even as Cirque stripped away some of the traditional circus offerings, it injected new elements drawn from the world of theater. For instance, unlike traditional circuses featuring a series of unrelated acts, each Cirque creation resembles a theater performance in that it has a theme and story line. Although the themes are intentionally vague, they bring harmony and an intellectual element to the acts. Cirque also borrows ideas from Broadway. For example, rather than putting on the traditional "once and for all" show, Cirque mounts multiple productions based on different themes and story lines. As with Broadway productions, too, each Cirque show has an original musical score, which drives the performance, lighting, and timing of the acts, rather than the other way around. The productions feature abstract and spiritual dance, an idea derived from theater and ballet. By introducing these factors, Cirque has created highly sophisticated entertainments. And by staging multiple productions, Cirque gives people reason to come to the circus more often, thereby increasing revenues.

Cirque offers the best of both circus and theater. And by eliminating many of the most expensive elements of the circus, it has been able to dramatically reduce its cost structure, achieving both differentiation and low cost. (For a depiction of the economics underpinning blue ocean strategy, see "The simultaneous pursuit of differentiation and low cost.")

By driving down costs while simultaneously driving up value for buyers, a company can achieve a leap in value for both itself and its customers. Since buyer value comes from the utility and price a company offers, and a company generates value for itself through cost structure and price, blue ocean strategy is achieved only when the whole system of a company's utility, price, and cost activities is properly aligned. It is this whole-system approach that makes the creation of blue oceans a sustainable strategy. Blue ocean strategy integrates the range of a firm's functional and operational activities.

A rejection of the trade-off between low cost and differentiation implies a fundamental change in strategic mind-set—we cannot emphasize enough how fundamental a shift it is. The red ocean assumption that industry structural conditions are a given and firms are forced to compete within them is based on an intellectual worldview that academics call the *structuralist* view, or *environmental determinism*. According to this view, companies and managers are largely at the mercy of economic forces greater than themselves. Blue ocean strategies, by contrast, are based on a worldview in which market boundaries and industries can be reconstructed by the actions and beliefs of industry players. We call this the *reconstructionist* view.

The founders of Cirque du Soleil clearly did not feel constrained to act within the confines of their industry. Indeed, is Cirque really a circus with all that it has eliminated, reduced, raised, and created? Or is it theater? If it is theater, then what genre—Broadway show, opera, ballet? The magic of Cirque was created through a reconstruction of elements drawn from all of these alternatives. In the end, Cirque is none of them and a little of all of them. From within the red oceans of theater and circus, Cirque has created a blue ocean of uncontested market space that has, as yet, no name.

Barriers to Imitation

Companies that create blue oceans usually reap the benefits without credible challenges for ten to 15 years, as was the case with Cirque du Soleil, Home Depot, Federal Express, Southwest Airlines, and CNN, to name just a few. The reason is that blue ocean strategy creates considerable economic and cognitive barriers to imitation.

The simultaneous pursuit of differentiation and low cost

A blue ocean is created in the region where a company's actions favorably affect both its cost structure and its value proposition to buyers. Cost savings are made from eliminating and reducing the factors an industry competes on. Buyer value is lifted by raising and creating elements the industry has never offered. Over time, costs are reduced further as scale economies kick in, due to the high sales volumes that superior value generates.

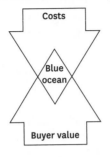

For a start, adopting a blue ocean creator's business model is easier to imagine than to do. Because blue ocean creators immediately attract customers in large volumes, they are able to generate scale economies very rapidly, putting would-be imitators at an immediate and continuing cost disadvantage. The huge economies of scale in purchasing that Wal-Mart enjoys, for example, have significantly discouraged other companies from imitating its business model. The immediate attraction of large numbers of customers can also create network externalities. The more customers eBay has online, the more attractive the auction site becomes for both sellers and buyers of wares, giving users few incentives to go elsewhere.

When imitation requires companies to make changes to their whole system of activities, organizational politics may impede a would-be competitor's ability to switch to the divergent business model of a blue ocean strategy. For instance, airlines trying to follow Southwest's example of offering the speed of air travel with the flexibility and cost of driving would have faced major revisions in routing, training, marketing, and pricing, not to mention culture. Few established airlines had the flexibility to make such extensive organizational and operating changes overnight. Imitating a whole-system approach is not an easy feat.

The cognitive barriers can be just as effective. When a company offers a leap in value, it rapidly earns brand buzz and a loyal following in the marketplace. Experience shows that even the most expensive marketing campaigns struggle to unseat a blue ocean creator. Microsoft, for example, has been trying for more than ten years to occupy the center of the blue ocean that Intuit created with its financial software product Quicken. Despite all of its efforts and all of its investment, Microsoft has not been able to unseat Intuit as the industry leader.

In other situations, attempts to imitate a blue ocean creator conflict with the imitator's existing brand image. The Body Shop, for example, shuns top models and makes no promises of eternal youth and beauty. For the established cosmetic brands like Estée Lauder and L'Oréal, imitation was very difficult, because it would have signaled a complete invalidation of their current images, which are based on promises of eternal youth and beauty.

A Consistent Pattern

While our conceptual articulation of the pattern may be new, blue ocean strategy has always existed, whether or not companies have been conscious of the fact. Just consider the striking parallels between the Cirque du Soleil theater-circus experience and Ford's creation of the Model T.

At the end of the nineteenth century, the automobile industry was small and unattractive. More than 500 automakers in America competed in turning out handmade luxury cars that cost around $1,500 and were enormously *un*popular with all but the very rich. Anticar activists tore up roads, ringed parked cars with barbed wire, and organized boycotts of car-driving businessmen and politicians. Woodrow Wilson caught the spirit of the times when he said in 1906 that "nothing has spread socialistic feeling more than the automobile." He called it "a picture of the arrogance of wealth."

Instead of trying to beat the competition and steal a share of existing demand from other automakers, Ford reconstructed the industry boundaries of cars and horse-drawn carriages to create a blue ocean. At the time, horse-drawn carriages were the primary means of local transportation across America. The carriage had two distinct advantages over cars. Horses could easily negotiate the bumps and mud that stymied cars—especially in rain and snow—on the nation's ubiquitous dirt roads. And horses and carriages were much easier to maintain than the luxurious autos of the time, which frequently broke down, requiring expert repairmen who were expensive and in short supply. It was Henry Ford's understanding of these advantages that showed him how he could break away from the competition and unlock enormous untapped demand.

Ford called the Model T the car "for the great multitude, constructed of the best materials." Like Cirque, the Ford Motor Company made the competition irrelevant. Instead of creating fashionable, customized cars for weekends in the countryside, a luxury few could justify, Ford built a car that, like the horse-drawn carriage, was for everyday use. The Model T came in just one color, black, and there were few optional extras. It was reliable and durable, designed to travel effortlessly over dirt roads in rain, snow, or sunshine. It was easy to use and fix. People could learn to drive it in a day. And like Cirque, Ford went outside the industry for a price point, looking at horse-drawn carriages ($400), not other autos. In 1908, the first Model T cost $850; in 1909, the price dropped to $609, and by 1924 it was down to $290. In this way, Ford converted buyers of horse-drawn carriages into car buyers—just as Cirque turned theatergoers into circusgoers. Sales of the Model T boomed. Ford's market share surged from 9% in 1908 to 61% in 1921, and by 1923, a majority of American households had a car.

Even as Ford offered the mass of buyers a leap in value, the company also achieved the lowest cost structure in the industry, much as Cirque did later. By keeping the cars highly standardized with limited options and interchangeable parts, Ford was able to scrap the prevailing manufacturing system in which cars were constructed by skilled craftsmen who swarmed around one workstation and built a car piece by piece from start to finish. Ford's revolutionary assembly line replaced craftsmen with unskilled laborers, each of whom worked quickly and efficiently on one small task. This allowed Ford to make a car in just four days—21 days was the industry norm—creating huge cost savings.

Blue and red oceans have always coexisted and always will. Practical reality, therefore, demands that companies understand the strategic logic of both types of oceans. At present, competing in red oceans dominates the field of strategy in theory and in practice, even as businesses' need to create blue oceans intensifies. It is time to even the scales in the field of strategy with a better balance of efforts across both oceans. For although blue ocean strategists have always existed, for the most part their strategies have been largely unconscious. But once corporations realize that the strategies for creating and capturing blue oceans have a different underlying logic from red ocean strategies, they will be able to create many more blue oceans in the future.

Originally published in October 2004. Reprint R0401D.

The Secrets to Successful Strategy Execution

by Gary L. Neilson, Karla L. Martin, and Elizabeth Powers

A BRILLIANT STRATEGY, blockbuster product, or breakthrough technology can put you on the competitive map, but only solid execution can keep you there. You have to be able to deliver on your intent. Unfortunately, the majority of companies aren't very good at it, by their own admission. Over the past five years, we have invited many thousands of employees (about 25% of whom came from executive ranks) to complete an online assessment of their organizations' capabilities, a process that's generated a database of 125,000 profiles representing more than 1,000 companies, government agencies, and not-for-profits in over 50 countries. Employees at three out of every five companies rated their organization weak at execution—that is, when asked if they agreed with the statement "Important strategic and operational decisions are quickly translated into action," the majority answered no.

Execution is the result of thousands of decisions made every day by employees acting according to the information they have and their own self-interest. In our work helping more than 250 companies learn to execute more effectively, we've identified four fundamental building blocks executives can use to influence those actions—clarifying decision rights, designing information flows, aligning motivators, and making changes to structure. (For simplicity's sake we refer to them as decision rights, information, motivators, and structure.)

In efforts to improve performance, most organizations go right to structural measures because moving lines around the org chart seems the most obvious solution and the changes are visible and concrete. Such steps generally reap some short-term efficiencies quickly, but in so doing address only the symptoms of dysfunction, not its root causes. Several years later, companies usually end up in the same place they started. Structural change can and should be part of the path to improved execution, but it's best to think of it as the capstone, not the cornerstone, of any organizational transformation. In fact, our research shows that actions having to do with decision rights and information are far more important—about twice as effective—as improvements made to the other two building blocks. (See "What matters most to strategy execution.")

Take, for example, the case of a global consumer packaged-goods company that lurched down the reorganization path in the early 1990s. (We have altered identifying details in this and other cases that follow.) Disappointed with company performance, senior management did what most companies were doing at that time: They restructured. They eliminated some layers of management and broadened spans of control. Management-staffing costs quickly fell by 18%. Eight years later, however, it was déjà vu. The layers had crept back in, and spans of control had once again narrowed. In addressing only structure, management had attacked the visible symptoms of poor performance but not the underlying cause—how people made decisions and how they were held accountable.

This time, management looked beyond lines and boxes to the mechanics of how work got done. Instead of searching for ways to strip out costs, they focused on improving execution—and in the process discovered the true reasons for the performance shortfall. Managers didn't have a clear sense of their respective roles and responsibilities. They did not intuitively understand which decisions were

Idea in Brief

A brilliant strategy may put you on the competitive map. But only solid execution keeps you there. Unfortunately, most companies struggle with implementation. That's because they overrely on structural changes, such as reorganization, to execute their strategy.

Though structural change has its place in execution, it produces only short-term gains. For example, one company reduced its management layers as part of a strategy to address disappointing performance. Costs plummeted initially, but the layers soon crept back in.

Research by Neilson, Martin, and Powers shows that execution exemplars focus their efforts on two levers far more powerful than structural change:

- **Clarifying decision rights**—for instance, specifying who "owns" each decision and who must provide input

- **Ensuring information flows where it's needed**—such as promoting managers laterally so they build networks needed for the cross-unit collaboration critical to a new strategy

Tackle decision rights and information flows first, and only then **alter organizational structures** and **realign incentives** to *support* those moves.

Q2

theirs to make. Moreover, the link between performance and rewards was weak. This was a company long on micromanaging and second-guessing, and short on accountability. Middle managers spent 40% of their time justifying and reporting upward or questioning the tactical decisions of their direct reports.

Armed with this understanding, the company designed a new management model that established who was accountable for what and made the connection between performance and reward. For instance, the norm at this company, not unusual in the industry, had been to promote people quickly, within 18 months to two years, before they had a chance to see their initiatives through. As a result, managers at every level kept doing their old jobs even after they had been promoted, peering over the shoulders of the direct reports who were now in charge of their projects and, all too frequently,

Idea in Practice

The following levers matter *most* for successful strategy execution:

Decision Rights

- Ensure that everyone in your company knows which decisions and actions they're responsible for.

  Example: In one global consumer-goods company, decisions made by divisional and geographic leaders were overridden by corporate functional leaders who controlled resource allocations. Decisions stalled. Overhead costs mounted as divisions added staff to create bulletproof cases for challenging corporate decisions. To support a new strategy hinging on sharper customer focus, the CEO designated accountability for profits unambiguously to the divisions.

- Encourage higher-level managers to delegate operational decisions.

Example: At one global charitable organization, country-level managers' inability to delegate led to decision paralysis. So the leadership team encouraged country managers to delegate standard operational tasks. This freed these managers to focus on developing the strategies needed to fulfill the organization's mission.

Information Flow

- Make sure important information about the competitive environment flows quickly to corporate headquarters. That way, the top team can identify patterns and promulgate best practices throughout the company.

Example: At one insurance company, accurate information about projects' viability was censored as it moved up the hierarchy. To improve information flow to senior levels of management, the company took steps

taking over. Today, people stay in their positions longer so they can follow through on their own initiatives, and they're still around when the fruits of their labors start to kick in. What's more, results from those initiatives continue to count in their performance reviews for some time after they've been promoted, forcing managers to live with the expectations they'd set in their previous jobs. As a consequence, forecasting has become more accurate and reliable. These actions did yield a structure with fewer layers and greater to create a more open, informal culture. Top executives began mingling with unit leaders during management meetings and held regular brown-bag lunches where people discussed the company's most pressing issues.

- Facilitate information flow across organizational boundaries.

  Example: To better manage relationships with large, cross-product customers, a B2B company needed its units to talk with one another. It charged its newly created customer-focused marketing group with encouraging cross-company communication. The group issued regular reports showing performance against targets (by product and geography) and supplied root-cause analyses of performance gaps. Quarterly performance-management meetings further

fostered the trust required for collaboration.

- Help field and line employees understand how their day-to-day choices affect your company's bottom line.

  Example: At a financial services firm, salespeople routinely crafted customized one-off deals with clients that cost the company more than it made in revenues. Sales didn't understand the cost and complexity implications of these transactions. Management addressed the information misalignment by adopting a "smart customization" approach to sales. For customized deals, it established standardized back-office processes (such as risk assessment). It also developed analytical support tools to arm salespeople with accurate information on the cost implications of their proposed transactions. Profitability improved.

spans of control, but that was a side effect, not the primary focus, of the changes.

The Elements of Strong Execution

Our conclusions arise out of decades of practical application and intensive research. Nearly five years ago, we and our colleagues set out to gather empirical data to identify the actions that were most effective in enabling an organization to implement strategy. What particular ways of restructuring, motivating, improving information flows, and clarifying decision rights mattered the most? We started by drawing up a list of 17 traits, each corresponding to one or more of the four building blocks we knew could enable effective execution—traits like the free flow of information across organizational boundaries or the degree to which senior leaders refrain from getting involved in operating decisions. With these factors in mind, we developed an online profiler that allows individuals to assess the execution capabilities of their organizations. Over the next four years or so, we collected data from many thousands of profiles, which in turn allowed us to more precisely calibrate the impact of each trait on an organization's ability to execute. That allowed us to rank all 17 traits in order of their relative influence. (See "The 17 fundamental traits of organizational effectiveness.")

Ranking the traits makes clear how important decision rights and information are to effective strategy execution. The first eight traits map directly to decision rights and information. Only three of the 17 traits relate to structure, and none of those ranks higher than 13th. We'll walk through the top five traits here.

1. Everyone has a good idea of the decisions and actions for which he or she is responsible

In companies strong on execution, 71% of individuals agree with this statement; that figure drops to 32% in organizations weak on execution.

Blurring of decision rights tends to occur as a company matures. Young organizations are generally too busy getting things done to define roles and responsibilities clearly at the outset. And why should they? In a small company, it's not so difficult to know what other people are up to. So for a time, things work out well enough. As the company grows, however, executives come and go, bringing in with them and taking away different expectations, and over time the approval process gets ever more convoluted and murky. It becomes increasingly unclear where one person's accountability begins and another's ends.

One global consumer-durables company found this out the hard way. It was so rife with people making competing and conflicting decisions that it was hard to find anyone below the CEO who felt truly accountable for profitability. The company was organized into 16 product divisions aggregated into three geographic groups—North America, Europe, and International. Each of the divisions was charged with reaching explicit performance targets, but functional staff at corporate headquarters controlled spending targets—how R&D dollars were allocated, for instance. Decisions made by divisional and geographic leaders were routinely overridden by functional leaders. Overhead costs began to mount as the divisions added staff to help them create bulletproof cases to challenge corporate decisions.

Decisions stalled while divisions negotiated with functions, each layer weighing in with questions. Functional staffers in the divisions (financial analysts, for example) often deferred to their higher-ups in corporate rather than their division vice president, since functional leaders were responsible for rewards and promotions. Only the CEO and his executive team had the discretion to resolve disputes. All of these symptoms fed on one another and collectively hampered execution—until a new CEO came in.

The new chief executive chose to focus less on cost control and more on profitable growth by redefining the divisions to focus on consumers. As part of the new organizational model, the CEO designated accountability for profits unambiguously to the divisions and also gave them the authority to draw on functional activities to support their goals (as well as more control of the budget). Corporate functional roles and decision rights were recast to better support the divisions' needs and also to build the cross-divisional links necessary for developing the global capabilities of the business as a whole. For the most part, the functional leaders understood the market realities—and that change entailed some adjustments to the operating model of the business. It helped that the CEO brought them into the organizational redesign process, so that the new model wasn't something imposed on them as much as it was something they engaged in and built together.

2. Important information about the competitive environment gets to headquarters quickly

On average, 77% of individuals in strong-execution organizations agree with this statement, whereas only 45% of those in weak-execution organizations do.

Headquarters can serve a powerful function in identifying patterns and promulgating best practices throughout business segments and geographic regions. But it can play this coordinating role only if it has accurate and up-to-date market intelligence. Otherwise, it will tend to impose its own agenda and policies rather than defer to operations that are much closer to the customer.

Consider the case of heavy-equipment manufacturer Caterpillar.[1] Today it is a highly successful $45 billion global company, but a generation ago, Caterpillar's organization was so badly misaligned that its very existence was threatened. Decision rights were hoarded at the top by functional general offices located at headquarters in Peoria, Illinois, while much of the information needed to make those decisions resided in the field with sales managers. "It just took a long time to get decisions going up and down the functional silos, and they really weren't good business decisions; they were more functional decisions," noted one field executive. Current CEO Jim Owens, then a managing director in Indonesia, told us that such information that did make it to the top had been "whitewashed and varnished several times over along the way." Cut off from information about the external market, senior executives focused on the organization's internal workings, overanalyzing issues and second-guessing decisions made at lower levels, costing the company opportunities in fast-moving markets.

Pricing, for example, was based on cost and determined not by market realities but by the pricing general office in Peoria. Sales representatives across the world lost sale after sale to Komatsu, whose competitive pricing consistently beat Caterpillar's. In 1982, the company posted the first annual loss in its almost-60-year history. In 1983 and 1984, it lost $1 million a day, seven days a week. By the end of 1984, Caterpillar had lost a billion dollars. By 1988, then-CEO George Schaefer stood atop an entrenched bureaucracy that was, in

What matters most to strategy execution

When a company fails to execute its strategy, the first thing managers often think to do is restructure. But our research shows that the fundamentals of good execution start with clarifying decision rights and making sure information flows where it needs to go. If you get those right, the correct structure and motivators often become obvious.

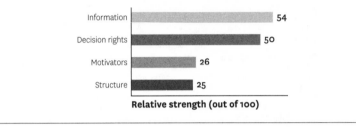

Relative strength (out of 100)

his words, "telling me what I wanted to hear, not what I needed to know." So, he convened a task force of "renegade" middle managers and tasked them with charting Caterpillar's future.

Ironically, the way to ensure that the right information flowed to headquarters was to make sure the right decisions were made much further down the organization. By delegating operational responsibility to the people closer to the action, top executives were free to focus on more global strategic issues. Accordingly, the company reorganized into business units, making each accountable for its own P&L statement. The functional general offices that had been all-powerful ceased to exist, literally overnight. Their talent and expertise, including engineering, pricing, and manufacturing, were parceled out to the new business units, which could now design their own products, develop their own manufacturing processes and schedules, and set their own prices. The move dramatically decentralized decision rights, giving the units control over market decisions. The business unit P&Ls were now measured consistently across the enterprise, as return on assets became the universal measure of success. With this accurate, up-to-date, and directly comparable information, senior decision makers at headquarters could make smart strategic choices and trade-offs rather than use

The 17 fundamental traits of organizational effectiveness

From our survey research drawn from more than 26,000 people in 31 companies, we have distilled the traits that make organizations effective at implementing strategy. Here they are, in order of importance.

Rank	Organization Trait	Strength Index (Out of 100)
1	Everyone has a good idea of the decisions and actions for which he or she is responsible.	81
2	Important information about the competitive environment gets to headquarters quickly.	68
3	Once made, decisions are rarely second-guessed.	58
4	Information flows freely across organizational boundaries.	58
5	Field and line employees usually have the information they need to understand the bottom-line impact of their day-to-day choices.	55
6	Line managers have access to the metrics they need to measure the key drivers of their business.	48
7	Managers up the line get involved in operating decisions.	32
8	Conflicting messages are rarely sent to the market.	32
9	The individual performance-appraisal process differentiates among high, adequate, and low performers.	32
10	The ability to deliver on performance commitments strongly influences career advancement and compensation.	32
11	It is more accurate to describe the culture of this organization as "persuade and cajole" than "command and control."	29
12	The primary role of corporate staff here is to support the business units rather than to audit them.	29
13	Promotions can be lateral moves (from one position to another on the same level in the hierarchy).	29
14	Fast-track employees here can expect promotions more frequently than every three years.	23
15	On average, middle managers here have five or more direct reports.	19
16	If the firm has a bad year, but a particular division has a good year, the division head would still get a bonus.	13
17	Besides pay, many other things motivate individuals to do a good job.	10

Building Blocks ■ Decision rights ☐ Information ■ Motivators ■ Structure outdated sales data to make ineffective, tactical marketing decisions.

Within 18 months, the company was working in the new model. "This was a revolution that became a renaissance," Owens recalls, "a spectacular transformation of a kind of sluggish company into one that actually has entrepreneurial zeal. And that transition was very quick because it was decisive and it was complete; it was thorough; it was universal, worldwide, all at one time."

3. Once made, decisions are rarely second-guessed

Whether someone is second-guessing depends on your vantage point. A more senior and broader enterprise perspective can add value to a decision, but managers up the line may not be adding incremental value; instead, they may be stalling progress by redoing their subordinates' jobs while, in effect, shirking their own. In our research, 71% of respondents in weak-execution companies thought that decisions were being second-guessed, whereas only 45% of those from strong-execution organizations felt that way.

Recently, we worked with a global charitable organization dedicated to alleviating poverty. It had a problem others might envy: It was suffering from the strain brought on by a rapid growth in donations and a corresponding increase in the depth and breadth of its program offerings. As you might expect, this nonprofit was populated with people on a mission who took intense personal ownership of projects. It did not reward the delegation of even the most mundane administrative tasks. Country-level managers, for example, would personally oversee copier repairs. Managers' inability to delegate led to decision paralysis and a lack of accountability as the organization grew. Second-guessing was an art form. When there was doubt over who was empowered to make a decision, the default was often to have a series of meetings in which no decision was reached. When decisions were finally made, they had generally been vetted by so many parties that no one person could be held accountable. An effort to expedite decision-making through restructuring—by collocating key leaders with subject-matter experts in newly established central and regional centers of excellence—became instead another logjam. Key managers still weren't sure of their right to take advantage of these centers, so they didn't.

The nonprofit's management and directors went back to the drawing board. We worked with them to design a decision-making map, a tool to help identify where different types of decisions should be taken, and with it they clarified and enhanced decision rights at all levels of management. All managers were then actively encouraged to delegate standard operational tasks. Once people had a clear idea of what decisions they should and should not be making, holding them accountable for decisions felt fair. What's more, now they could focus their energies on the organization's mission. Clarifying decision rights and responsibilities also improved the organization's ability to track individual achievement, which helped it chart new and appealing career-advancement paths.

4. Information flows freely across organizational boundaries

When information does not flow horizontally across different parts of the company, units behave like silos, forfeiting economies of scale and the transfer of best practices. Moreover, the organization as a whole loses the opportunity to develop a cadre of up-and-coming managers well versed in all aspects of the company's operations. Our research indicates that only 21% of respondents from weak-execution companies thought information flowed freely across organizational boundaries whereas 55% of those from strong-execution firms did. Since scores for even the strong companies are pretty low, though, this is an issue that most companies can work on.

A cautionary tale comes from a business-to-business company whose customer and product teams failed to collaborate in serving a key segment: large, cross-product customers. To manage relationships with important clients, the company had established a customer-focused marketing group, which developed customer outreach programs, innovative pricing models, and tailored promotions and discounts. But this group issued no clear and consistent reports of its initiatives and progress to the product units and had difficulty securing time with the regular cross-unit management to discuss key performance issues. Each product unit communicated and planned in its own way, and it took tremendous energy for the customer group to understand the units' various priorities and tailor communications to each one. So the units were not aware, and had little faith, that this new division was making constructive inroads into a key customer segment. Conversely (and predictably), the customer team felt the units paid only perfunctory attention to its plans and couldn't get their cooperation on issues critical to multiproduct customers, such as potential trade-offs and volume discounts.

Historically, this lack of collaboration hadn't been a problem because the company had been the dominant player in a high-margin market. But as the market became more competitive, customers began to view the firm as unreliable and, generally, as a difficult supplier, and they became increasingly reluctant to enter into favorable relationships.

Once the issues became clear, though, the solution wasn't terribly complicated, involving little more than getting the groups to talk to one another. The customer division became responsible for issuing regular reports to the product units showing performance against targets, by product and geographic region, and for supplying a supporting root-cause analysis. A standing performance-management meeting was placed on the schedule every quarter, creating a forum for exchanging information face-to-face and discussing outstanding issues. These moves bred the broader organizational trust required for collaboration.

5. Field and line employees usually have the information they need to understand the bottom-line impact of their day-to-day choices

Rational decisions are necessarily bounded by the information available to employees. If managers don't understand what it will cost to capture an incremental dollar in revenue, they will always pursue the incremental revenue. They can hardly be faulted, even if their decision is—in the light of full information—wrong. Our research shows that 61% of individuals in strong-execution organizations agree that field and line employees have the information they need to understand the bottom-line impact of their decisions. This figure plummets to 28% in weak-execution organizations.

We saw this unhealthy dynamic play out at a large, diversified financial-services client, which had been built through a series of successful mergers of small regional banks. In combining operations, managers had chosen to separate front-office bankers who sold loans from back-office support groups who did risk assessments, placing each in a different reporting relationship and, in many cases, in different locations. Unfortunately, they failed to institute the necessary information and motivation links to ensure smooth operations. As a result, each pursued different, and often competing, goals.

For example, salespeople would routinely enter into highly customized one-off deals with clients that cost the company more than they made in revenues. Sales did not have a clear understanding of the cost and complexity implications of these transactions. Without sufficient information, sales staff believed that the back-end people were sabotaging their deals, while the support groups considered the front-end people to be cowboys. At year's end, when the data were finally reconciled, management would bemoan the sharp increase in operational costs, which often erased the profit from these transactions.

Executives addressed this information misalignment by adopting a "smart customization" approach to sales. They standardized the end-to-end processes used in the majority of deals and allowed for customization only in select circumstances. For these customized deals, they established clear back-office processes and analytical support tools to arm salespeople with accurate information on the cost implications of the proposed transactions. At the same time, they rolled out common reporting standards and tools for both the front- and back-office operations to ensure that each group had access to the same data and metrics when making decisions. Once each side understood the business realities confronted by the other, they cooperated more effectively, acting in the whole company's best interests—and there were no more year-end surprises.

About the Data

WE TESTED ORGANIZATIONAL effectiveness by having people fill out an online diagnostic, a tool comprising 19 questions (17 that describe organizational traits and two that describe outcomes).

To determine which of the 17 traits in our profiler are most strongly associated with excellence in execution, we looked at 31 companies in our database for which we had responses from at least 150 individual (anonymously completed) profiles, for a total of 26,743 responses. Applying regression analysis to each of the 31 data sets, we correlated the 17 traits with our measure of organizational effectiveness, which we defined as an affirmative response to the outcome statement, "Important strategic and operational decisions are quickly translated into action." Then we ranked the traits in order, according to the number of data sets in which the trait exhibited a significant correlation with our measure of success within a 90% confidence interval. Finally, we indexed the result to a 100-point scale. The top trait—"Everyone has a good idea of the decisions and actions for which he or she is responsible"— exhibited a significant positive correlation with our success indicator in 25 of the 31 data sets, for an index score of 81.

Creating a Transformation Program

The four building blocks that managers can use to improve strategy execution—decision rights, information, structure, and motivators— are inextricably linked. Unclear decision rights not only paralyze decision making but also impede information flow, divorce performance from rewards, and prompt workarounds that subvert formal reporting lines. Blocking information results in poor decisions, limited career development, and a reinforcement of structural silos. So what to do about it?

Since each organization is different and faces a unique set of internal and external variables, there is no universal answer to that question. The first step is to identify the sources of the problem. In our work, we often begin by having a company's employees take our profiling survey and consolidating the results. The more people in the organization who take the survey, the better.

Once executives understand their company's areas of weakness, they can take any number of actions. "Mapping improvements to the building blocks: Some sample tactics" shows 15 possible steps that can have an impact on performance. (The options listed represent only a sampling of the dozens of choices managers might make.) All of these actions are geared toward strengthening one or more of the 17 traits. For example, if you were to take steps to "clarify and streamline decision making" you could potentially strengthen two traits: "Everyone has a good idea of the decisions and actions for which he or she is responsible," and "Once made, decisions are rarely second-guessed."

You certainly wouldn't want to put 15 initiatives in a single transformation program. Most organizations don't have the managerial capacity or organizational appetite to take on more than five or six at a time. And as we've stressed, you should first take steps to address decision rights and information, and then design the necessary changes to motivators and structure to support the new design.

To help companies understand their shortcomings and construct the improvement program that will have the greatest impact, we have developed an organizational-change simulator. This interactive tool accompanies the profiler, allowing you to try out different elements of a change program virtually, to see which ones will best target your company's particular area of weakness. (For an overview of the simulation process, see the sidebar "Test Drive Your Organization's Transformation.")

To get a sense of the process from beginning to end—from taking the diagnostic profiler, to formulating your strategy, to launching your organizational transformation—consider the experience of a leading insurance company we'll call Goodward Insurance. Goodward was a successful company with strong capital reserves and steady revenue and customer growth. Still, its leadership wanted to further enhance execution to deliver on an ambitious five-year strategic agenda that included aggressive targets in customer growth, revenue increases, and cost reduction, which would require a new level of teamwork. While there were pockets of cross-unit collaboration within the company, it was far more common for each unit to focus on its own goals, making it difficult to spare resources to support another unit's goals. In many cases there was little

Mapping improvements to the building blocks: some sample tactics

Companies can take a host of steps to improve their ability to execute strategy. The 15 here are only some of the possible examples. Every one strengthens one or more of the building blocks executives can use to improve their strategy-execution capability: clarifying decision rights, improving information, establishing the right motivators, and restructuring the organization.

Focus corporate staff on supporting business-unit decision making.

Clarify and streamline decision making at each operating level.

Focus headquarters on important strategic questions.

Create centers of excellence by consolidating similar functions into a single organizational unit.

Assign process owners to coordinate activities that span organizational functions.

Establish individual performance measures.

Improve field-to-headquarters information flow.

Define and distribute daily operating metrics to the field or line.

Create cross-functional teams.

Introduce differentiating performance awards.

Expand nonmonetary rewards to recognize exceptional performers.

Increase position tenure.

Institute lateral moves and rotations.

Broaden spans of control.

Building blocks ■ Decision rights ☐ Information ■ Motivators ■ Structure incentive to do so anyway: Unit A's goals might require the involvement of Unit B to succeed, but Unit B's goals might not include supporting Unit A's effort.

The company had initiated a number of enterprisewide projects over the years, which had been completed on time and on budget, but these often had to be reworked because stakeholder needs hadn't been sufficiently taken into account. After launching a shared-services center, for example, the company had to revisit its operating model and processes when units began hiring shadow staff to focus on priority work that the center wouldn't expedite. The center might decide what technology applications, for instance, to develop on its own rather than set priorities according to what was most important to the organization.

In a similar way, major product launches were hindered by insufficient coordination among departments. The marketing department would develop new coverage options without asking the claims-processing group whether it had the ability to process the claims. Since it didn't, processors had to create expensive manual work-arounds when the new kinds of claims started pouring in. Nor did marketing ask the actuarial department how these products would affect the risk profile and reimbursement expenses of the company, and for some of the new products, costs did indeed increase.

To identify the greatest barriers to building a stronger execution culture, Goodward Insurance gave the diagnostic survey to all of its 7,000-plus employees and compared the organization's scores on the 17 traits with those from strong-execution companies. Numerous previous surveys (employee-satisfaction, among others) had elicited qualitative comments identifying the barriers to execution excellence. But the diagnostic survey gave the company quantifiable data that it could analyze by group and by management level to determine which barriers were most hindering the people actually charged with execution. As it turned out, middle management was far more pessimistic than the top executives in their assessment of the organization's execution ability. Their input became especially critical to the change agenda ultimately adopted.

Through the survey, Goodward Insurance uncovered impediments to execution in three of the most influential organizational traits:

Information did not flow freely across organizational boundaries. Sharing information was never one of Goodward's hallmarks, but managers had always dismissed the mounting anecdotal evidence of poor cross-divisional information flow as "some other group's problem." The organizational diagnostic data, however, exposed such plausible deniability as an inadequate excuse. In fact, when the CEO reviewed the profiler results with his direct reports, he held up the chart on cross-group information flows and declared, "We've been discussing this problem for several years, and yet you always say that it's so-and-so's problem, not mine. Sixty-seven percent of [our] respondents said that they do not think information flows freely across divisions. This is not so-and-so's problem—it's our problem. You just don't get results that low [unless it comes] from everywhere. We are all on the hook for fixing this."

Contributing to this lack of horizontal information flow was a dearth of lateral promotions. Because Goodward had always promoted up rather than over and up, most middle and senior managers remained within a single group. They were not adequately apprised of the activities of the other groups, nor did they have a network of contacts across the organization.

Important information about the competitive environment did not get to headquarters quickly. The diagnostic data and subsequent surveys and interviews with middle management revealed that the wrong information was moving up the org chart. Mundane day-to-day decisions were escalated to the executive level—the top team had to approve midlevel hiring decisions, for instance, and bonuses of $1,000—limiting Goodward's agility in responding to competitors' moves, customers' needs, and changes in the broader marketplace. Meanwhile, more important information was so heavily filtered as it moved up the hierarchy that it was all but worthless for rendering key verdicts. Even if lower-level managers knew that a certain project could never work for highly valid reasons, they would not

Test-Drive Your Organization's Transformation

YOU KNOW YOUR ORGANIZATION could perform better. You are faced with dozens of levers you could conceivably pull if you had unlimited time and resources. But you don't. You operate in the real world.

How, then, do you make the most-educated and cost-efficient decisions about which change initiatives to implement? We've developed a way to test the efficacy of specific actions (such as clarifying decision rights, forming cross-functional teams, or expanding nonmonetary rewards) without risking significant amounts of time and money. You can go to www.simulatororgeffectiveness.com to assemble and try out various five-step organizational-change programs and assess which would be the most effective and efficient in improving execution at your company.

You begin the simulation by selecting one of seven organizational profiles that most resembles the current state of your organization. If you're not sure, you can take a five-minute diagnostic survey. This online survey automatically generates an organizational profile and baseline execution-effectiveness score. (Although 100 is a perfect score, nobody is perfect; even the most effective companies often score in the 60s and 70s.)

Having established your baseline, you use the simulator to chart a possible course you'd like to take to improve your execution capabilities by selecting five out of a possible 28 actions. Ideally, these moves should directly address the weakest links in your organizational profile. To help you make the right choices, the simulator offers insights that shed further light on how a proposed action influences particular organizational elements.

Once you have made your selections, the simulator executes the steps you've elected and processes them through a web-based engine that evaluates them using empirical relationships identified from 31 companies representing more than 26,000 data observations. It then generates a bar chart indicating how much your organization's execution score has improved and where it now

communicate that dim view to the top team. Nonstarters not only started, they kept going. For instance, the company had a project under way to create new incentives for its brokers. Even though this approach had been previously tried without success, no one spoke up in meetings or stopped the project because it was a priority for one of the top-team members.

stands in relation to the highest-performing companies from our research and the scores of other people like you who have used the simulator starting from the same original profile you did. If you wish, you may then advance to the next round and pick another five actions. What you will see is illustrated below.

The beauty of the simulator is its ability to consider—consequence-free—the impact on execution of endless combinations of possible actions. Each simulation includes only two rounds, but you can run the simulation as many times as you like. The simulator has also been used for team competition within organizations, and we've found that it engenders very engaging and productive dialogue among senior executives.

While the simulator cannot capture all of the unique situations an organization might face, it is a useful tool for assessing and building a targeted and effective organization-transformation program. It serves as a vehicle to stimulate thinking about the impact of various changes, saving untold amounts of time and resources in the process.

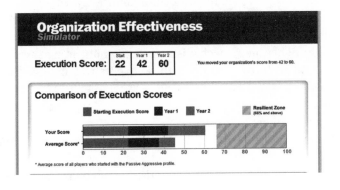

No one had a good idea of the decisions and actions for which he or she was responsible. The general lack of information flow extended to decision rights, as few managers understood where their authority ended and another's began. Accountability even for day-to-day decisions was unclear, and managers did not know whom to ask for clarification. Naturally, confusion over decision rights led to second-guessing. Fifty-five percent of respondents felt that decisions were regularly second-guessed at Goodward.

To Goodward's credit, its top executives immediately responded to the results of the diagnostic by launching a change program targeted at all three problem areas. The program integrated early, often symbolic, changes with longer-term initiatives, in an effort to build momentum and galvanize participation and ownership. Recognizing that a passive-aggressive attitude toward people perceived to be in power solely as a result of their position in the hierarchy was hindering information flow, they took immediate steps to signal their intention to create a more informal and open culture. One symbolic change: the seating at management meetings was rearranged. The top executives used to sit in a separate section, the physical space between them and the rest of the room fraught with symbolism. Now they intermingled, making themselves more accessible and encouraging people to share information informally. Regular brown-bag lunches were established with members of the C-suite, where people had a chance to discuss the overall culture-change initiative, decision rights, new mechanisms for communicating across the units, and so forth. Seating at these events was highly choreographed to ensure that a mix of units was represented at each table. Icebreaker activities were designed to encourage individuals to learn about other units' work.

Meanwhile, senior managers commenced the real work of remedying issues relating to information flows and decision rights. They assessed their own informal networks to understand how people making key decisions got their information, and they identified critical gaps. The outcome was a new framework for making important decisions that clearly specifies who owns each decision, who must provide input, who is ultimately accountable for the results, and how results are defined. Other longer-term initiatives include:

- Pushing certain decisions down into the organization to better align decision rights with the best available information. Most hiring and bonus decisions, for instance, have been delegated to immediate managers, so long as they are within preestablished boundaries relating to numbers hired and salary levels. Being clear about who needs what information is encouraging cross-group dialogue.

- Identifying and eliminating duplicative committees.

- Pushing metrics and scorecards down to the group level, so that rather than focus on solving the mystery of *who* caused a problem, management can get right to the root cause of *why* the problem occurred. A well-designed scorecard captures not only outcomes (like sales volume or revenue) but also leading indicators of those outcomes (such as the number of customer calls or completed customer plans). As a result, the focus of management conversations has shifted from trying to explain the past to charting the future—anticipating and preventing problems.

- Making the planning process more inclusive. Groups are explicitly mapping out the ways their initiatives depend on and affect one another; shared group goals are assigned accordingly.

- Enhancing the middle management career path to emphasize the importance of lateral moves to career advancement.

Goodward Insurance has just embarked on this journey. The insurer has distributed ownership of these initiatives among various groups and management levels so that these efforts don't become silos in themselves. Already, solid improvement in the company's execution is beginning to emerge. The early evidence of success has come from employee-satisfaction surveys: Middle management responses to the questions about levels of cross-unit collaboration and clarity of decision making have improved as much as 20 to 25 percentage points. And high performers are already reaching across boundaries to gain a broader understanding of the full business, even if it doesn't mean a better title right away.

———————

Execution is a notorious and perennial challenge. Even at the companies that are best at it—what we call "resilient organizations"— just two-thirds of employees agree that important strategic and operational decisions are quickly translated into action. As long as companies continue to attack their execution problems primarily or solely with structural or motivational initiatives, they will continue to fail. As we've seen, they may enjoy short-term results, but they will inevitably slip back into old habits because they won't have addressed the root causes of failure. Such failures can almost always be fixed by ensuring that people truly understand what they are responsible for and who makes which decisions—and then giving them the information they need to fulfill their responsibilities. With these two building blocks in place, structural and motivational elements will follow.

Originally published in June 2008. Reprint R0806C.

Notes

1. The details for this example have been taken from Gary L. Neilson and Bruce A. Pasternack, *Results: Keep What's Good, Fix What's Wrong, and Unlock Great Performance* (Random House, 2005).

Using the Balanced Scorecard as a Strategic Management System

by Robert S. Kaplan and David P. Norton

AS COMPANIES AROUND the world transform themselves for competition that is based on information, their ability to exploit intangible assets has become far more decisive than their ability to invest in and manage physical assets. Several years ago, in recognition of this change, we introduced a concept we called the *balanced scorecard*. The balanced scorecard supplemented traditional financial measures with criteria that measured performance from three additional perspectives—those of customers, internal business processes, and learning and growth. (See "Translating vision and strategy: Four perspectives.") It therefore enabled companies to track financial results while simultaneously monitoring progress in building the capabilities and acquiring the intangible assets they would need for future growth. The scorecard wasn't a replacement for financial measures; it was their complement.

Recently, we have seen some companies move beyond our early vision for the scorecard to discover its value as the cornerstone of a new strategic management system. Used this way, the scorecard addresses a serious deficiency in traditional management systems: their inability to link a company's long-term strategy with its short-term actions.

Most companies' operational and management control systems are built around financial measures and targets, which bear little relation to the company's progress in achieving long-term strategic objectives. Thus the emphasis most companies place on short-term financial measures leaves a gap between the development of a strategy and its implementation.

Managers using the balanced scorecard do not have to rely on short-term financial measures as the sole indicators of the company's performance. The scorecard lets them introduce four new management processes that, separately and in combination, contribute to linking long-term strategic objectives with short-term actions. (See "Managing strategy: Four processes.")

The first new process—*translating the vision*—helps managers build a consensus around the organization's vision and strategy. Despite the best intentions of those at the top, lofty statements about becoming "best in class," "the number one supplier," or an "empowered organization" don't translate easily into operational terms that provide useful guides to action at the local level. For people to act on the words in vision and strategy statements, those statements must be expressed as an integrated set of objectives and measures, agreed upon by all senior executives, that describe the long-term drivers of success.

The second process—*communicating and linking*—lets managers communicate their strategy up and down the organization and link it to departmental and individual objectives. Traditionally, departments are evaluated by their financial performance, and individual incentives are tied to short-term financial goals. The scorecard gives managers a way of ensuring that all levels of the organization understand the long-term strategy and that both departmental and individual objectives are aligned with it.

The third process—*business planning*—enables companies to integrate their business and financial plans. Almost all organizations today are implementing a variety of change programs, each with its own champions, gurus, and consultants, and each competing for

Idea in Brief

Why do budgets often bear little direct relation to a company's long-term strategic objectives? Because they don't take enough into consideration. A balanced scorecard augments traditional financial measures with benchmarks for performance in three key nonfinancial areas:

- a company's relationship with its customers

- its key internal processes

- its learning and growth.

When performance measures for these areas are added to the financial metrics, the result is not only a broader perspective on the company's health and activities, it's also a powerful organizing framework. A sophisticated instrument panel for coordinating and fine-tuning a company's operations and businesses so that all activities are aligned with its strategy.

senior executives' time, energy, and resources. Managers find it difficult to integrate those diverse initiatives to achieve their strategic goals—a situation that leads to frequent disappointments with the programs' results. But when managers use the ambitious goals set for balanced scorecard measures as the basis for allocating resources and setting priorities, they can undertake and coordinate only those initiatives that move them toward their long-term strategic objectives.

The fourth process—*feedback and learning*—gives companies the capacity for what we call strategic learning. Existing feedback and review processes focus on whether the company, its departments, or its individual employees have met their budgeted financial goals. With the balanced scorecard at the center of its management systems, a company can monitor short-term results from the three additional perspectives—customers, internal business processes, and learning and growth—and evaluate strategy in the light of recent performance. The scorecard thus enables companies to modify strategies to reflect real-time learning.

Idea in Practice

The balanced scorecard relies on four processes to bind short-term activities to long-term objectives:

1. Translating the Vision

By relying on measurement, the scorecard forces managers to come to agreement on the metrics they will use to operationalize their lofty visions.

> *Example:* A bank had articulated its strategy as providing "superior service to targeted customers." But the process of choosing operational measures for the four areas of the scorecard made executives realize that they first needed to reconcile divergent views of who the targeted customers were and what constituted superior service.

2. Communicating and Linking

When a scorecard is disseminated up and down the organizational chart, strategy becomes a tool available to everyone. As the high-level scorecard cascades down to individual business units, overarching strategic objectives and measures are translated into objectives and measures appropriate to each particular group. Tying these targets to individual performance and compensation systems yields "personal scorecards." Thus, individual employees understand how their own productivity supports the overall strategy.

None of the more than 100 organizations that we have studied or with which we have worked implemented their first balanced scorecard with the intention of developing a new strategic management system. But in each one, the senior executives discovered that the scorecard supplied a framework and thus a focus for many critical management processes: departmental and individual goal setting, business planning, capital allocations, strategic initiatives, and feedback and learning. Previously, those processes were uncoordinated and often directed at short-term operational goals. By building the scorecard, the senior executives started a process of change that has gone well beyond the original idea of simply broadening the company's performance measures.

For example, one insurance company—let's call it National Insurance—developed its first balanced scorecard to create a new vision for itself as an underwriting specialist. But once National started to

3. Business Planning

Most companies have separate procedures (and sometimes units) for strategic planning and budgeting. Little wonder, then, that typical long-term planning is, in the words of one executive, where "the rubber meets the sky." The discipline of creating a balanced scorecard forces companies to integrate the two functions, thereby ensuring that financial budgets do indeed support strategic goals. After agreeing on performance measures for the four scorecard perspectives, companies identify the most influential "drivers" of the desired outcomes and then set milestones for gauging the progress they make with these drivers.

4. Feedback and Learning

By supplying a mechanism for strategic feedback and review, the balanced scorecard helps an organization foster a kind of learning often missing in companies: the ability to reflect on inferences and adjust theories about cause-and-effect relationships.

Feedback about products and services. New learning about key internal processes. Technological discoveries. All this information can be fed into the scorecard, enabling strategic refinements to be made continually. Thus, at any point in the implementation, managers can know whether the strategy is working—and if not, why.

use it, the scorecard allowed the CEO and the senior management team not only to introduce a new strategy for the organization but also to overhaul the company's management system. The CEO subsequently told employees in a letter addressed to the whole organization that National would thenceforth use the balanced scorecard and the philosophy that it represented to manage the business.

National built its new strategic management system step-by-step over 30 months, with each step representing an incremental improvement. (See "How one company built a strategic management system . . .") The iterative sequence of actions enabled the company to reconsider each of the four new management processes two or three times before the system stabilized and became an established part of National's overall management system. Thus the CEO was able to transform the company so that everyone could focus on

Translation vision and strategy: four perspectives

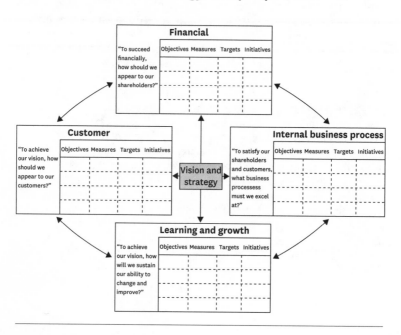

achieving long-term strategic objectives—something that no purely financial framework could do.

Translating the Vision

The CEO of an engineering construction company, after working with his senior management team for several months to develop a mission statement, got a phone call from a project manager in the field. "I want you to know," the distraught manager said, "that I believe in the mission statement. I want to act in accordance with the mission statement. I'm here with my customer. What am I supposed to do?"

Managing strategy: four processes

The mission statement, like those of many other organizations, had declared an intention to "use high-quality employees to provide services that surpass customers' needs." But the project manager in the field with his employees and his customer did not know how to translate those words into the appropriate actions. The phone call convinced the CEO that a large gap existed between the mission statement and employees' knowledge of how their day-to-day actions could contribute to realizing the company's vision.

Metro Bank (not its real name), the result of a merger of two competitors, encountered a similar gap while building its balanced scorecard. The senior executive group thought it had reached

How one company built a strategic management system . . .

2A *Communicate to middle managers.* The top three layers of management (100 people) are brought together to learn about and discuss the new strategy. The balanced scorecard is the communication vehicle. *(months 4–5)*

2B *Develop business unit scorecards.* Using the corporate scorecard as a template, each business unit translates its strategy into its own scorecard. *(months 6–9)*

5 *Refine the vision.* The review of business unit scorecards identifies several cross-business issues not initially included in the corporate strategy. The corporate scorecard is updated. *(month 12)*

Time frame *(in months)*

0	1	2	3	4	5	6	7	8	9	10	11	12

Actions:

1 *Clarify the vision.* Ten members of a newly formed executive team work together for three months. A balanced scorecard is developed to translate a generic vision into a strategy that is understood and can be communicated. The process helps build consensus and commitment to the strategy.

3A *Eliminate nonstrategic investments.* The corporate scorecard, by clarifying strategic priorities, identifies many active programs that are not contributing to the strategy. *(month 6)*

3B *Launch corporate change programs.* The corporate scorecard identifies the need for cross-business change programs. They are launched while the business units prepare their scorecards. *(month 6)*

4 *Review business unit scorecards.* The CEO and the executive team review the individual business units' scorecards. The review permits the CEO to participate knowledgeably in shaping business unit strategy. *(months 9–11)*

7 Update long-range plan and budget. Five-year goals are established for each measure. The investments required to meet those goals are identified and funded. The first year of the five-year plan becomes the annual budget. *(months 15–17)*

9 Conduct annual strategy review. At the start of the third year, the initial strategy has been achieved and the corporate strategy requires updating. The executive committee lists ten strategic issues. Each business unit is asked to develop a position on each issue as a prelude to updating its strategy and scorecard. *(months 25–26)*

13	14	15	16	17	18	19	20	21	22	23	24	25	26

6A Communicate the balanced scorecard to the entire company. At the end of one year, when the management teams are comfortable with the strategic approach, the scorecard is disseminated to the entire organization. *(month 12–ongoing)*

6B Establish individual performance objectives. The top three layers of management link their individual objectives and incentive compensation to their scorecards. *(months 13–14)*

8 Conduct monthly and quarterly reviews. After corporate approval of the business unit scorecards, a monthly review process, supplemented by quarterly reviews that focus more heavily on strategic issues, begins. *(month 18–ongoing)*

10 Link everyone's performance to the balanced scorecard. All employees are asked to link their individual objectives to the balanced scorecard. The entire organization's incentive compensation is linked to the scorecard. *(months 25–26)*

> Note: Steps 7, 8, 9, and 10 are performed on a regular schedule. The balanced scorecard is now a routine part of the management process.

. . . around the balanced scorecard

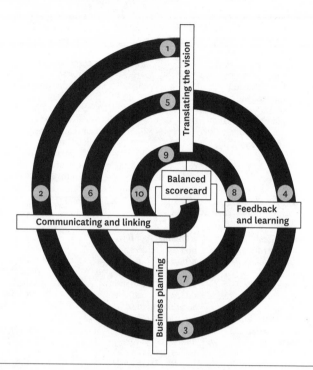

agreement on the new organization's overall strategy: "to provide superior service to targeted customers." Research had revealed five basic market segments among existing and potential customers, each with different needs. While formulating the measures for the customer-perspective portion of their balanced scorecard, however, it became apparent that although the 25 senior executives agreed on the words of the strategy, each one had a different definition of *superior service* and a different image of the *targeted customers*.

The exercise of developing operational measures for the four perspectives on the bank's scorecard forced the 25 executives to clarify the meaning of the strategy statement. Ultimately, they agreed to stimulate revenue growth through new products and services and also agreed on the three most desirable customer segments. They developed scorecard measures for the specific products and services that should be delivered to customers in the targeted segments as well as for the relationship the bank should build with customers in each segment. The scorecard also highlighted gaps in employees' skills and in information systems that the bank would have to close in order to deliver the selected value propositions to the targeted customers. Thus, creating a balanced scorecard forced the bank's senior managers to arrive at a consensus and then to translate their vision into terms that had meaning to the people who would realize the vision.

Communicating and Linking

"The top ten people in the business now understand the strategy better than ever before. It's too bad," a senior executive of a major oil company complained, "that we can't put this in a bottle so that everyone could share it." With the balanced scorecard, he can.

One company we have worked with deliberately involved three layers of management in the creation of its balanced scorecard. The senior executive group formulated the financial and customer objectives. It then mobilized the talent and information in the next two levels of managers by having them formulate the internal-business-process and learning-and-growth objectives that would drive the achievement of the financial and customer goals. For example, knowing the importance of satisfying customers' expectations of on-time delivery, the broader group identified several internal business processes—such as order processing, scheduling, and fulfillment— in which the company had to excel. To do so, the company would have to retrain frontline employees and improve the information systems available to them. The group developed performance measures for those critical processes and for staff and systems capabilities.

Broad participation in creating a scorecard takes longer, but it offers several advantages: Information from a larger number of managers is incorporated into the internal objectives; the managers gain a better understanding of the company's long-term strategic goals; and such broad participation builds a stronger commitment to achieving those goals. But getting managers to buy into the scorecard is only a first step in linking individual actions to corporate goals.

The balanced scorecard signals to everyone what the organization is trying to achieve for shareholders and customers alike. But to align employees' individual performances with the overall strategy, scorecard users generally engage in three activities: communicating and educating, setting goals, and linking rewards to performance measures.

Communicating and educating

Implementing a strategy begins with educating those who have to execute it. Whereas some organizations opt to hold their strategy close to the vest, most believe that they should disseminate it from top to bottom. A broad-based communication program shares with all employees the strategy and the critical objectives they have to meet if the strategy is to succeed. Onetime events such as the distribution of brochures or newsletters and the holding of "town meetings" might kick off the program. Some organizations post bulletin boards that illustrate and explain the balanced scorecard measures, then update them with monthly results. Others use groupware and electronic bulletin boards to distribute the scorecard to the desktops of all employees and to encourage dialogue about the measures. The same media allow employees to make suggestions for achieving or exceeding the targets.

The balanced scorecard, as the embodiment of business unit strategy, should also be communicated upward in the organization—to corporate headquarters and to the corporate board of directors. With the scorecard, business units can quantify and communicate their long-term strategies to senior executives using a comprehensive set of linked financial and nonfinancial measures. Such communication informs the executives and the board in specific terms that long-term strategies designed for competitive success are in place. The measures also provide the basis for feedback and accountability. Meeting short-term financial targets should not constitute satisfactory performance when other measures indicate that the long-term strategy is either not working or not being implemented well.

Should the balanced scorecard be communicated beyond the boardroom to external shareholders? We believe that as senior executives gain confidence in the ability of the scorecard measures to monitor strategic performance and predict future financial performance, they will find ways to inform outside investors about those measures without disclosing competitively sensitive information.

Skandia, an insurance and financial services company based in Sweden, issues a supplement to its annual report called "The Business Navigator"—"an instrument to help us navigate into the future and thereby stimulate renewal and development." The supplement describes Skandia's strategy and the strategic measures the company uses to communicate and evaluate the strategy. It also provides a report on the company's performance along those measures during the year. The measures are customized for each operating unit and include, for example, market share, customer satisfaction and retention, employee competence, employee empowerment, and technology deployment.

Communicating the balanced scorecard promotes commitment and accountability to the business's long-term strategy. As one executive at Metro Bank declared, "The balanced scorecard is both motivating and obligating."

Setting goals

Mere awareness of corporate goals, however, is not enough to change many people's behavior. Somehow, the organization's high-level strategic objectives and measures must be translated into objectives and measures for operating units and individuals.

The exploration group of a large oil company developed a technique to enable and encourage individuals to set goals for themselves that were consistent with the organization's. It created a small, fold-up, personal scorecard that people could carry in their shirt pockets or wallets. (See "The personal scorecard.") The scorecard contains three levels of information. The first describes corporate objectives, measures, and targets. The second leaves room for translating corporate targets into targets for each business unit. For the third level, the company asks both individuals and teams to articulate which of their own objectives would be consistent with the business unit and corporate objectives, as well as what initiatives they would take to achieve their objectives. It also asks them to define up to five performance measures for their objectives and to set targets for each measure. The personal scorecard helps to communicate corporate and business unit objectives to the people and teams performing the work, enabling them to translate the objectives into meaningful tasks and targets for themselves. It also lets them keep that information close at hand—in their pockets.

Linking rewards to performance measures

Should compensation systems be linked to balanced scorecard measures? Some companies, believing that tying financial compensation to performance is a powerful lever, have moved quickly to establish such a linkage. For example, an oil company that we'll call Pioneer Petroleum uses its scorecard as the sole basis for computing incentive compensation. The company ties 60% of its executives' bonuses to their achievement of ambitious targets for a weighted average of four financial indicators: return on capital, profitability, cash flow, and operating cost. It bases the remaining 40% on indicators of customer satisfaction, dealer satisfaction, employee satisfaction, and environmental responsibility (such as a percentage change in the level of emissions to water and air). Pioneer's CEO says that linking compensation to the scorecard has helped to align the company with its strategy. "I know of no competitor," he says, "who has this degree of alignment. It is producing results for us."

As attractive and as powerful as such linkage is, it nonetheless carries risks. For instance, does the company have the right measures on the scorecard? Does it have valid and reliable data for the selected

The personal scorecard

Corporate objectives

☐ Double our corporate value in seven years.
☐ Increase our earnings by an average of 20% per year.
☐ Achieve an internal rate of return 2% above the cost of capital.
☐ Increase both production and reserves by 20% in the next decade.

Corporate targets					Scorecard measures	Business unit targets					Team/individual objectives and initiatives
1995	1996	1997	1998	1999		1995	1996	1997	1998	1999	
					Financial						1.
100	120	160	180	250	Earnings (in $ millions)						
100	450	200	210	225	Net cash flow						
100	85	80	75	70	Overhead and operating expenses						2.
					Operating						
100	75	73	70	64	Production costs per barrel						
100	97	93	90	82	Development costs per barrel						3.
100	105	108	108	110	Total annual production						
Team/individual measures						**Targets**					
1.											4.
2.											
3.											
4.											5.
5.											

Name:

Location:

measures? Could unintended or unexpected consequences arise from the way the targets for the measures are achieved? Those are questions that companies should ask.

Furthermore, companies traditionally handle multiple objectives in a compensation formula by assigning weights to each objective and calculating incentive compensation by the extent to which each weighted objective was achieved. This practice permits substantial incentive compensation to be paid if the business unit overachieves on a few objectives even if it falls far short on others. A better approach would be to establish minimum threshold levels for a critical subset of the strategic measures. Individuals would earn no incentive compensation if performance in a given period fell short of any threshold. This requirement should motivate people to achieve a more balanced performance across short- and long-term objectives.

Some organizations, however, have reduced their emphasis on short-term, formula-based incentive systems as a result of introducing the balanced scorecard. They have discovered that dialogue among executives and managers about the scorecard—both the formulation of the measures and objectives and the explanation of actual versus targeted results—provides a better opportunity to observe managers' performance and abilities. Increased knowledge of their managers' abilities makes it easier for executives to set incentive rewards subjectively and to defend those subjective evaluations—a process that is less susceptible to the game playing and distortions associated with explicit, formula-based rules.

One company we have studied takes an intermediate position. It bases bonuses for business unit managers on two equally weighted criteria: their achievement of a financial objective—economic value added—over a three-year period and a subjective assessment of their performance on measures drawn from the customer, internal-business-process, and learning-and-growth perspectives of the balanced scorecard.

That the balanced scorecard has a role to play in the determination of incentive compensation is not in doubt. Precisely what that role should be will become clearer as more companies experiment with linking rewards to scorecard measures.

Business Planning

"Where the rubber meets the sky": That's how one senior executive describes his company's long-range-planning process. He might have said the same of many other companies because their financially based management systems fail to link change programs and resource allocation to long-term strategic priorities.

The problem is that most organizations have separate procedures and organizational units for strategic planning and for resource allocation and budgeting. To formulate their strategic plans, senior executives go off-site annually and engage for several days in active discussions facilitated by senior planning and development managers or external consultants. The outcome of this exercise is a strategic plan articulating where the company expects (or hopes or prays) to be in three, five, and ten years. Typically, such plans then sit on executives' bookshelves for the next 12 months.

Meanwhile, a separate resource-allocation and budgeting process run by the finance staff sets financial targets for revenues, expenses, profits, and investments for the next fiscal year. The budget it produces consists almost entirely of financial numbers that generally bear little relation to the targets in the strategic plan.

Which document do corporate managers discuss in their monthly and quarterly meetings during the following year? Usually only the budget, because the periodic reviews focus on a comparison of actual and budgeted results for every line item. When is the strategic plan next discussed? Probably during the next annual off-site meeting, when the senior managers draw up a new set of three-, five-, and ten-year plans.

The very exercise of creating a balanced scorecard forces companies to integrate their strategic planning and budgeting processes and therefore helps to ensure that their budgets support their strategies. Scorecard users select measures of progress from all four scorecard perspectives and set targets for each of them. Then they determine which actions will drive them toward their targets, identify the measures they will apply to those drivers from the four perspectives, and establish the short-term milestones that will mark their progress along the strategic paths they have selected. Building a scorecard thus enables a company to link its financial budgets with its strategic goals.

For example, one division of the Style Company (not its real name) committed to achieving a seemingly impossible goal articulated by the CEO: to double revenues in five years. The forecasts built into the organization's existing strategic plan fell $1 billion short of this objective. The division's managers, after considering various scenarios, agreed to specific increases in five different performance drivers: the number of new stores opened, the number of new customers attracted into new and existing stores, the percentage of shoppers in each store converted into actual purchasers, the portion of existing customers retained, and average sales per customer.

By helping to define the key drivers of revenue growth and by committing to targets for each of them, the division's managers eventually grew comfortable with the CEO's ambitious goal.

The process of building a balanced scorecard—clarifying the strategic objectives and then identifying the few critical drivers— also creates a framework for managing an organization's various change programs. These initiatives—reengineering, employee empowerment, time-based management, and total quality management, among others—promise to deliver results but also compete with one another for scarce resources, including the scarcest resource of all: senior managers' time and attention.

Shortly after the merger that created it, Metro Bank, for example, launched more than 70 different initiatives. The initiatives were intended to produce a more competitive and successful institution, but they were inadequately integrated into the overall strategy. After building their balanced scorecard, Metro Bank's managers dropped many of those programs—such as a marketing effort directed at individuals with very high net worth—and consolidated others into initiatives that were better aligned with the company's strategic objectives. For example, the managers replaced a program aimed at enhancing existing low-level selling skills with a major initiative aimed at retraining salespersons to become trusted financial advisers, capable of selling a broad range of newly introduced products to the three selected customer segments. The bank made both changes because the scorecard enabled it to gain a better understanding of the programs required to achieve its strategic objectives.

Once the strategy is defined and the drivers are identified, the scorecard influences managers to concentrate on improving or reengineering those processes most critical to the organization's strategic success. That is how the scorecard most clearly links and aligns action with strategy.

The final step in linking strategy to actions is to establish specific short-term targets, or milestones, for the balanced scorecard measures. Milestones are tangible expressions of managers' beliefs about when and to what degree their current programs will affect those measures.

In establishing milestones, managers are expanding the traditional budgeting process to incorporate strategic as well as financial goals. Detailed financial planning remains important, but financial goals taken by themselves ignore the three other balanced scorecard perspectives. In an integrated planning and budgeting process, executives continue to budget for short-term financial performance, but they also introduce short-term targets for measures in the customer, internal-business-process, and learning-and-growth perspectives. With those milestones established, managers can continually test both the theory underlying the strategy and the strategy's implementation.

At the end of the business-planning process, managers should have set targets for the long-term objectives they would like to achieve in all four scorecard perspectives; they should have identified the strategic initiatives required and allocated the necessary resources to those initiatives; and they should have established milestones for the measures that mark progress toward achieving their strategic goals.

Feedback and Learning

"With the balanced scorecard," a CEO of an engineering company told us, "I can continually test my strategy. It's like performing real-time research." That is exactly the capability that the scorecard should give senior managers: the ability to know at any point in its implementation whether the strategy they have formulated is, in fact, working, and if not, why.

The first three management processes—translating the vision, communicating and linking, and business planning—are vital for implementing strategy, but they are not sufficient in an unpredictable world. Together they form an important single-loop-learning process—single-loop in the sense that the objective remains constant, and any departure from the planned trajectory is seen as a defect to be remedied. This single-loop process does not require or even facilitate reexamination of either the strategy or the techniques used to implement it in light of current conditions.

Most companies today operate in a turbulent environment with complex strategies that, though valid when they were launched, may lose their validity as business conditions change. In this kind of environment, where new threats and opportunities arise constantly, companies must become capable of what Chris Argyris calls *double-loop learning*—learning that produces a change in people's assumptions and theories about cause-and-effect relationships. (See "Teaching Smart People How to Learn," HBR May–June 1991.)

Budget reviews and other financially based management tools cannot engage senior executives in double-loop learning—first, because these tools address performance from only one perspective, and second, because they don't involve strategic learning. Strategic learning consists of gathering feedback, testing the hypotheses on which strategy was based, and making the necessary adjustments.

The balanced scorecard supplies three elements that are essential to strategic learning. First, it articulates the company's shared vision, defining in clear and operational terms the results that the company, as a team, is trying to achieve. The scorecard communicates a holistic model that links individual efforts and accomplishments to business unit objectives.

Second, the scorecard supplies the essential strategic feedback system. A business strategy can be viewed as a set of hypotheses about cause-and-effect relationships. A strategic feedback system should be able to test, validate, and modify the hypotheses embedded in a business unit's strategy. By establishing short-term goals, or milestones, within the business-planning process, executives are forecasting the relationship between changes in performance drivers and the associated changes in one or more specified goals. For example, executives at Metro Bank estimated the amount of time it would take for improvements in training and in the availability of information systems before employees could sell multiple financial products effectively to existing and new customers. They also estimated how great the effect of that selling capability would be.

Another organization attempted to validate its hypothesized cause-and-effect relationships in the balanced scorecard by measuring the strength of the linkages among measures in the different perspectives. (See the exhibit "How one company linked measures from the four perspectives.") The company found significant correlations between employees' morale, a measure in the learning-and-growth perspective, and customer satisfaction, an important customer perspective measure. Customer satisfaction, in turn, was correlated with faster payment of invoices—a relationship that led to a substantial reduction in accounts receivable and hence a higher return on capital employed. The company also found correlations between employees' morale and the number of suggestions made by employees (two learning-and-growth measures) as well as between an increased number of suggestions and lower rework (an internal-business-process measure). Evidence of such strong correlations help to confirm the organization's business strategy. If, however, the expected correlations are not found over time, it should be an indication to executives that the theory underlying the unit's strategy may not be working as they had anticipated.

Especially in large organizations, accumulating sufficient data to document significant correlations and causation among balanced scorecard measures can take a long time—months or years. Over the short term, managers' assessment of strategic impact may have to rest on subjective and qualitative judgments. Eventually, however, as more evidence accumulates, organizations may be able to provide more objectively grounded estimates of cause-and-effect relationships. But just getting managers to think systematically about the

How one company linked measures from the four perspectives

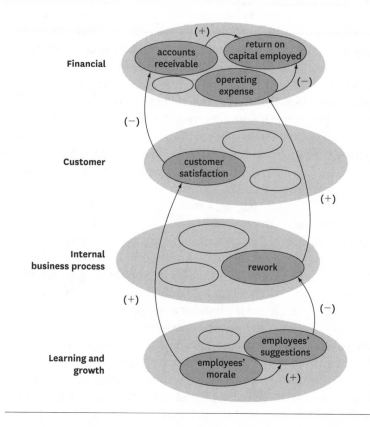

assumptions underlying their strategy is an improvement over the current practice of making decisions based on short-term operational results.

Third, the scorecard facilitates the strategy review that is essential to strategic learning. Traditionally, companies use the monthly or quarterly meetings between corporate and division executives to analyze the most recent period's financial results. Discussions focus on past performance and on explanations of why financial objectives were not achieved. The balanced scorecard, with its specification of the causal relationships between performance drivers and objectives, allows corporate and business unit executives to use their periodic review sessions to evaluate the validity of the unit's strategy and the quality of its execution. If the unit's employees and managers have delivered on the performance drivers (retraining of employees, availability of information systems, and new financial products and services, for instance), then their failure to achieve the expected outcomes (higher sales to targeted customers, for example) signals that the theory underlying the strategy may not be valid. The disappointing sales figures are an early warning.

Managers should take such disconfirming evidence seriously and reconsider their shared conclusions about market conditions, customer value propositions, competitors' behavior, and internal capabilities. The result of such a review may be a decision to reaffirm their belief in the current strategy but to adjust the quantitative relationship among the strategic measures on the balanced scorecard. But they also might conclude that the unit needs a different strategy (an example of double-loop learning) in light of new knowledge about market conditions and internal capabilities. In any case, the scorecard will have stimulated key executives to learn about the viability of their strategy. This capacity for enabling organizational learning at the executive level—strategic learning—is what distinguishes the balanced scorecard, making it invaluable for those who wish to create a strategic management system.

Toward a New Strategic Management System

Many companies adopted early balanced scorecard concepts to improve their performance measurement systems. They achieved tangible but narrow results. Adopting those concepts provided clarification, consensus, and focus on the desired improvements in performance. More recently, we have seen companies expand their use of the balanced scorecard, employing it as the foundation of an integrated and iterative strategic management system. Companies are using the scorecard to

- clarify and update strategy;

- communicate strategy throughout the company;

- align unit and individual goals with the strategy;

- link strategic objectives to long-term targets and annual budgets;

- identify and align strategic initiatives; and

- conduct periodic performance reviews to learn about and improve strategy.

The balanced scorecard enables a company to align its management processes and focuses the entire organization on implementing long-term strategy. At National Insurance, the scorecard provided the CEO and his managers with a central framework around which they could redesign each piece of the company's management system. And because of the cause-and-effect linkages inherent in the scorecard framework, changes in one component of the system reinforced earlier changes made elsewhere. Therefore, every change made over the 30-month period added to the momentum that kept the organization moving forward in the agreed-upon direction.

Without a balanced scorecard, most organizations are unable to achieve a similar consistency of vision and action as they attempt to change direction and introduce new strategies and processes. The balanced scorecard provides a framework for managing the implementation of strategy while also allowing the strategy itself to evolve in response to changes in the company's competitive, market, and technological environments.

Originally published in January 1996. Reprint R0707M.

Transforming Corner-Office Strategy into Frontline Action

by Orit Gadiesh and James L. Gilbert

WE ALL KNOW THE BENEFITS of pushing decision making from the CEO's office out to the far reaches of an organization. Fleeting business opportunities can be seized quickly. Products and services better reflect subtle shifts in customers' preferences. Empowered workers are motivated to innovate and take risks.

But while the value of such an approach is clear, particularly in a volatile business environment, there is also a built-in risk: an organization in which everyone is a decision maker has the potential to spin out of control. Within a single company, it's tricky to achieve both decentralized decision making and coherent strategic action. Still, some companies—think General Electric, America Online, Vanguard, Dell, Wal-Mart, Southwest Airlines, and eBay—have done just that.

These companies employ what we call a *strategic principle,* a memorable and actionable phrase that distills a company's corporate strategy into its unique essence and communicates it throughout the organization. (For a list of companies' strategic principles, see "It's all in a phrase.")

This tool—which we have observed in use at about a dozen companies, even though they don't label it as such—would always serve a company well. But it has become particularly useful in today's rapidly and constantly changing business environment. Indeed, in our conversations and work with more than 50 CEOs over the past two years, we have come to appreciate the strategic principle's power—its ability to help companies maintain strategic focus while fostering the flexibility among employees that permits innovation and a rapid response to opportunities. Strategic principles are likely to become even more crucial to corporate success in the years ahead.

Distillation and Communication

To better understand what a strategic principle is and how it can be used, it may be helpful to look at a military analogy: the rules of engagement for battle. For example, Admiral Lord Nelson's crews in Britain's eighteenth-century wars against the French were guided by a simple strategic principle: whatever you do, get alongside an enemy ship.

The Royal Navy's seamanship, training, and experience gave it the advantage every time it engaged one-on-one against any of Europe's lesser fleets. So Nelson rejected as impractical the common practice of an admiral attempting to control a fleet through the use of flag signals. Instead, he gave his captains strategic parameters—they knew they had to battle rival ships one-on-one—leaving them to determine exactly how to engage in such combat. By using a strategic principle instead of explicit signals to direct his forces, Nelson consistently defeated the French, including a great victory in the dark of night, when signals would have been useless. Nelson's rule of engagement was simple enough for every one of his officers and sailors to know by heart. And it was enduring, a valid directive that was good until the relative naval capabilities of Britain and its rivals changed.

The distillation of a company's strategy into a pithy, memorable, and prescriptive phrase is important because a brilliant business strategy, like an insightful approach to warfare, is of little use unless

Idea in Brief

Southwest Airlines keeps soaring. Its stock price rose a compounded 21,000% between 1972 and 1992 and leapt 300% between 1995 and 2000.

Why does Southwest succeed while so many other airlines fail? Because it sticks to its powerful **strategic principle:** "Meet customers' short-haul travel needs at fares competitive with the cost of automobile travel." This pithy, memorable, action-oriented phrase distills Southwest's unique strategy and communicates it throughout the company.

An effective **strategic principle** lets a company simultaneously:

- maintain strategic focus,

- empower workers to innovate and take risks,

- seize fleeting opportunities,

- create products and services that meet subtle shifts in customers' needs.

In today's rapidly changing world, companies must integrate decentralized decision making *with* coherent, strategic action. A well-crafted, skillfully implemented **strategic principle** lets them strike that delicate balance.

people understand it well enough to apply it—both to anticipated decisions and unforeseen opportunities. In our work, we often see evidence of what we call the 80-100 rule: you're better off with a strategy that is 80% right and 100% implemented than one that is 100% right but doesn't drive consistent action throughout the company. A strategic principle can help a company balance that ratio.

The beauty of having a corporate strategic principle—a company should have only one—is that everyone in an organization, the executives in the front office as well as people in the operating units, can knowingly work toward the same strategic objective without being rigid about how they do so. Decisions don't always have to make the slow trip to and from the executive suite. When a strategic principle is well crafted and effectively communicated, managers at all levels can be trusted to make decisions that advance rather than undermine company strategy.

Idea in Practice

Hallmarks of Powerful Strategic Principles

A successful strategic principle:

- Forces trade-offs between competing resources.

  Example: Southwest Airlines' 1983 expansion to the high-traffic Denver area *seemed* sensible. But unusually long delays there due to bad weather and taxi time would have forced Southwest to increase ticket prices—preventing it from adhering to its strategic principle of offering air fares competitive with the cost of auto travel. The company pulled out of Denver.

- Tests the strategic soundness of particular decisions by linking leaders' strategic insights with line operators' pragmatic sense.

  Example: AOL's strategic principle,"Consumer connectivity first—anytime, anywhere," tested the wisdom of a powerful business decision: expanding AOL's global network through alliances with local partners, rather than using its own technology everywhere. Partners' understanding of local culture greatly increased customers' connectivity.

- Sets clear boundaries within which employees operate and experiment.

  Example: At mutual-fund giant The Vanguard Group, frontline employees conceived a potent idea: Let customers access their accounts on-line, but limit on-line trading. This move kept Vanguard's costs low, enabling the company to

---

Given what we've said so far, a strategic principle might seem to be a mission statement by another name. But while both help employees understand a company's direction, the two are different tools that communicate different things. A mission statement informs a company's *culture*. A strategic principle drives a company's *strategy*. A mission statement is *aspirational*: it gives people something to strive for. A strategic principle is *action oriented*: it enables people to do something now. A mission statement is meant to *inspire* frontline workers. A strategic principle enables them to *act* quickly by giving them explicit guidance to make strategically consistent choices.

stick to its strategic principle: creating "unmatchable value for investors/owners."

Creating and Communicating Your Strategic Principle

Capturing and communicating the essence of your company's strategy in a simple, memorable, actionable phrase isn't easy. These steps can help:

1. **Draft a working strategic principle.** Summarize your *corporate strategy*—your plan to allocate scarce resources in order to create value that distinguishes you from competitors—in a brief phrase. That phrase becomes your working *strategic principle*.

2. **Test its endurance.** A good strategic principle endures. Ask: Does our working strategic principle capture the timeless essence of our company's unique competitive value?

3. **Test its communicative power.** Ask: Is the phrase clear, concise, memorable? Would you feel proud to paint it on the side of your firm's trucks, as Wal-Mart does?

4. **Test its ability to promote and guide action.** Ask: Does the principle exhibit the three essential attributes: forcing trade-offs, testing the wisdom of business moves, setting boundaries for employees' experimentation?

5. **Communicate it.** Communicate your strategic principle consistently, simply, and repeatedly. You'll know you've succeeded when employees— as well as business writers, MBA students, and competitors— all "chant the rant."

Consider the difference between GE's mission statement and its strategic principle. The company's mission statement exhorts GE's leaders—"always with unyielding integrity"—to be "passionately focused on driving customer success" and to "create an environment of 'stretch,' excitement, informality, and trust," among other things. The language is aspirational and emotional. By contrast, GE's well-known strategic principle—"Be number one or number two in every industry in which we compete, or get out"—is action oriented. The first part of the phrase is an explicit strategic challenge, and the second part leaves no question in line managers' minds about what they should do.

Three Defining Attributes

A strategic principle, as the distillation of a company's strategy, should guide a company's allocation of scarce resources—capital, time, management's attention, labor, and brand—in order to build a sustainable competitive advantage. It should tell a company what to do and, just as important, what not to do. More specifically, an effective strategic principle does the following:

- It forces trade-offs between competing resource demands;

- It tests the strategic soundness of a particular action;

- It sets clear boundaries within which employees must operate while granting them freedom to experiment within those constraints.

These three qualities can be seen in America Online's strategic principle. CEO Steve Case says personal interaction on-line is the soul of the Internet, and he has positioned AOL to create that interaction. Thus, AOL's strategic principle in the years leading up to its recent merger with Time Warner has been "Consumer connectivity first—anytime, anywhere."

This strategic principle has helped AOL make tough choices when allocating its resources. For example, in 1997, the company needed cash to grow, so it sold off its network infrastructure and outsourced that capability—a risky move at a time when it appeared that network ownership might be the key to success on the Internet. In keeping with its strategic principle, AOL instead spent its time and cash on improving connectivity at its Web site, focusing particularly on access, navigation, and interaction. As a result, it avoided investing capital in what turned out to be a relatively low-return business.

Its strategic principle has also helped AOL test whether a given business move makes strategic sense. For instance, the Internet company has chosen to expand its global network through alliances with local partners, even though that approach can take longer than simply transplanting AOL's own technology and know-how.

AOL acknowledges that a local partner better understands the native culture and community, which is essential for connecting with customers.

Finally, AOL's strategic principle has spurred focused experimentation in the field by clearly defining employees' latitude for making moves. For example, AOL's former vice president of marketing, Jan Brandt, mailed more than 250 million AOL diskettes to consumers nationwide. The innovative campaign turned the company into one of the best-known names in cyberspace—all because Brandt, now AOL's vice chair and chief marketing officer, guided by the principle of connecting consumers, put her resources into empowering AOL's target community rather than sinking time and money into slick advertising.

As AOL's experience illustrates, a strong strategic principle can inform high-level corporate decisions—those involving divestitures, for example—as well as decisions made by department heads or others further down in an organization. It also frees up CEOs from constant involvement in the implementation of their strategic mandates. "The genius of a great leader is to leave behind him a situation that common sense, without the grace of genius, can deal with successfully," said journalist and political thinker Walter Lippman. Scratch the surface of a number of high-performing companies, and you'll find that strategic principles are connecting the strategic insights—if not always the genius—of leaders with the pragmatic sense of line operators.

Now More Than Ever

In the past, a strategic principle was nice to have but was hardly required, unless a company found itself in a trying business situation. Today, many companies simultaneously face four situations that make a strategic principle crucial for success: decentralization, rapid growth, technological change, and institutional turmoil.

For the reasons mentioned above, *decentralization* is becoming common at companies of all stripes; thus, there is a corresponding need for a mechanism to ensure coherent strategic action. Especially in the case of diversified conglomerates, where strategy is formed in each of the business units, a strategic principle can help executives maintain consistency while giving unit managers the freedom to tailor their strategies to meet their own needs. It can also clarify the value of the center at such far-flung companies. For example, GE's long-standing strategic principle of always being number one or number two in an industry offers a powerful rationale for how a conglomerate can create value but still give individual units considerable strategic freedom.

A strategic principle is also crucial when a company is experiencing *rapid growth*. During such times, it's increasingly the case that less-experienced managers are forced to make decisions about nettlesome issues for which there may be no precedent. A clear and precise strategic principle can help counteract this shortage of experience. This is particularly true when a start-up company is growing rapidly in an established industry. For instance, as Southwest Airlines began to grow quickly, it might have been tempted to mimic its rivals' ultimately unsuccessful strategies if it hadn't had its own strategic principle to follow: "Meet customers' short-haul travel needs at fares competitive with the cost of automobile travel." Likewise, eBay, whose principle is "Focus on trading communities," might have been tempted, like many Internet marketplaces, to diversify into all sorts of services. But eBay has chosen to outsource certain services—for instance, management of the photos that sellers post on the site to illustrate the items they put up for bid—while it continues to invest in services like Billpoint, which lets sellers accept credit-card payments from bidders. EBay's strategic principle has ensured that the entire company stays focused on the core trading business.

The staggering pace of *technological change* over the past decade has been costly for companies that don't have a strategic principle. Never before in business has there been more uncertainty combined with so great an emphasis on speed. Managers in high-tech industries in particular must react immediately to sudden and unexpected developments. Often, the sum of the reactions across the

It's all in a phrase

A handful of companies have distilled their strategy into a phrase and have used it to drive consistent strategic action throughout their organizations.

Company	Strategic Principle
America Online	*Consumer connectivity first—anytime, anywhere*
Dell	*Be direct*
eBay	*Focus on trading communities*
General Electric	*Be number one or number two in every industry in which we compete, or get out*
Southwest Airlines	*Meet customers' short-haul travel needs at fares competitive with the cost of automobile travel*
Vanguard	*Unmatchable value for the investor-owner*
Wal-Mart	*Low prices, every day*

organization ends up defining the company's strategic course. A strategic principle—for example, Dell's mandate to sell direct to end users—helps ensure that the decisions made by frontline managers in such circumstances add up to a consistent, coherent strategy.

Finally, a strategic principle can help provide continuity during periods of *organizational turmoil*. An increasingly common example of turmoil in this era of short-term CEOs is leadership succession. A new CEO can bring with him or her a new strategy—but not necessarily a new strategic principle. For instance, when Jack Brennan took over as chairman and CEO at Vanguard five years ago, the strategic transition was seamless, despite some tension around the leadership transition. He maintained the mutual fund company's strategic principle—"Unmatchable value for the investor-owner"—thereby allowing managers to pursue their strategic objectives without many of the distractions so often associated with leadership changes. (For our own experience with organizational turmoil and strategic principles, see the sidebar "Bain & Company: Case Study of a Strategic Principle.")

Bain & Company: Case Study of a Strategic Principle

I LEARNED THE MOST ABOUT strategic principles in the trenches at Bain & Company when, a decade ago, we almost went bankrupt.

Bill Bain founded Bain & Company nearly 30 years ago on the basis of a simple but powerful notion: "The product of a consultant should be results for clients—not reports." Over time, this mandate to deliver results through strategy became Bain's strategic principle. It remains so today.

This directive fosters specific action, as an effective strategic principle should. It means that, from the very beginning of an assignment, you are constantly thinking about how a recommendation will get implemented. It also requires you to tell clients the truth, even if it's difficult, because you can't achieve results by whitewashing problems. And this strategic principle has teeth: Bain has always measured partners' performance according to the results they achieve for their clients, not just on billings to the firm.

That was the company I joined. And for many years it grew rapidly, all the time guided by its strategic principle. Then, just over a decade ago, the founding partners decided to get their money out and sold 30% of the firm to an employee stock-option plan. This saddled us with hundreds of millions of dollars of debt and tens of millions of dollars of interest payments. The move, whose details initially were not disclosed to the rest of us, was based on the assumption that the company would continue its historic growth rate of 50% a year, which couldn't be sustained at the size we had become. When growth slowed, the details came to light.

The nonfounding partners faced a critical choice. Everybody had attractive offers. Competitors and the press predicted we wouldn't survive. Recruits

Strategic Principles in Action

Strategic principles and their benefits can best be understood by seeing the results they create.

Forcing trade-offs at Southwest Airlines

Southwest Airlines is one of the air-travel industry's great success stories. It is the only airline that hasn't lost money in the past 25 years. Its stock price rose a compounded 21,000% between 1972 and 1992, and it is up 300% over the past five years, which have been and clients were watchful. To make a long story short, we sat down around a conference table and resolved to turn the company around. The key to doing that, we decided, was to stick with our strategic principle.

What followed was a couple of years during which adhering to that goal was achingly difficult. But doing so forced important trade-offs. In one case, right in the middle of the crisis, we pulled out of a major assignment that was inconsistent with our principle. We believed the projects that the client was determined to undertake could not produce significant results for the company. Today, we all believe that had we veered from our principle in that instance, we would not be around.

More recently, our strategic principle has freed us to explore other ventures. Seven years ago, for instance, we became interested in private equity consulting, quite a different business from serving corporate clients. We initially struggled with the notion but quickly realized that it fit our strategic principle of delivering results through strategy, only to a new client segment. We knew that we could trust our colleagues forming the practice area to act consistently with the company's broader goals because the strategic principle was fundamental to their perspective. The strength of our shared principle permitted us to experiment and ultimately develop a successful new practice area.

Our principle continues to let partners develop new practices, markets, and interests quickly and without splintering the firm. It has given us the capacity to evolve and endure.

—*Orit Gadiesh*

difficult ones in the airline industry. For most companies, such rapid growth would cause problems: legions of frontline employees taking up the mantle of decision making from core executives and, inevitably, stumbling. But in Southwest's case, employees have consistently made trade-offs in keeping with the company's strategic principle.

The process for making important and complicated decisions about things like network design, service offerings, route selection and pricing, cabin design, and ticketing procedures is straightforward. That's because the trade-offs required by the strategic principle are clear. For instance, in 1983, Southwest initiated service to Denver, a potentially high-traffic destination and a seemingly sensible expansion of the company's presence in the Southwestern United States. However, the airline experienced longer and more consistent delays at Denver's Stapleton airport than it did anywhere else. These delays were caused not by slow turnaround at the gate but by increased taxi time on the runway and planes circling in the air because of bad weather. Southwest had to decide whether the potential growth from serving the Denver market was worth the higher costs associated with the delays, which would ultimately be reflected in higher ticket prices. The company turned to its strategic principle: would the airline be able to maintain fares competitive with the cost of automobile travel? Clearly, in Denver at least, it couldn't. Southwest pulled out of Stapleton three years after inaugurating the service there and has not returned.

Testing action at AOL

A large part of AOL's ability to move so far and so fast across untrod ground lies in its practice of testing potential moves against its strategic principle. Employees who see attractive opportunities can ask themselves whether seizing one or several will lead to deeper consumer connectivity or broader distribution. Take, for example, line manager Katherine Borescnik, now president of programming at AOL. Several years ago she noticed increased activity—call it consumer connectivity—around the bulletin-board folders created on the site by two irreverent stock analysts and AOL subscribers. She offered the analysts the chance to create their own financial site, which became Motley Fool, a point of connection and information for do-it-yourself investors.

And AOL's strategic principle reaches even deeper into the organization. The hundreds of acquisitions and deals that AOL has made in the past few years have involved numerous employees. While top officers make final decisions, employees on the ground first screen opportunities against the company's strategic principle.

Furthermore, the integration efforts following acquisitions, while choreographed at the top, are executed by a coterie of managers who ensure that the plans comply with the company's strategic principle. "We have succeeded, both in our deal making and in our integration, because our acquisitions have all been driven by our focus on how our customers communicate and connect," says Ken Novack, AOL Time Warner's vice chairman.

AOL's massive merger with Time Warner clearly furthers AOL's strategic principle of enabling consumer connections "anytime, anywhere" by adding TV and cable access to the Internet company's current dial-up access on the personal computer. But integrating this merger, which will involve hundreds of employees making and executing thousands of decisions, may be the ultimate test of AOL's strategic principle.

Experimenting within boundaries at Vanguard

The Vanguard Group, with $565 billion in assets under management, has quietly become a giant in the mutual fund industry. The company's strategy is a response to the inability of most mutual funds to beat the market, often because of the cost of their marketing activities, overhead, and frequent transactions. To counter this, Vanguard discourages investors from making frequent trades and keeps its own overhead and advertising costs far below the industry average. It passes the savings directly to investors, who, because Vanguard is a mutual rather than a public company, are the fund's owners.

While this was Vanguard's founding strategy, for years the company didn't communicate it widely to employees. As a result, they often suggested initiatives that were out of sync with the company's core strategy. "Midlevel managers would walk in holding the newspaper saying, 'Look at what Fidelity just did. How about if we do that?'" Jack Brennan says. It wasn't apparent to them that Vanguard's strategy was very different from that of its rival, which has higher costs and isn't mutually owned. Over the years, Vanguard has invested considerable energy in crafting a strategic principle and using it to disseminate the company's strategy. Now, because employees understand the strategy, top management trusts them to initiate moves on their own.

Consider Vanguard's response to a major trend in retail fund distribution: the emergence of the on-line channel. Industry surveys indicated that most investors wanted Internet access to their accounts and that on-line traders were more active than off-line traders. So Vanguard chose to integrate the Internet into its service in a way that furthered its strategy of keeping costs low: basically, it lets customers access their accounts on-line, but it limits Web-based trading. It should be noted that the original ideas for Vanguard's on-line initiatives, including early ventures with AOL, were conceived by frontline employees, not senior executives.

Brennan says the company's strategic principle affects the entire management process, including hiring, training, performance measurement, and incentives. He points to a hidden benefit of having a strong strategic principle: "You're more efficient and can run with a leaner management team because everyone is on the same page."

Creating a Strategic Principle

Many of the best and most conspicuous examples of strategic principles come from companies that were founded on them, companies such as eBay, Dell, Vanguard, Southwest Airlines, and Wal-Mart ("Low prices, every day"). The founders of those companies espoused a clear guiding principle that summarized the essence of what would become a full-blown business strategy. They attracted investors who believed it, hired employees who bought into it, and targeted customers who wanted it.

Leaders of long-standing multinationals, like GE, crafted their strategic principles at a critical juncture: when increasing corporate complexity threatened to confuse priorities on the front line and obscure the essence that truly differentiated their strategy from that of their rivals.

Companies in this second category, which represents most of the companies that are likely to contemplate creating a strategic principle, face a demanding exercise. It probably comes as no surprise that identifying the essence of your strategy so it can be translated into a simple, memorable phrase is no easy task. It's a bit like corporate genomics: the principle must isolate and capture the corporate equivalent of the genetic code that differentiates your company from its competitors. This is somewhat like identifying the 2% of DNA that separates man from monkey—or, even more difficult and more apt, the .1% of DNA that differentiates each human being.

There are different ways to identify the elements that must be captured in a strategic principle, but keep in mind that a corporate strategy represents a plan to effectively allocate scarce resources to achieve sustainable competitive advantage. Managers need to ask themselves: how does my company allocate those resources to create value in a unique way, one that differentiates my company from competitors? Try to summarize the answer in a brief phrase that captures the essence of your company's point of differentiation.

Once that idea has been expressed in a phrase, test the strategic principle for its enduring nature. Does it capture what you intend to do for only the next three to five years, or does it capture a more timeless essence: the genetic code of your company's competitive differentiation? Then test the strategic principle for its communicative power. Is it clear, concise, and memorable? Would you feel proud to paint it on the side of a truck, as Wal-Mart does?

Finally, test the principle for its ability to promote and guide action. In particular, assess whether it exhibits the three attributes of an effective strategic principle. Will it force trade-offs? Will it serve as a test for the wisdom of a particular business move, especially one that might promote short-term profits at the expense of long-term strategy? Does it set boundaries within which people will nonetheless be free to experiment?

Given the importance of getting your strategic principle right, it is wise to gather feedback on these questions from executives and other employees during an incubation period. Once you are satisfied that the statement is accurate and compelling, disseminate it throughout the organization.

Of course, just as a brilliant strategy is worthless unless it is implemented, a powerful strategic principle is of no use unless it is communicated effectively. When CEO Jack Welch talks about aligning employees around GE's strategy and values, he emphasizes the need for consistency, simplicity, and repetition. The approach is neither flashy nor complicated, but it takes enormous discipline and could scarcely be more important. Welch has so broadly evangelized GE's "Be number one or number two" strategic principle that employees are not the only ones to chant the rant. So can most business writers, MBA students, and managers at other companies.

When Rethinking Is Required

No strategy is eternal, nor is any strategic principle. But even if the elements of your strategy change, the very essence of it is likely to remain the same. Thus, your strategy may shift substantially as your customers' demographics and needs change. It may have to be modified in light of your company's changing costs and assets compared with those of competitors. Strategic half-lives are shortening, and, in general, strategy should be reviewed every quarter and updated every year. But while it's worth revisiting your strategic principle every time you reexamine your strategy, it is likely to change only when there is a significant shift in the basic economics and opportunities of your market caused by, say, legislation or a completely new technology or business model.

Even then, your strategic principle may need only refining or expanding. GE's strategic principle has been enhanced, but not replaced, since Welch articulated it in 1981. Similarly, AOL's strategic principle will need to be broadened, but not necessarily jettisoned, following its merger with Time Warner. Ultimately, the merged company's strategic principle will also need to embody the importance of high-quality and relevant content, Time Warner's hallmark.

Vanguard takes explicit steps to ensure that the direction provided by its strategic principle remains current. For example, as part of an internal "devil's advocacy" process, managers are divided into groups to critique and defend past decisions and current policies. Recently, the group reconsidered two major strategic policies: the prohibitions against opening branch offices and against acquiring money management firms. After considerable discussion, the policies remained in place. According to CEO Brennan, "Sometimes the greatest value [of revisiting our strategic principle] is reconfirming what we're already doing." At the same time, Vanguard has the process to identify when change is needed.

Fundamental Principles

Respondents to Bain's annual survey of executives on the usefulness of management tools repeatedly cite the key role a mission statement can play in a company's success. We agree that a mission statement is crucial for promulgating a company's values and building a robust corporate culture. But it still leaves a large gap in a company's management communications portfolio. At least as important as a mission statement is something that promulgates a company's strategy—that is, a strategic principle.

The ability of frontline employees to execute a company's strategy without close central oversight is vital as the pace of technological change accelerates and as companies grow rapidly and become increasingly decentralized. To drive such behavior, a company needs to give employees a mandate broad enough to encourage enterprising behavior but specific enough to align employees' initiatives with company strategy.

While not a perfect analogy, the U.S. Constitution is in some ways like a strategic principle. It articulates and embodies the essence of the country's "strategy"—to guarantee liberty and justice for all of its citizens—while providing direction to those drafting the laws and regulations that implement the strategy. While no corporate strategy has liberty and justice at its heart, the elements of an effective strategy are just as central to the success of a company as those concepts are to the prosperity of the United States. And in neither case will success be realized unless the core strategy is communicated broadly and effectively.

Bain consultant Coleman Mark assisted with this article.

Originally published in May 2001. Reprint R0105D.

Turning Great Strategy into Great Performance

by Michael C. Mankins and Richard Steele

THREE YEARS AGO, THE LEADERSHIP team at a major manufacturer spent months developing a new strategy for its European business. Over the prior half-decade, six new competitors had entered the market, each deploying the latest in low-cost manufacturing technology and slashing prices to gain market share. The performance of the European unit—once the crown jewel of the company's portfolio—had deteriorated to the point that top management was seriously considering divesting it.

To turn around the operation, the unit's leadership team had recommended a bold new "solutions strategy"—one that would leverage the business's installed base to fuel growth in after-market services and equipment financing. The financial forecasts were exciting—the strategy promised to restore the business's industry-leading returns and growth. Impressed, top management quickly approved the plan, agreeing to provide the unit with all the resources it needed to make the turnaround a reality.

Today, however, the unit's performance is nowhere near what its management team had projected. Returns, while better than before, remain well below the company's cost of capital. The revenues and profits that managers had expected from services and financing have not materialized, and the business's cost position still lags behind that of its major competitors.

At the conclusion of a recent half-day review of the business's strategy and performance, the unit's general manager remained steadfast and vowed to press on. "It's all about execution," she declared. "The strategy we're pursuing is the right one. We're just not delivering the numbers. All we need to do is work harder, work smarter."

The parent company's CEO was not so sure. He wondered: Could the unit's lackluster performance have more to do with a mistaken strategy than poor execution? More important, what should he do to get better performance out of the unit? Should he do as the general manager insisted and stay the course—focusing the organization more intensely on execution—or should he encourage the leadership team to investigate new strategy options? If execution was the issue, what should he do to help the business improve its game? Or should he just cut his losses and sell the business? He left the operating review frustrated and confused—not at all confident that the business would ever deliver the performance its managers had forecast in its strategic plan.

Talk to almost any CEO, and you're likely to hear similar frustrations. For despite the enormous time and energy that goes into strategy development at most companies, many have little to show for the effort. Our research suggests that companies on average deliver only 63% of the financial performance their strategies promise. Even worse, the causes of this strategy-to-performance gap are all but invisible to top management. Leaders then pull the wrong levers in their attempts to turn around performance—pressing for better execution when they actually need a better strategy, or opting to change direction when they really should focus the organization on execution. The result: wasted energy, lost time, and continued underperformance.

But, as our research also shows, a select group of high-performing companies have managed to close the strategy-to-performance gap through better planning *and* execution. These companies—Barclays, Cisco Systems, Dow Chemical, 3M, and Roche, to name a few—develop

Idea in Brief

Most companies' strategies deliver only 63% of their promised financial value. Why? Leaders press for better execution when they really need a sounder strategy. Or they craft a new strategy when execution is the true weak spot.

How to avoid these errors? View strategic planning and execution as inextricably linked—then raise the bar for both simultaneously. Start by applying seven deceptively straightforward rules, including: keeping your strategy simple and concrete, making resource-allocation decisions early in the planning process, and continuously monitoring performance as you roll out your strategic plan.

By following these rules, you reduce the likelihood of performance shortfalls. And even if your strategy still stumbles, you quickly determine whether the fault lies with the strategy itself, your plan for pursuing it, or the execution process. The payoff? You make the *right* midcourse corrections—promptly. And as high-performing companies like Cisco Systems, Dow Chemical, and 3M have discovered, you boost your company's financial performance 60% to 100%.

realistic plans that are solidly grounded in the underlying economics of their markets and then use the plans to drive execution. Their disciplined planning and execution processes make it far less likely that they will face a shortfall in actual performance. And, if they do fall short, their processes enable them to discern the cause quickly and take corrective action. While these companies' practices are broad in scope—ranging from unique forms of planning to integrated processes for deploying and tracking resources—our experience suggests that they can be applied by any business to help craft great plans and turn them into great performance.

The Strategy-to-Performance Gap

In the fall of 2004, our firm, Marakon Associates, in collaboration with the Economist Intelligence Unit, surveyed senior executives from 197 companies worldwide with sales exceeding $500 million. We wanted to see how successful companies are at translating their strategies into performance. Specifically, how effective are they at

Idea in Practice

Seven rules for successful strategy execution:

- **Keep it simple.** Avoid drawn-out descriptions of lofty goals. Instead, clearly describe what your company will and won't do.

  Example: Executives at European investment-banking giant Barclays Capital stated they wouldn't compete with large U.S. investment banks or in unprofitable equity-market segments. Instead, they'd position Barclays for investors' burgeoning need for fixed income.

- **Challenge assumptions.** Ensure that the assumptions underlying your long-term strategic plans reflect real market economics and your organization's actual performance relative to rivals'.

  Example: Struggling conglomerate Tyco commissioned cross-functional teams in each business unit to continuously analyze their markets' profitability and their offerings, costs, and price positioning relative to competitors'. Teams met with corporate executives biweekly to discuss their findings. The revamped process generated more realistic plans and contributed to Tyco's dramatic turnaround.

- **Speak the same language.** Unit leaders and corporate strategy, marketing, and finance teams must agree on a common framework for assessing performance. For example, some high-performing companies use benchmarking to estimate the size of the profit pool available in each market their company serves, the pool's

meeting the financial projections set forth in their strategic plans? And when they fall short, what are the most common causes, and what actions are most effective in closing the strategy-to-performance gap? Our findings were revealing—and troubling.

While the executives we surveyed compete in very different product markets and geographies, they share many concerns about planning and execution. Virtually all of them struggle to produce the financial performance forecasts in their long-range plans. Furthermore, the processes they use to develop plans and monitor potential growth, and the company's likely portion of that pool, given its market share and profitability. By using the shared approach, executives easily agree on financial projections.

- **Discuss resource deployments early.** Challenge business units about when they'll need new resources to execute their strategy. By asking questions such as, "How fast can you deploy the new sales force?" and "How quickly will competitors respond?" you create more feasible forecasts and plans.

- **Identify priorities.** Delivering planned performance requires a few key actions taken at the right time, in the right way. Make strategic priorities explicit, so everyone knows what to focus on.

- **Continuously monitor performance.** Track real-time results against your plan, resetting planning assumptions and reallocating resources as needed. You'll remedy flaws in your plan *and* its execution—and avoid confusing the two.

- **Develop execution ability.** No strategy can be better than the people who must implement it. Make selection and development of managers a priority.

Example: Barclays' top executive team takes responsibility for all hiring. Members vet each others' potential hires and reward talented newcomers for superior execution. And stars aren't penalized if their business enters new markets with lower initial returns.

performance make it difficult to discern whether the strategy-to-performance gap stems from poor planning, poor execution, both, or neither. Specifically, we discovered:

Companies rarely track performance against long-term plans
In our experience, less than 15% of companies make it a regular practice to go back and compare the business's results with the performance forecast for each unit in its prior years' strategic plans. As a result, top managers can't easily know whether the projections that underlie their

Where the performance goes

This chart shows the average performance loss implied by the importance ratings that managers in our survey gave to specific breakdowns in the planning and execution process.

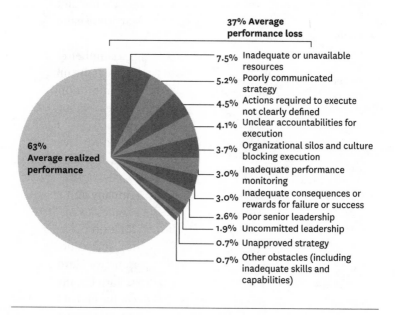

37% Average performance loss

- 7.5% Inadequate or unavailable resources
- 5.2% Poorly communicated strategy
- 4.5% Actions required to execute not clearly defined
- 4.1% Unclear accountabilities for execution
- 3.7% Organizational silos and culture blocking execution
- 3.0% Inadequate performance monitoring
- 3.0% Inadequate consequences or rewards for failure or success
- 2.6% Poor senior leadership
- 1.9% Uncommitted leadership
- 0.7% Unapproved strategy
- 0.7% Other obstacles (including inadequate skills and capabilities)

63% Average realized performance

capital-investment and portfolio-strategy decisions are in any way predictive of actual performance. More important, they risk embedding the same disconnect between results and forecasts in their future investment decisions. Indeed, the fact that so few companies routinely monitor actual versus planned performance may help explain why so many companies seem to pour good money after bad—continuing to fund losing strategies rather than searching for new and better options.

Multiyear results rarely meet projections

When companies do track performance relative to projections over a number of years, what commonly emerges is a picture one of our clients recently described as a series of "diagonal venetian blinds," where each year's performance projections, when viewed side by side, resemble venetian blinds hung diagonally. (See "The venetian blinds of business.") If things are going reasonably well, the starting point for each year's new "blind" may be a bit higher than the prior year's starting point, but rarely does performance match the prior year's projection. The obvious implication: year after year of under-performance relative to plan.

The venetian blinds phenomenon creates a number of related problems. First, because the plan's financial forecasts are unreliable, senior management cannot confidently tie capital approval to strategic planning. Consequently, strategy development and re-source allocation become decoupled, and the annual operating plan (or budget) ends up driving the company's long-term investments and strategy. Second, portfolio management gets derailed. Without credible financial forecasts, top management cannot know whether a particular business is worth more to the company and its share-holders than to potential buyers. As a result, businesses that destroy shareholder value stay in the portfolio too long (in the hope that their performance will eventually turn around), and value-creating businesses are starved for capital and other resources. Third, poor fi-nancial forecasts complicate communications with the investment community. Indeed, to avoid coming up short at the end of the quar-ter, the CFO and head of investor relations frequently impose a "con-tingency" or "safety margin" on top of the forecast produced by consolidating the business-unit plans. Because this top-down con-tingency is wrong just as often as it is right, poor financial forecasts run the risk of damaging a company's reputation with analysts and investors.

A lot of value is lost in translation

Given the poor quality of financial forecasts in most strategic plans, it is probably not surprising that most companies fail to realize their strategies' potential value. As we've mentioned, our survey indi-cates that, on average, most strategies deliver only 63% of their po-tential financial performance. And more than one-third of the

---

The venetian blinds of business

This figure illustrates a dynamic common to many companies. In January 2001, management approves a strategic plan (Plan 2001) that projects modest performance for the first year and a high rate of performance thereafter, as shown in the first solid line. For beating the first year's projection, the unit management is both commended and handsomely rewarded. A new plan is then prepared, projecting uninspiring results for the first year and once again promising a fast rate of performance improvement thereafter, as shown by the second solid line (Plan 2002). This, too, succeeds only partially, so another plan is drawn up, and so on. The actual rate of performance improvement can be seen by joining the start points of each plan (the dotted line).

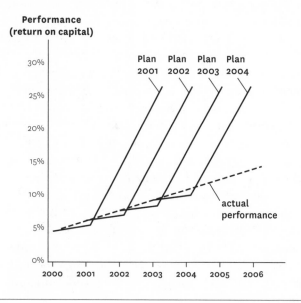

---

executives surveyed placed the figure at less than 50%. Put differently, if management were to realize the full potential of its current strategy, the increase in value could be as much as 60% to 100%!

As illustrated in "Where the performance goes," the strategy-to-performance gap can be attributed to a combination of factors, such as poorly formulated plans, misapplied resources, breakdowns in communication, and limited accountability for results. To elaborate, management starts with a strategy it believes will generate a certain level of financial performance and value over time (100%, as noted in the exhibit). But, according to the executives we surveyed, the failure to have the right resources in the right place at the right time strips away some 7.5% of the strategy's potential value. Some 5.2% is lost to poor communications, 4.5% to poor action planning, 4.1% to blurred accountabilities, and so on. Of course, these estimates reflect the average experience of the executives we surveyed and may not be representative of every company or every strategy. Nonetheless, they do highlight the issues managers need to focus on as they review their companies' processes for planning and executing strategies.

What emerges from our survey results is a sequence of events that goes something like this: Strategies are approved but poorly communicated. This, in turn, makes the translation of strategy into specific actions and resource plans all but impossible. Lower levels in the organization don't know what they need to do, when they need to do it, or what resources will be required to deliver the performance senior management expects. Consequently, the expected results never materialize. And because no one is held responsible for the shortfall, the cycle of underperformance gets repeated, often for many years.

Performance bottlenecks are frequently invisible to top management

The processes most companies use to develop plans, allocate resources, and track performance make it difficult for top management to discern whether the strategy-to-performance gap stems from poor planning, poor execution, both, or neither. Because so many plans incorporate overly ambitious projections, companies frequently write off performance shortfalls as "just another hockey-stick forecast." And when plans are realistic and performance falls short, executives have few early-warning signals. They often have no way of knowing whether critical actions were carried out as expected, resources were deployed on schedule, competitors responded as anticipated, and so on. Unfortunately, without clear information on how and why performance is falling short, it is virtually impossible for top management to take appropriate corrective action.

The strategy-to-performance gap fosters a culture of underperformance

In many companies, planning and execution breakdowns are reinforced—even magnified—by an insidious shift in culture. In our experience, this change occurs subtly but quickly, and once it has taken root it is very hard to reverse. First, unrealistic plans create the expectation throughout the organization that plans simply will not be fulfilled. Then, as the expectation becomes experience, it becomes the norm that performance commitments won't be kept. So commitments cease to be binding promises with real consequences. Rather than stretching to ensure that commitments are kept, managers, expecting failure, seek to protect themselves from the eventual fallout. They spend time covering their tracks rather than identifying actions to enhance performance. The organization becomes less self-critical and less intellectually honest about its shortcomings. Consequently, it loses its capacity to perform.

Closing the Strategy-to-Performance Gap

As significant as the strategy-to-performance gap is at most companies, management can close it. A number of high-performing companies have found ways to realize more of their strategies' potential. Rather than focus on improving their planning and execution processes separately to close the gap, these companies work both sides of the equation, raising standards for both planning and execution simultaneously and creating clear links between them.

Our research and experience in working with many of these companies suggests they follow seven rules that apply to planning and execution. Living by these rules enables them to objectively assess any performance shortfall and determine whether it stems from the strategy, the plan, the execution, or employees' capabilities. And the same rules that allow them to spot problems early also help them prevent performance shortfalls in the first place. These rules may seem simple—even obvious—but when strictly and collectively observed, they can transform both the quality of a company's strategy and its ability to deliver results.

Rule 1: Keep it simple, make it concrete

At most companies, strategy is a highly abstract concept—often confused with vision or aspiration—and is not something that can be easily communicated or translated into action. But without a clear sense of where the company is headed and why, lower levels in the organization cannot put in place executable plans. In short, the link between strategy and performance can't be drawn because the strategy itself is not sufficiently concrete.

To start off the planning and execution process on the right track, high-performing companies avoid long, drawn-out descriptions of lofty goals and instead stick to clear language describing their course of action. Bob Diamond, CEO of Barclays Capital, one of the fastest-growing and best-performing investment banking operations in Europe, puts it this way: "We've been very clear about what we will and will not do. We knew we weren't going to go head-to-head with U.S. bulge bracket firms. We communicated that we wouldn't compete in this way and that we wouldn't play in unprofitable segments within the equity markets but instead would invest to position ourselves for the euro, the burgeoning need for fixed income, and the end of Glass-Steigel. By ensuring everyone knew the strategy and how it was different, we've been able to spend more time on tasks that are key to executing this strategy."

By being clear about what the strategy is and isn't, companies like Barclays keep everyone headed in the same direction. More important, they safeguard the performance their counterparts lose to ineffective communications; their resource and action planning becomes more effective; and accountabilities are easier to specify.

Rule 2: Debate assumptions, not forecasts

At many companies, a business unit's strategic plan is little more than a negotiated settlement—the result of careful bargaining with the corporate center over performance targets and financial forecasts.

Planning, therefore, is largely a political process—with unit management arguing for lower near-term profit projections (to secure higher annual bonuses) and top management pressing for more long-term stretch (to satisfy the board of directors and other external constituents). Not surprisingly, the forecasts that emerge from these negotiations almost always understate what each business unit can deliver in the near term and overstate what can realistically be expected in the long-term—the hockey-stick charts with which CEOs are all too familiar.

Even at companies where the planning process is isolated from the political concerns of performance evaluation and compensation, the approach used to generate financial projections often has built-in biases. Indeed, financial forecasting frequently takes place in complete isolation from the marketing or strategy functions. A business unit's finance function prepares a highly detailed line-item forecast whose short-term assumptions may be realistic, if conservative, but whose long-term assumptions are largely uninformed. For example, revenue forecasts are typically based on crude estimates about average pricing, market growth, and market share. Projections of long-term costs and working capital requirements are based on an assumption about annual productivity gains—expediently tied, perhaps, to some companywide efficiency program. These forecasts are difficult for top management to pick apart. Each line item may be completely defensible, but the overall plan and projections embed a clear upward bias—rendering them useless for driving strategy execution.

High-performing companies view planning altogether differently. They want their forecasts to drive the work they actually do. To make this possible, they have to ensure that the assumptions underlying their long-term plans reflect both the real economics of their markets and the performance experience of the company relative to competitors. Tyco CEO Ed Breen, brought in to turn the company around in July 2002, credits a revamped plan-building process for contributing to Tyco's dramatic recovery. When Breen joined the company, Tyco was a labyrinth of 42 business units and several hundred profit centers, built up over many years through countless acquisitions. Few of Tyco's businesses had complete plans, and virtually none had reliable financial forecasts.

To get a grip on the conglomerate's complex operations, Breen assigned cross-functional teams at each unit, drawn from strategy, marketing, and finance, to develop detailed information on the profitability of Tyco's primary markets as well as the product or service offerings, costs, and price positioning relative to the competition. The teams met with corporate executives biweekly during Breen's first six months to review and discuss the findings. These discussions focused on the assumptions that would drive each unit's long-term financial performance, not on the financial forecasts themselves. In fact, once assumptions about market trends were agreed on, it was relatively easy for Tyco's central finance function to prepare externally oriented and internally consistent forecasts for each unit.

Separating the process of building assumptions from that of preparing financial projections helps to ground the business unit–corporate center dialogue in economic reality. Units can't hide behind specious details, and corporate center executives can't push for unrealistic goals. What's more, the fact-based discussion resulting from this kind of approach builds trust between the top team and each unit and removes barriers to fast and effective execution. "When you understand the fundamentals and performance drivers in a detailed way," says Bob Diamond, "you can then step back, and you don't have to manage the details. The team knows which issues it can get on with, which it needs to flag to me, and which issues we really need to work out together."

Rule 3: Use a rigorous framework, speak a common language
To be productive, the dialogue between the corporate center and the business units about market trends and assumptions must be conducted within a rigorous framework. Many of the companies we advise use the concept of profit pools, which draws on the competition theories of Michael Porter and others. In this framework, a business's long-term financial performance is tied to the total profit pool available in each of the markets it serves and its share of each profit

pool—which, in turn, is tied to the business's market share and relative profitability versus competitors in each market.

In this approach, the first step is for the corporate center and the unit team to agree on the size and growth of each profit pool. Fiercely competitive markets, such as pulp and paper or commercial airlines, have small (or negative) total profit pools. Less competitive markets, like soft drinks or pharmaceuticals, have large total profit pools. We find it helpful to estimate the size of each profit pool directly—through detailed benchmarking—and then forecast changes in the pool's size and growth. Each business unit then assesses what share of the total profit pool it can realistically capture over time, given its business model and positioning. Competitively advantaged businesses can capture a large share of the profit pool—by gaining or sustaining a high market share, generating above-average profitability, or both. Competitively disadvantaged businesses, by contrast, typically capture a negligible share of the profit pool. Once the unit and the corporate center agree on the likely share of the pool the business will capture over time, the corporate center can easily create the financial projections that will serve as the unit's road map.

In our view, the specific framework a company uses to ground its strategic plans isn't all that important. What is critical is that the framework establish a common language for the dialogue between the corporate center and the units—one that the strategy, marketing, and finance teams all understand and use. Without a rigorous framework to link a business's performance in the product markets with its financial performance over time, it is very difficult for top management to ascertain whether the financial projections that accompany a business unit's strategic plan are reasonable and realistically achievable. As a result, management can't know with confidence whether a performance shortfall stems from poor execution or an unrealistic and ungrounded plan.

Rule 4: Discuss resource deployments early

Companies can create more realistic forecasts and more executable plans if they discuss up front the level and timing of critical resource deployments. At Cisco Systems, for example, a cross-functional team reviews the level and timing of resource deployments early in the planning stage. These teams regularly meet with John Chambers (CEO), Dennis Powell (CFO), Randy Pond (VP of operations), and the other members of Cisco's executive team to discuss their findings and make recommendations. Once agreement is reached on re-source allocation and timing at the unit level, those elements are factored into the company's two-year plan. Cisco then monitors each unit's actual resource deployments on a monthly basis (as well as its performance) to make sure things are going according to plan and that the plan is generating the expected results.

Challenging business units about when new resources need to be in place focuses the planning dialogue on what actually needs to happen across the company in order to execute each unit's strategy. Critical questions invariably surface, such as: How long will it take us to change customers' purchase patterns? How fast can we deploy our new sales force? How quickly will competitors respond? These are tough questions. But answering them makes the forecasts and the plans they accompany more feasible.

What's more, an early assessment of resource needs also informs discussions about market trends and drivers, improving the quality of the strategic plan and making it far more executable. In the course of talking about the resources needed to expand in the rapidly grow-ing cable market, for example, Cisco came to realize that additional growth would require more trained engineers to improve existing products and develop new features. So, rather than relying on the functions to provide these resources from the bottom up, corporate management earmarked a specific number of trained engineers to support growth in cable. Cisco's financial-planning organization carefully monitors the engineering head count, the pace of feature development, and revenues generated by the business to make sure the strategy stays on track.

Rule 5: Clearly identify priorities
To deliver any strategy successfully, managers must make thousands of tactical decisions and put them into action. But not all tactics are equally important. In most instances, a few key steps must be

taken—at the right time and in the right way—to meet planned performance. Leading companies make these priorities explicit so that each executive has a clear sense of where to direct his or her efforts.

At Textron, a $10 billion multi-industrial conglomerate, each business unit identifies "improvement priorities" that it must act upon to realize the performance outlined in its strategic plan. Each improvement priority is translated into action items with clearly defined accountabilities, timetables, and key performance indicators (KPIs) that allow executives to tell how a unit is delivering on a priority. Improvement priorities and action items cascade to every level at the company—from the management committee (consisting of Textron's top five executives) down to the lowest levels in each of the company's ten business units. Lewis Campbell, Textron's CEO, summarizes the company's approach this way: "Everyone needs to know: 'If I have only one hour to work, here's what I'm going to focus on.' Our goal deployment process makes each individual's accountabilities and priorities clear."

The Swiss pharmaceutical giant Roche goes as far as to turn its business plans into detailed performance contracts that clearly specify the steps needed and the risks that must be managed to achieve the plans. These contracts all include a "delivery agenda" that lists the five to ten critical priorities with the greatest impact on performance. By maintaining a delivery agenda at each level of the company, Chairman and CEO Franz Humer and his leadership team make sure "everyone at Roche understands exactly what we have agreed to do at a strategic level and that our strategy gets translated into clear execution priorities. Our delivery agenda helps us stay the course with the strategy decisions we have made so that execution is actually allowed to happen. We cannot control implementation from HQ, but we can agree on the priorities, communicate relentlessly, and hold managers accountable for executing against their commitments."

Rule 6: Continuously monitor performance

Seasoned executives know almost instinctively whether a business has asked for too much, too little, or just enough resources to deliver the goods. They develop this capability over time—essentially through trial and error. High-performing companies use real-time Q4 performance tracking to help accelerate this trial-and-error process. They continuously monitor their resource deployment patterns and their results against plan, using continuous feedback to reset planning assumptions and reallocate resources. This real-time information allows management to spot and remedy flaws in the plan and shortfalls in execution—and to avoid confusing one with the other.

At Textron, for example, each KPI is carefully monitored, and regular operating reviews percolate performance shortfalls—or "red light" events—up through the management ranks. This provides CEO Lewis Campbell, CFO Ted French, and the other members of Textron's management committee with the information they need to spot and fix breakdowns in execution.

A similar approach has played an important role in the dramatic revival of Dow Chemical's fortunes. In December 2001, with performance in a free fall, Dow's board of directors asked Bill Stavropoulos (Dow's CEO from 1993 to 1999) to return to the helm. Stavropoulos and Andrew Liveris (the current CEO, then COO) immediately focused Dow's entire top leadership team on execution through a project they called the Performance Improvement Drive. They began by defining clear performance metrics for each of Dow's 79 business units. Performance on these key metrics was tracked against plans on a weekly basis, and the entire leadership team discussed any serious discrepancies first thing every Monday morning. As Liveris told us, the weekly monitoring sessions "forced everyone to live the details of execution" and let "the entire organization know how we were performing."

Continuous monitoring of performance is particularly important in highly volatile industries, where events outside anyone's control can render a plan irrelevant. Under CEO Alan Mulally, Boeing Commercial Airplanes' leadership team holds weekly business performance reviews to track the division's results against its multiyear plan. By tracking the deployment of resources as a leading indicator of whether a plan is being executed effectively, BCA's leadership team can make course corrections each week rather than waiting for quarterly results to roll in.

Furthermore, by proactively monitoring the primary drivers of performance (such as passenger traffic patterns, airline yields and load factors, and new aircraft orders), BCA is better able to develop and deploy effective countermeasures when events throw its plans off course. During the SARS epidemic in late 2002, for example, BCA's leadership team took action to mitigate the adverse consequences of the illness on the business's operating plan within a week of the initial outbreak. The abrupt decline in air traffic to Hong Kong, Singapore, and other Asian business centers signaled that the number of future aircraft deliveries to the region would fall—perhaps precipitously. Accordingly, BCA scaled back its medium-term production plans (delaying the scheduled ramp-up of some programs and accelerating the shutdown of others) and adjusted its multiyear operating plan to reflect the anticipated financial impact.

Rule 7: Reward and develop execution capabilities

No list of rules on this topic would be complete without a reminder that companies have to motivate and develop their staffs; at the end of the day, no process can be better than the people who have to make it work. Unsurprisingly, therefore, nearly all of the companies we studied insisted that the selection and development of management was an essential ingredient in their success. And while improving the capabilities of a company's workforce is no easy task—often taking many years—these capabilities, once built, can drive superior planning and execution for decades.

For Barclays' Bob Diamond, nothing is more important than "ensuring that [the company] hires only A players." In his view, "the hidden costs of bad hiring decisions are enormous, so despite the fact that we are doubling in size, we insist that as a top team we take responsibility for all hiring. The jury of your peers is the toughest judgment, so we vet each others' potential hires and challenge each other to keep raising the bar." It's equally important to make sure that talented hires are rewarded for superior execution. To reinforce its core values of "client," "meritocracy," "team," and "integrity," Barclays Capital has innovative pay schemes that "ring fence" rewards. Stars don't lose out just because the business is entering new markets with lower returns during the growth phase. Says Diamond: "It's so bad for the culture if you don't deliver what you promised to people who have delivered. . . . You've got to make sure you are consistent and fair, unless you want to lose your most productive people."

Companies that are strong on execution also emphasize development. Soon after he became CEO of 3M, Jim McNerney and his top team spent 18 months hashing out a new leadership model for the company. Challenging debates among members of the top team led to agreement on six "leadership attributes"—namely, the ability to "chart the course," "energize and inspire others," "demonstrate ethics, integrity, and compliance," "deliver results," "raise the bar," and "innovate resourcefully." 3M's leadership agreed that these six attributes were essential for the company to become skilled at execution and known for accountability. Today, the leaders credit this model with helping 3M to sustain and even improve its consistently strong performance.

The prize for closing the strategy-to-performance gap is huge—an increase in performance of anywhere from 60% to 100% for most companies. But this almost certainly understates the true benefits. Companies that create tight links between their strategies, their plans, and, ultimately, their performance often experience a cultural multiplier effect. Over time, as they turn their strategies into great performance, leaders in these organizations become much more confident in their own capabilities and much more willing to make the stretch commitments that inspire and transform large companies. In turn, individual managers who keep their commitments are rewarded—with faster progression and fatter paychecks—reinforcing the behaviors needed to drive any company forward.

Eventually, a culture of overperformance emerges. Investors start giving management the benefit of the doubt when it comes to bold moves and performance delivery. The result is a performance premium on the company's stock—one that further rewards stretch commitments and performance delivery. Before long, the company's reputation among potential recruits rises, and a virtuous circle is created in which talent begets performance, performance begets rewards, and rewards beget even more talent. In short, closing the strategy-to-performance gap is not only a source of immediate performance improvement but also an important driver of cultural change with a large and lasting impact on the organization's capabilities, strategies, and competitiveness.

Originally published in July 2005. Reprint R0507E.

Who Has the D?

How Clear Decision Roles Enhance Organizational Performance. *by Paul Rogers and Marcia Blenko*

DECISIONS ARE THE COIN of the realm in business. Every success, every mishap, every opportunity seized or missed is the result of a decision that someone made or failed to make. At many companies, decisions routinely get stuck inside the organization like loose change. But it's more than loose change that's at stake, of course; it's the performance of the entire organization. Never mind what industry you're in, how big and well known your company may be, or how clever your strategy is. If you can't make the right decisions quickly and effectively, and execute those decisions consistently, your business will lose ground.

Indeed, making good decisions and making them happen quickly are the hallmarks of high-performing organizations. When we surveyed executives at 350 global companies about their organizational effectiveness, only 15% said that they have an organization that helps the business outperform competitors. What sets those top performers apart is the quality, speed, and execution of their decision making. The most effective organizations score well on the major strategic decisions—which markets to enter or exit, which businesses to buy or sell, where to allocate capital and talent. But they truly shine when it comes to the critical operating decisions requiring consistency and speed—how to drive product innovation, the best way to position brands, how to manage channel partners.

Even in companies respected for their decisiveness, however, there can be ambiguity over who is accountable for which decisions.

As a result, the entire decision-making process can stall, usually at one of four bottlenecks: global versus local, center versus business unit, function versus function, and inside versus outside partners.

The first of these bottlenecks, *global versus local* decision making, can occur in nearly every major business process and function. Decisions about brand building and product development frequently get snared here, when companies wrestle over how much authority local businesses should have to tailor products for their markets. Marketing is another classic global versus local issue—should local markets have the power to determine pricing and advertising?

The second bottleneck, *center versus business unit* decision making, tends to afflict parent companies and their subsidiaries. Business units are on the front line, close to the customer; the center sees the big picture, sets broad goals, and keeps the organization focused on winning. Where should the decision-making power lie? Should a major capital investment, for example, depend on the approval of the business unit that will own it, or should headquarters make the final call?

Function versus function decision making is perhaps the most common bottleneck. Every manufacturer, for instance, faces a balancing act between product development and marketing during the design of a new product. Who should decide what? Cross-functional decisions too often result in ineffective compromise solutions, which frequently need to be revisited because the right people were not involved at the outset.

The fourth decision-making bottleneck, *inside versus outside partners,* has become familiar with the rise of outsourcing, joint ventures, strategic alliances, and franchising. In such arrangements, companies need to be absolutely clear about which decisions can be owned by the external partner (usually those about the execution of strategy) and which must continue to be made internally (decisions about the strategy itself). In the case of outsourcing, for instance, brand-name apparel and foot-wear marketers once assumed that overseas suppliers could be responsible for decisions about plant employees' wages and working conditions. Big mistake.

Idea in Brief

Decisions are the coin of the realm in business. Every success, every mishap, every opportunity seized or missed stems from a decision someone made—or failed to make. Yet in many firms, decisions routinely stall inside the organization—hurting the entire company's performance.

The culprit? Ambiguity over who's accountable for which decisions. In one auto manufacturer that was missing milestones for rolling out new models, marketers *and* product developers each thought they were responsible for deciding new models' standard features and colors. Result? Conflict over who had final say, endless revisiting of decisions—and missed deadlines that led to lost sales.

How to clarify decision accountability? Assign clear roles for the decisions that most affect your firm's performance—such as which markets to enter, where to allocate capital, and how to drive product innovation. Think "RAPID": Who should recommend a course of action on a key decision? Who must agree to a recommendation before it can move forward? Who will perform the actions needed to implement the decision? Whose input is needed to determine the proposal's feasibility? Who decides—brings the decision to closure and commits the organization to implement it?

When you clarify decision roles, you make the *right* choices— swiftly and effectively.

Clearing the Bottlenecks

The most important step in unclogging decision-making bottlenecks is assigning clear roles and responsibilities. Good decision makers recognize which decisions really matter to performance. They think through who should recommend a particular path, who needs to agree, who should have input, who has ultimate responsibility for making the decision, and who is accountable for follow-through. They make the process routine. The result: better coordination and quicker response times.

Companies have devised a number of methods to clarify decision roles and assign responsibilities. We have used an approach called RAPID, which has evolved over the years, to help hundreds of companies develop clear decision-making guidelines. It is, for sure, not a

Idea in Practice

The RAPID Decision Model

For every strategic decision, assign the following roles and responsibilities:

People Who . . .	Are Responsible For . . .
Recommend	• Making a proposal on a key decision, gathering input, and providing data and analysis to make a sensible choice in a timely fashion • Consulting with input providers—hearing and incorporating their views, and winning their buy-in
Agree	• Negotiating a modified proposal with the recommender if they have concerns about the original proposal • Escalating unresolved issues to the decider if the "A" and "R" can't resolve differences • If necessary, exercising veto power over the recommendation
Perform	• Executing a decision once it's made • Seeing that the decision is implemented promptly and effectively
Input	• Providing relevant facts to the recommender that shed light on the proposal's feasibility and practical implications
Decide	• Serving as the single point of accountability • Bringing the decision to closure by resolving any impasse in the decision-making process • Committing the organization to implementing the decision

panacea (an indecisive decision maker, for example, can ruin any good system), but it's an important start. The letters in RAPID stand for the primary roles in any decision-making process, although these roles are not performed exactly in this order: recommend, agree, perform, input, and decide—the "D." (See the sidebar "A Decision-Making Primer.")

Decision-Role Pitfalls

In assigning decision roles:

- Ensure that only one person "has the D." If two or more people think they're in charge of a particular decision, a tug-of-war results.

- Watch for a proliferation of "A's." Too many people with veto power can paralyze recommenders. If many people must agree, you probably haven't pushed decisions down far enough in your organization.

- Avoid assigning too many "I's." When many people give input, at least some of them aren't making meaningful contributions.

The RAPID Model in Action

Example: At British department-store chain John Lewis, company buyers wanted to increase sales and reduce complexity by offering fewer salt and pepper mill models. The company launched the streamlined product set without involving the sales staff. And sales fell. Upon visiting the stores, buyers saw that salespeople (not understanding the strategy behind the recommendation) had halved shelf space to match the reduction in product range, rather than maintaining the same space but stocking more of the products.

To fix the problem, the company "gave buyers the D" on how much space product categories would have. Sales staff "had the A": If space allocations didn't make sense to them, they could force additional negotiations. They also "had the P," implementing product layouts in stores.

Once decision roles were clarified, sales of salt and pepper mills exceeded original levels.

The people who *recommend* a course of action are responsible for making a proposal or offering alternatives. They need data and analysis to support their recommendations, as well as common sense about what's reasonable, practical, and effective.

The people who *agree* to a recommendation are those who need to sign off on it before it can move forward. If they veto a proposal, they must either work with the recommender to come up with an alternative or elevate the issue to the person with the D. For decision making to function smoothly, only a few people should have such veto power. They may be executives responsible for legal or regulatory compliance or the heads of units whose operations will be significantly affected by the decision.

People with *input* responsibilities are consulted about the recommendation. Their role is to provide the relevant facts that are the basis of any good decision: How practical is the proposal? Can manufacturing accommodate the design change? Where there's dissent or contrasting views, it's important to get these people to the table at the right time. The recommender has no obligation to act on the input he or she receives but is expected to take it into account—particularly since the people who provide input are generally among those who must implement a decision. Consensus is a worthy goal, but as a decision-making standard, it can be an obstacle to action or a recipe for lowest-common-denominator compromise. A more practical objective is to get everyone involved to buy in to the decision.

Eventually, one person will *decide*. The decision maker is the single point of accountability who must bring the decision to closure and commit the organization to act on it. To be strong and effective, the person with the D needs good business judgment, a grasp of the relevant trade-offs, a bias for action, and a keen awareness of the organization that will execute the decision.

The final role in the process involves the people who will *perform* the decision. They see to it that the decision is implemented promptly and effectively. It's a crucial role. Very often, a good decision executed quickly beats a brilliant decision implemented slowly or poorly.

RAPID can be used to help redesign the way an organization works or to target a single bottleneck. Some companies use the approach for the top ten to 20 decisions, or just for the CEO and his or her direct reports. Other companies use it throughout the organization—to improve customer service by clarifying decision roles on the front line, for instance. When people see an effective process for making decisions, they spread the word. For example, after senior managers at a major U.S. retailer used RAPID to sort out a particularly thorny set of corporate decisions, they promptly built the process into their own functional organizations.

To see the process in action, let's look at the way four companies have worked through their decision-making bottlenecks.

Global Versus Local

Every major company today operates in global markets, buying raw materials in one place, shipping them somewhere else, and selling finished products all over the world. Most are trying simultaneously to build local presence and expertise, and to achieve economies of scale. Decision making in this environment is far from straightforward. Frequently, decisions cut across the boundaries between global and local managers, and sometimes across a regional layer in between: What investments will streamline our supply chain? How far should we go in standardizing products or tailoring them for local markets?

The trick in decision making is to avoid becoming either mindlessly global or hopelessly local. If decision-making authority tilts too far toward global executives, local customers' preferences can easily be overlooked, undermining the efficiency and agility of local operations. But with too much local authority, a company is likely to miss out on crucial economies of scale or opportunities with global clients.

To strike the right balance, a company must recognize its most important sources of value and make sure that decision roles line up with them. This was the challenge facing Martin Broughton, the former CEO and chairman of British American Tobacco, the second-largest tobacco company in the world. In 1993, when Broughton was appointed chief executive, BAT was losing ground to its nearest competitor. Broughton knew that the company needed to take better advantage of its global scale, but decision roles and responsibilities were at odds with this goal. Four geographic operating units ran themselves autonomously, rarely collaborating and sometimes even competing. Achieving consistency across global brands proved difficult, and cost

A Decision-Making Primer

GOOD DECISION MAKING DEPENDS on assigning clear and specific roles. This sounds simple enough, but many companies struggle to make decisions because lots of people feel accountable—or no one does. RAPID and other tools used to analyze decision making give senior management teams a method for assigning roles and involving the relevant people. The key is to be clear who has input, who gets to decide, and who gets it done.

The five letters in RAPID correspond to the five critical decision-making roles: recommend, agree, perform, input, and decide. As you'll see, the roles are not carried out lockstep in this order—we took some liberties for the sake of creating a useful acronym.

Recommend

People in this role are responsible for making a proposal, gathering input, and providing the right data and analysis to make a sensible decision in a timely fashion. In the course of developing a proposal, recommenders consult with the people who provide input, not just hearing and incorporating their views but also building buy in along the way. Recommenders must have analytical skills, common sense, and organizational smarts.

Agree

Individuals in this role have veto power—yes or no—over the recommendation. Exercising the veto triggers a debate between themselves and the recommenders, which should lead to a modified proposal. If that takes too long, or if the two parties simply can't agree, they can escalate the issue to the person who has the D.

Input

These people are consulted on the decision. Because the people who provide input are typically involved in implementation, recommenders have a strong interest in taking their advice seriously. No input is binding, but this

---

synergies across the operating units were elusive. Industry insiders joked that "there are seven major tobacco companies in the world—and four of them are British American Tobacco." Broughton vowed to change the punch line.

The chief executive envisioned an organization that could take advantage of the opportunities a global business offers—global brands that could compete with established winners such as Altria Group's Marlboro; global purchasing of important raw materials,

shouldn't undermine its importance. If the right people are not involved and motivated, the decision is far more likely to falter during execution.

Decide

The person with the D is the formal decision maker. He or she is ultimately accountable for the decision, for better or worse, and has the authority to resolve any impasse in the decision-making process and to commit the organization to action.

Perform

Once a decision is made, a person or group of people will be responsible for executing it. In some instances, the people responsible for implementing a decision are the same people who recommended it.

Writing down the roles and assigning accountability are essential steps, but good decision making also requires the right process. Too many rules can cause the process to collapse under its own weight. The most effective process is grounded in specifics but simple enough to adapt if necessary.

When the process gets slowed down, the problem can often be traced back to one of three trouble spots. First is a lack of clarity about who has the D. If more than one person think they have it for a particular decision, that decision will get caught up in a tug-of-war. The flip side can be equally damaging: No one is accountable for crucial decisions, and the business suffers. Second, a proliferation of people who have veto power can make life tough for recommenders. If a company has too many people in the "agree" role, it usually means that decisions are not pushed down far enough in the organization. Third, if there are a lot of people giving input, it's a signal that at least some of them aren't making a meaningful contribution.

including tobacco; and more consistency in innovation and customer management. But Broughton didn't want the company to lose its nimbleness and competitive hunger in local markets by shifting too much decision-making power to global executives.

The first step was to clarify roles for the most important decisions. Procurement became a proving ground. Previously, each operating unit had identified its own suppliers and negotiated contracts for all materials. Under Broughton, a global procurement team was set up in headquarters and given authority to choose suppliers and negotiate pricing and quality for global materials, including bulk tobacco and certain types of packaging. Regional procurement teams were now given input into global materials strategies but ultimately had to implement the team's decision. As soon as the global team signed contracts with suppliers, responsibility shifted to the regional teams, who worked out the details of delivery and service with the suppliers in their regions. For materials that did not offer global economies of scale (mentholated filters for the North American market, for example), the regional teams retained their decision-making authority.

As the effort to revamp decision making in procurement gained momentum, the company set out to clarify roles in all its major decisions. The process wasn't easy. A company the size of British American Tobacco has a huge number of moving parts, and developing a practical system for making decisions requires sweating lots of details. What's more, decision-making authority is power, and people are often reluctant to give it up.

It's crucial for the people who will live with the new system to help design it. At BAT, Broughton created working groups led by people earmarked, implicitly or explicitly, for leadership roles in the future. For example, Paul Adams, who ultimately succeeded Broughton as chief executive, was asked to lead the group charged with redesigning decision making for brand and customer management. At the time, Adams was a regional head within one of the operating units. With other senior executives, including some of his own direct reports, Broughton specified that their role was to provide input, not to veto recommendations. Broughton didn't make the common mistake of seeking consensus, which is often an obstacle to action. Instead, he made it clear that the objective was not deciding whether to change the decision-making process but achieving buy in about how to do so as effectively as possible.

The new decision roles provided the foundation the company needed to operate successfully on a global basis while retaining flexibility at the local level. The focus and efficiency of its decision making were reflected in the company's results: After the decision-making overhaul, British American Tobacco experienced nearly ten years of growth well above the levels of its competitors in sales, profits, and market value. The company has gone on to have one of the best-performing stocks on the UK market and has reemerged as a major global player in the tobacco industry.

Center Versus Business Unit

The first rule for making good decisions is to involve the right people at the right level of the organization. For BAT, capturing economies of scale required its global team to appropriate some decision-making powers from regional divisions. For many companies, a similar balancing act takes place between executives at the center and managers in the business units. If too many decisions flow to the center, decision making can grind to a halt. The problem is different but no less critical if the decisions that are elevated to senior executives are the wrong ones.

Companies often grow into this type of problem. In small and midsize organizations, a single management team—sometimes a single leader—effectively handles every major decision. As a company grows and its operations become more complex, however, senior executives can no longer master the details required to make decisions in every business.

A change in management style, often triggered by the arrival of a new CEO, can create similar tensions. At a large British retailer, for example, the senior team was accustomed to the founder making all critical decisions. When his successor began seeking consensus on important issues, the team was suddenly unsure of its role, and many decisions stalled. It's a common scenario, yet most management teams and boards of directors don't specify how decision-making authority should change as the company does.

A growth opportunity highlighted that issue for Wyeth (then known as American Home Products) in late 2000. Through organic growth, acquisitions, and partnerships, Wyeth's pharmaceutical division had developed three sizable businesses: biotech, vaccines, and traditional pharmaceutical products. Even though each business had its own market dynamics, operating requirements, and research focus, most important decisions were pushed up to one group of senior executives. "We were using generalists across all issues," said Joseph M. Mahady, president of North American and global businesses for Wyeth Pharmaceuticals. "It was a signal that we weren't getting our best decision making."

The problem crystallized for Wyeth when managers in the biotech business saw a vital—but perishable—opportunity to establish a leading position with Enbrel, a promising rheumatoid arthritis drug. Competitors were working on the same class of drug, so Wyeth needed to move quickly. This meant expanding production capacity by building a new plant, which would be located at the Grange Castle Business Park in Dublin, Ireland.

The decision, by any standard, was a complex one. Once approved by regulators, the facility would be the biggest biotech plant in the world—and the largest capital investment Wyeth had ever undertaken. Yet peak demand for the drug was not easy to determine. What's more, Wyeth planned to market Enbrel in partnership with Immunex (now a part of Amgen). In its deliberations about the plant, therefore, Wyeth needed to factor in the requirements of building up its technical expertise, technology transfer issues, and an uncertain competitive environment.

Input on the decision filtered up slowly through a gauze of overlapping committees, leaving senior executives hungry for a more detailed grasp of the issues. Given the narrow window of opportunity, Wyeth acted quickly, moving from a first look at the Grange Castle project to implementation in six months. But in the midst of this process, Wyeth Pharmaceuticals' executives saw the larger issue: The company needed a system that would push more decisions down to the business units, where operational knowledge was greatest, and elevate the decisions that required the senior team's input, such as marketing strategy and manufacturing capacity.

In short order, Wyeth gave authority for many decisions to business unit managers, leaving senior executives with veto power over some of the more sensitive issues related to Grange Castle. But after that investment decision was made, the D for many subsequent decisions about the Enbrel business lay with Cavan Redmond, the executive vice president and general manager of Wyeth's biotech division, and his new management team. Redmond gathered input from managers in biotech manufacturing, marketing, forecasting, finance, and R&D, and quickly set up the complex schedules needed to collaborate with Immunex. Responsibility for execution rested firmly with the business unit, as always. But now Redmond, supported by his team, also had authority to make important decisions.

Grange Castle is paying off so far. Enbrel is among the leading brands for rheumatoid arthritis, with sales of $1.7 billion through the first half of 2005. And Wyeth's metabolism for making decisions has increased. Recently, when the U.S. Food and Drug Administration granted priority review status to another new drug, Tygacil, because of the antibiotic's efficacy against drug-resistant infections, Wyeth displayed its new reflexes. To keep Tygacil on a fast track, the company had to orchestrate a host of critical steps—refining the process technology, lining up supplies, ensuring quality control, allocating manufacturing capacity. The vital decisions were made one or two levels down in the biotech organization, where the expertise resided. "Instead of debating whether you can move your product into my shop, we had the decision systems in place to run it up and down the business units and move ahead rapidly with Tygacil," said Mahady. The drug was approved by the FDA in June 2005 and moved into volume production a mere three days later.

Function Versus Function

Decisions that cut across functions are some of the most important a company faces. Indeed, cross-functional collaboration has become an axiom of business, essential for arriving at the best answers for the company and its customers. But fluid decision making across functional teams remains a constant challenge, even for companies known for doing it well, like Toyota and Dell. For instance, a team that thinks it's more efficient to make a decision without consulting other functions may wind up missing out on relevant input or being overruled by another team that believes—rightly or wrongly—it

A Recipe for a Decision-Making Bottleneck

AT ONE AUTOMAKER WE STUDIED, marketers and product developers were confused about who was responsible for making decisions about new models.

When we asked, "Who has the right to decide which features will be standard?"

64% of product developers said, "We do."

83% of marketers said, "We do."

When we asked, "Who has the right to decide which colors will be offered?"

77% of product developers said, "We do."

61% of marketers said, "We do."

Not surprisingly, the new models were delayed.

Q6

should have been included in the process. Many of the most important cross-functional decisions are, by their very nature, the most difficult to orchestrate, and that can string out the process and lead to sparring between fiefdoms and costly indecision.

The theme here is a lack of clarity about who has the D. For example, at a global auto manufacturer that was missing its milestones for rolling out new models—and was paying the price in falling sales—it turned out that marketers and product developers were confused about which function was responsible for making decisions about standard features and color ranges for new models. When we asked the marketing team who had the D about which features should be standard, 83% said the marketers did. When we posed the same question to product developers, 64% said the responsibility rested with them. (See "A Recipe for a Decision-Making Bottleneck.")

The practical difficulty of connecting functions through smooth decision making crops up frequently at retailers. John Lewis, the leading department store chain in the United Kingdom, might reasonably expect to overcome this sort of challenge more readily than other retailers. Spedan Lewis, who built the business in the early twentieth century, was a pioneer in employee ownership. A strong connection between managers and employees permeated every aspect of the store's operations and remained vital to the company as it grew into the largest employee-owned business in the United Kingdom, with 59,600 employees and more than £5 billion in revenues in 2004.

Even at John Lewis, however, with its heritage of cooperation and teamwork, cross-functional decision making can be hard to sustain. Take salt and pepper mills, for instance. John Lewis, which prides itself on having great selection, stocked nearly 50 SKUs of salt and pepper mills, while most competitors stocked around 20. The company's buyers saw an opportunity to increase sales and reduce complexity by offering a smaller number of popular and well-chosen products in each price point and style.

When John Lewis launched the new range, sales fell. This made no sense to the buyers until they visited the stores and saw how the merchandise was displayed. The buyers had made their decision without fully involving the sales staff, who therefore did not understand the strategy behind the new selection. As a result, the sellers had cut shelf space in half to match the reduction in range, rather than devoting the same amount of shelf space to stocking more of each product.

To fix the communication problem, John Lewis needed to clarify decision roles. The buyers were given the D on how much space to allocate to each product category. If the space allocation didn't make sense to the sales staff, however, they had the authority to raise their concerns and force a new round of negotiations. They also had responsibility for implementing product layouts in the stores. When the communication was sorted out and shelf space was restored, sales of the salt and pepper mills climbed well above original levels.

Crafting a decision-making process that connected the buying and selling functions for salt and pepper mills was relatively easy; rolling it out across the entire business was more challenging. Salt and pepper mills are just one of several hundred product categories for John Lewis. This element of scale is one reason why cross-functional bottlenecks are not easy to unclog. Different functions have different incentives and goals, which are often in conflict. When it comes down to a struggle between two functions, there may be good reasons to locate the D in either place—buying or selling, marketing or product development.

Here, as elsewhere, someone needs to think objectively about where value is created and assign decision roles accordingly. Eliminating cross-functional bottlenecks actually has less to do with shifting decision-making responsibilities between departments and more to do with ensuring that the people with relevant information are allowed to share it. The decision maker is important, of course, but more important is designing a system that aligns decision making and makes it routine.

Inside Versus Outside Partners

Decision making within an organization is hard enough. Trying to make decisions between separate organizations on different continents adds layers of complexity that can scuttle the best strategy. Companies that outsource capabilities in pursuit of cost and quality advantages face this very challenge. Which decisions should be made internally? Which can be delegated to outsourcing partners?

These questions are also relevant for strategic partners—a global bank working with an IT contractor on a systems development project, for example, or a media company that acquires content from a studio—and for companies conducting part of their business through franchisees. There is no right answer to who should have the power to decide what. But the wrong approach is to assume that contractual arrangements can provide the answer.

An outdoor-equipment company based in the United States discovered this recently when it decided to scale up production of gas patio heaters for the lower end of the market. The company had some success manufacturing high-end products in China. But with the advent of superdiscounters like Wal-Mart, Target, and Home Depot, the company realized it needed to move more of its production overseas to feed these retailers with lower-cost offerings. The timetable left little margin for error: The company started tooling up factories in April and June of 2004, hoping to be ready for the Christmas season.

The Decision-Driven Organization

THE DEFINING CHARACTERISTIC of high-performing organizations is their ability to make good decisions and to make them happen quickly. The companies that succeed tend to follow a few clear principles.

Some decisions matter more than others

The decisions that are crucial to building value in the business are the ones that matter most. Some of them will be the big strategic decisions, but just as important are the critical operating decisions that drive the business day to day and are vital to effective execution.

Action is the goal

Good decision making doesn't end with a decision; it ends with implementation. The objective shouldn't be consensus, which often becomes an obstacle to action, but buy in.

Ambiguity is the enemy

Clear accountability is essential: Who contributes input, who makes the decision, and who carries it out? Without clarity, gridlock and delay are the most likely outcomes. Clarity doesn't necessarily mean concentrating authority in a few people; it means defining who has responsibility to make decisions, who has input, and who is charged with putting them into action.

Speed and adaptability are crucial

A company that makes good decisions quickly has a higher metabolism, which allows it to act on opportunities and overcome obstacles. The best decision makers create an environment where people can come together quickly and efficiently to make the most important decisions.

Decision roles trump the organizational chart

No decision-making structure will be perfect for every decision. The key is to involve the right people at the right level in the right part of the organization at the right time.

A well-aligned organization reinforces roles

Clear decision roles are critical, but they are not enough. If an organization does not reinforce the right approach to decision making through its measures and incentives, information flows, and culture, the behavior won't become routine.

Practicing beats preaching

Involve the people who will live with the new decision roles in designing them. The very process of thinking about new decision behaviors motivates people to adopt them.

A Decision Diagnostic

CONSIDER THE LAST THREE MEANINGFUL decisions you've been involved in and ask yourself the following questions.

1. Were the decisions right?

2. Were they made with appropriate speed?

3. Were they executed well?

4. Were the right people involved, in the right way?

5. Was it clear for each decision

   - who would recommend a solution?

   - who would provide input?

   - who had the final say?

   - who would be responsible for following through?

6. Were the decision roles, process, and time frame respected?

7. Were the decisions based on appropriate facts?

8. To the extent that there were divergent facts or opinions, was it clear who had the D?

9. Were the decision makers at the appropriate level in the company?

10. Did the organization's measures and incentives encourage the people involved to make the right decisions?

Right away, there were problems. Although the Chinese manufacturing partners understood costs, they had little idea what American consumers wanted. When expensive designs arrived from the head office in the United States, Chinese plant managers made compromises to meet contracted cost targets. They used a lower grade material, which discolored. They placed the power switch in a spot that was inconvenient for the user but easier to build. Instead of making certain parts from a single casting, they welded materials together, which looked terrible.

To fix these problems, the U.S. executives had to draw clear lines around which decisions should be made on which side of the ocean. The company broke down the design and manufacturing process into five steps and analyzed how decisions were made at each step. The company was also much more explicit about what the manufacturing specs would include and what the manufacturer was expected to do with them. The objective was not simply to clarify decision roles but to make sure those roles corresponded directly to the sources of value in the business. If a decision would affect the look and feel of the finished product, headquarters would have to sign off on it. But if a decision would not affect the customer's experience, it could be made in China. If, for example, Chinese engineers found a less expensive material that didn't compromise the product's look, feel, and functionality, they could make that change on their own.

To help with the transition to this system, the company put a team of engineers on-site in China to ensure a smooth handoff of the specs and to make decisions on issues that would become complex and time-consuming if elevated to the home office. Marketing executives in the home office insisted that it should take a customer ten minutes and no more than six steps to assemble the product at home. The company's engineers in China, along with the Chinese manufacturing team, had input into this assembly requirement and were responsible for execution. But the D resided with headquarters, and the requirement became a major design factor. Decisions about logistics, however, became the province of the engineering team in China: It would figure out how to package the heaters so that one-third more boxes would fit into a container, which reduced shipping costs substantially.

If managers suddenly realize that they're spending less time sitting through meetings wondering why they are there, that's an early signal that companies have become better at making decisions. When meetings start with a common understanding about who is responsible for providing valuable input and who has the D, an organization's decision-making metabolism will get a boost.

No single lever turns a decision-challenged organization into a decision-driven one, of course, and no blueprint can provide for all the contingencies and business shifts a company is bound to encounter. The most successful companies use simple tools that help them recognize potential bottlenecks and think through decision roles and responsibilities with each change in the business environment. That's difficult to do—and even more difficult for competitors to copy. But by taking some very practical steps, any company can become more effective, beginning with its next decision.

Originally published in January 2006. Reprint R0601D.

About the Contributors

MICHAEL E. PORTER is the Bishop William Lawrence University Professor at Harvard Business School.

JAMES C. COLLINS operates a management research laboratory in Boulder, Colorado.

JERRY I. PORRAS is the Lane Professor, Emeritus, at Stanford University's Graduate School of Business.

MARK W. JOHNSON is the chairman and a cofounder of Innosight, a strategic innovation and investing company based in Boston.

CLAYTON M. CHRISTENSEN is the Robert and Jane Cizik Professor of Business Administration at Harvard Business School.

HENNING KAGERMANN is a former CEO of SAP AG, a software corporation based in Germany.

W. CHAN KIM is the Boston Consulting Group Bruce D. Henderson Chaired Professor of Strategy and International Management at Insead in France.

RENÉE MAUBORGNE is the Insead Distinguished Fellow and a professor of strategy at Insead in France.

GARY L. NEILSON is a senior vice president in the Chicago office of Booz & Company, a management consulting firm.

KARLA L. MARTIN is a principal in Booz & Company's San Francisco office.

ELIZABETH POWERS is a principal in Booz & Company's New York office.

ROBERT S. KAPLAN is the Baker Foundation Professor at Harvard Business School and codeveloper, with David P. Norton, of the balanced scorecard.

DAVID P. NORTON is the founder and president of the Balanced Scorecard Collaborative, Palladium Group, in Massachusetts.

ORIT GADIESH is the chairman of Bain & Company, a management consulting firm based in Boston.

JAMES L. GILBERT, a former director of Bain & Company, is an executive vice president of strategy and business development at Boston Scientific.

MICHAEL C. MANKINS is a managing partner in the San Francisco office of Marakon Associates, an international strategy consulting firm.

RICHARD STEELE is a partner in the New York office of The Bridgespan Group, a nonprofit consulting firm.

PAUL ROGERS is managing partner for the United Kingdom at Bain & Company's London office.

MARCIA BLENKO is a partner at Bain & Company in Boston and leads Bain's Global Organization practice.

Index

Smart advice and inspiration from a source you trust.

Whether you need help tackling today's most urgent work challenge or shaping your organization's strategy for the future, *Harvard Business Review* has got you covered.

HBR Guides Series

HOW-TO ESSENTIALS FROM LEADING EXPERTS

HBR Guide to Better Business Writing
HBR Guide to Finance Basics for Managers
HBR Guide to Getting the Right Work Done
HBR Guide to Managing Up and Across
HBR Guide to Persuasive Presentations
HBR Guide to Project Management

HBR's 10 Must Reads Series

IF YOU READ NOTHING ELSE, READ THESE DEFINITIVE ARTICLES FROM HARVARD BUSINESS REVIEW

HBR's 10 Must Reads on Change Management
HBR's 10 Must Reads on Leadership
HBR's 10 Must Reads on Managing People
HBR's 10 Must Reads on Managing Yourself
HBR's 10 Must Reads on Strategy
HBR's 10 Must Reads: The Essentials

Buy for your team, clients, or event.
Visit our site for quantity discount rates.

hbr.org/books/direct-and-bulk-sales

HAVE STUDENTS WORK
IN GROUPS TO WRITE A
CHAPTER SUMMARY IN
CLASS AND THEN REVISIT
IT LATER.